W9-CMQ-817

THE 51 DAY WAR

ALSO BY MAX BLUMENTHAL

*Republican Gomorrah: Inside the Movement
that Shattered the Party* (2009)

Goliath: Life and Loathing in Greater Israel (2013)

THE 51 DAY WAR

Ruin and Resistance in Gaza

MAX BLUMENTHAL

NATION
BOOKS
New York

Published by Nation Books
A Member of the Perseus Books Group
116 East 16th Street, 8th Floor
New York, NY 10003

Nation Books is a co-publishing venture of the Nation Institute and the Perseus
Books Group

Books published by Nation Books are available at special discounts
for bulk purchases in the United States by corporations, institutions,
and other organizations. For more information, please contact the Special
Markets Department at the Perseus Books Group, 2300 Chestnut Street,
Suite 200, Philadelphia, PA 19103, or call (800) 810-4145, ext. 5000,
or e-mail special.markets@perseusbooks.com.

Designed by *BackStory Design*

Library of Congress Control Number: 2015940023
ISBN: 978-1-56858-511-6 (HC)
ISBN: 978-1-56858-512-3 (EB)

10 9 8 7 6 5 4 3 2 1

For Eman

CONTENTS

CONTENTS

Tiny Feet

A mother looks at another—

a sea of small bodies

burnt or decapitated

around them—

and asks,

How do we mourn this?

—NATHALIE HANDAL

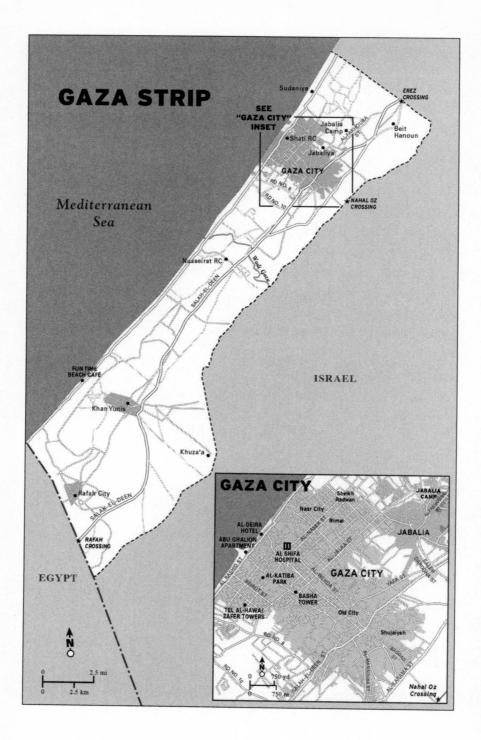

GAZA STRIP

Mediterranean
Sea

SEE
"GAZA CITY"
INSET

Sudaniya

EREZ
CROSSING

Jabalia
Camp

Shati RC

Beit
Hanoun

Jabaliya

GAZA CITY

RD NO. 8

RD NO. 10

NAHAL OZ
CROSSING

Nusseirat RC

Wadi Gaza

SALAH-EL-DEEN

ISRAEL

FUN TIME
BEACH CAFÉ

Khan Yunis

Khuza'a

Rafah City

SALAH-EL-DEEN

RAFAH
CROSSING

EGYPT

N

0   2.5 mi

0   2.5 km

GAZA CITY

Sheikh
Radwan

JABALIA
CAMP

Nasr City

Rimal

JABALIA

AL-DEIRA
HOTEL

ABU GHALION
APARTMENT

AL SHIFA
HOSPITAL

GAZA CITY

AL-KATIBA
PARK

BASHA
TOWER

TEL AL-HAWA/
ZAFER TOWERS

Old City

Shujaiyeh

RD NO. 8

RD NO. 10

N

0   750 yd

0   750 m

SALAH-EL-DEEN

Nahal Oz
Crossing

INTRODUCTION

Why Gaza?

The remote-controlled Israeli machine gun at the Erez Crossing. Photo by Dan Cohen.

The first thing a visitor sees upon entering the Gaza Strip through Israel's Erez border crossing is a remote-controlled machine gun perched atop a concrete wall that extends as far as the eye can see. The first thing a visitor hears is the hum of the Israeli drone that hovers constantly above Gaza and forms the sonic backdrop of its residents' lives. After just a few minutes in Gaza it becomes abundantly apparent that this is among the most closely surveilled and intensely controlled patches of earth on the planet.

The Gaza Strip is a ghetto of children. Of its 1.8 million residents, a majority are under the age of 18. Most have never left the 360 square kilometers where they were born, raised and confined. There is no discernible future for them beyond the Israeli military occupation that has endured nearly 50 years and a siege that was officially proclaimed in 2007. The formative years of these young people have been marked by three major military assaults. These are their rites of passage. The Palestinians of Gaza have no reason or experience to believe that a fourth war will not arrive soon.

The violence in Gaza has become a ritual that has confounded many outsiders, leading to the rise of simplistic explanations for the bloodshed as the product of religious extremism, endemic anti-Semitism and intractable conflict. But a brief look at the history leading up to the 51 Day War of 2014 presents a different reality.

Eighty percent of Gaza's residents are refugees from the State of Israel. Their families were among the 750,000 indigenous Palestinians who fled or were forcibly expelled in the period from November 1947 to late 1948 known to them as the Nakba, or the catastrophe. Since Israel was founded, every one of its governments has identified these refugees as a demographic threat whose repatriation would threaten Israel's Jewish majority and the Zionist project itself. Palestinians in Gaza are ultimately confined and excluded from Israel for one simple reason: They are not Jews. There is simply no place for them in an Israel that defines itself as an exclusive Jewish state, and that will not grant equal rights to these people. That is why Gaza has become a warehouse for a surplus population that the Israeli-American scholar Martin Kramer described as "superfluous young men." And that is why Gaza resists.

A stateless people with no internationally recognized right to organize an army, navy, or air force, Gaza's refugee population nonetheless embarked on an armed campaign against Israeli occupation that began in earnest in the early 1950s. Some prominent Israelis understood this. The famous 1956 eulogy by Moshe Dayan, then the Israeli army's Chief of Staff, for Roy Rotenberg, an Israeli kibbutz guard Palestinian fighters killed near the border of Gaza, was both unusually empathetic about the causes of the conflict and even more committed to continuing it. "Let us not cast the blame on the murderers today. Why should we declare their burning hatred for us?" Dayan asked. "For eight years they have been sitting in the refugee camps in Gaza, and before their eyes we have been transforming the lands and the villages, where they and their forefathers previously dwelled, into our home."

Summoning his countrymen to persevere in the face of ferocious resistance, Dayan declared, "We are a generation that settles the land and without the steel helmet and the cannon's muzzle, we will not be able to plant a tree and build a home... This is the fate of our generation. This is our life's choice—to be ready and armed, tough and hard, or else the sword shall fall from our hand and our lives will be cut short."

Dayan's eulogy was perhaps the clearest distillation of the mentality that has governed Israel's approach to the Palestinian people in general and to the Gaza Strip in particular for some sixty years. Just as he conceded Israel's colonial ambitions, he also clearly explained the motives behind Palestinian violence. By the end of 2003, as the Second Intifada approached its conclusion, both Israeli and Palestinian societies were near exhaustion. It was then that Prime Minister Ariel Sharon announced his intention to pursue "disengagement" with Gaza that would reorient the relationship between the two peoples by hardening their separation.

Because Sharon's maneuver entailed the forced evacuation of about 9,000 religious nationalist settlers from the strip, many proponents of a two-state solution to the crisis of Israel–Palestine were convinced that the right-wing warrior king had experienced a sudden change of heart. "[Sharon] realized that the land had to be partitioned between its two peoples, that the occupation could not continue, that the Palestinians would have their own state and that thousands of Israeli settlers would have to be evacuated from the Gaza Strip," David Grossman, the renowned novelist and voice of Israel's liberal "peace camp," wrote hopefully at the time. With support from liberal and centrist elements, Sharon secured approval for his plan.

The Prime Minister's advisors were adamant, however, that separating from Gaza should not be confused with peace. "The significance of the disengagement plan is the freezing of the peace process," senior Sharon advisor Dov Weisglass informed the Israeli paper *Haaretz* in October 2004. "And when you freeze that process, you prevent the establishment of a Palestinian state, and you prevent a discussion on the refugees, the borders and Jerusalem. Effectively, this whole package called the Palestinian state, with all that it entails, has been removed indefinitely from our agenda. And all this with authority and permission. All with a presidential blessing and the ratification of both houses of Congress."

Sharon's plan was conceived with substantial input from a notable academic named Arnon Soffer at the University of Haifa. A professor of "geostrategy" and consultant to successive governments, Soffer became so obsessed with the details of Israel's demographic trench war with the Palestinians that his colleagues referred to him as "Arnon the Arab counter." Like Weisglass, he advocated Gaza disengagement for reasons that had nothing to do with conflict resolution. "Unilateral separation doesn't guarantee 'peace,'" Soffer said in 2004, referring to Sharon's proposal. "It guarantees a Jewish-Zionist state with an overwhelming majority of Jews."

Soffer presciently predicted that disengagement would lead to Hamas assuming power in Gaza, and that the unilateral separation could only be enforced through overwhelming violence against Gaza's civilians. "We will tell the Palestinians that if a single missile is fired over the fence, we will fire ten in response. And women and children will be killed and houses will be destroyed," he warned. Soffer went on to predict that "when 2.5 million people live in a closed off Gaza, it's going to be a human catastrophe. Those people will be even bigger animals than they are today, with the aid of an insane fundamentalist Islam. The pressure at the border will be awful. It's going to be a terrible war. So, if we want to remain alive, we will have to kill and kill and kill. All day, every day."

In January 2006, in an election in occupied Palestinian territories judged "free and fair" by the US Congressional Research Service, Hamas, the Islamist organization that earned support through religious charity and armed struggle, won 56 percent of seats in the Palestinian Legislative Council. Fatah, the rival to Hamas and original standard-bearer of Palestinian nationalism, joined Hamas in a unity government that existed in name only. The two factions never cooperated. In practice, Fatah rejected the results of the election while Hamas refused arrangements that required it to share power. After months of bitter skirmishes that left scores of Palestinians dead, the US arranged for massive shipments of arms to the Fatah-controlled Preventive Security Services it had been training. On June 10, Fatah's forces battled for control of Gaza with Hamas's Al-Qassam Brigades. Fatah was easily routed. Four days later, Fatah leader Mahmoud Abbas declared emergency rule in the West Bank, where his security services coordinated with the Israeli army, while Hamas assumed power in Gaza, where the Al-Qassam Brigades maintained a war footing against the occupation.

Israel promptly placed Gaza under siege, restricting access to its border crossings, enforcing severe curbs on its exports, and devising complex mathematical formulas to regulate the caloric intake of each resident. A January 2008 Israeli military study called "Food Consumption in the Gaza Strip—The Red Lines," estimated the required daily calorie intake in Gaza at 2,279 per person "in order to maintain the basic fabric of life."

Everything that has happened since the implementation of the Gaza disengagement has borne out the predictions of Weisglass and Soffer: The peace process has been frozen. The prospect of a viable Palestinian state has been shattered. The settlements have expanded and the occupation entrenched. Violent resistance in Gaza has intensified. And the Israeli public has taken a hard right turn, electing governing coalitions filled with zealots clamoring for a war to end all wars.

Beginning in December 2008, Israel launched a military assault on Gaza that left more than 1,400 dead over the course of three weeks, most of them civilians. Violence erupted again in November 2012 with a military escalation that saw more than 400 killed in Gaza—mostly civilians—while Palestinian rockets reached Tel Aviv for the first time. But even after that battle was over, two years later another one loomed on the horizon, the fulfillment of Soffer's bloody prophecy—"kill and kill and kill."

CHAPTER 1

Rogues

As the summer of 2014 began, life continued as normal in the Gaza Strip. Israeli Hermes 450 drones hovered overhead at night, lending a persistent buzzing sound to the coastal enclave's sonic ambiance. Fishermen ran into the teeth of the Israeli navy whenever they attempted to pursue a school of sardines further than three miles into the Mediterranean. Farmers and scavengers risked falling under a hail of bullets if they dared cross into the so-called "buffer zone" that extended three hundred meters from the concrete walls encircling Gaza. Permits to enter and leave Gaza were more rare than ever, prompting hundreds of college students in the fall of the previous year to storm the Rafah crossing on the Egyptian border to make good on their scholarships abroad. Unemployment rates hovered above 40 percent and anemia was frequent in children under the age of two as Gaza residents still reeled from four major Israeli assaults in five years. The siege had become the new normal.

However, it was not in Gaza, but in occupied East Jerusalem and the West Bank where Prime Minister Benjamin Netanyahu's strategy of peace without peace, or perpetual occupation management, would face the first major disruption that summer. Negotiations over the US-led framework for a two-state solution broke down in late April in part because Economics Minister Naftali Bennett of the religious nationalist Jewish Home party—a key junior partner in Netanyahu's governing coalition—threatened to bolt from the government of Prime Minister Benjamin Netanyahu if Netanyahu agreed to US demands to release a fourth batch of Palestinian prisoners. Netanyahu acceded to the radical right-wing pressure, authorizing the construction of hundreds of new settlement units to mollify his junior partners while flouting the demand to release prisoners. US negotiator and longtime pro-Israel lobbyist Martin Indyk regarded Netanyahu's actions as flagrant perfidy. He turned to Nahum Barnea, one of Israel's most influential columnists, to anonymously blame Netanyahu's government for destroying the negotiations. (Indyk later made his views public.) Within weeks, the US negotiating team had moved out of its luxury suites in Jerusalem while Fatah and Hamas formed a unity government for which Washington offered its qualified endorsement. Rebuked by the Americans and defied by the Palestinians, Netanyahu and his inner circle reacted with outrage.

Meanwhile, in Hebron, in the West Bank, a rogue Hamas cell decided to stage a kidnapping. The members likely hoped the operation would lead to the kind of prisoner swap Israel had just rejected in negotiations. Cell members Marwan Qawasmeh and Amer Abu Aysha had spent years in Israeli prisons, subjected to prolonged isolation. Each had lost family members in the armed struggle against the occupation, and both were prepared to kill and die to achieve their desperate goals.

On June 12, Qawasmeh and Abu Aysha set out in a stolen car from Hebron towards a busy crossroads in Gush Etzion in the occupied West Bank. Three hitchhikers, students at a nearby yeshiva, entered the car, apparently believing the driver was an Israeli Jew like them. Hours later, they would be pronounced missing by the Israeli police. In callous acts of bloodletting and cynical deception that followed, the stage was set for the 51 Day War.

Bound and Gagged

The plan quickly unraveled when one of the students, Gilad Shaar, was caught calling the Israeli police from his cell phone to report his abduction. Qawasmeh and Abu Aysha shot the teens to death almost immediately, then buried their bodies in a shallow grave on property Qawasmeh's relative, Hussam, had purchased adjacent to his family's home near Hebron.

Prime Minister Netanyahu and his National Security Council received news of the kidnapping in its immediate aftermath from the Shin Bet and police investigators. They huddled together and listened to the eerie phone call Shaar placed to police, in which the sound of gunshots and the kidnappers' celebratory singing was audible in the background. (One of the killers can be heard exclaiming, "We got three!") Then they examined evidence gathered from inside the burned remnants of the kidnappers' stolen car—blood, bullets, DNA. All signs pointed to a case of triple homicide. Yet instead of announcing that the teens had likely been killed, or releasing the names of the suspects, which by that point they had in hand, then ordering a police action to catch them, Netanyahu engaged in an ambitious act of deception that set the stage for full-scale war.

According to Bat-Galim Shaar, Gilad's mother, police investigators convinced her that her son was still alive, insisting that gunshots she heard in the recorded call he placed to police were actually blanks. She was not informed that blood and bullets were found throughout the vehicle.

"When [Israeli officials] told me finally at 6:00 a.m. Friday that the army was on the job, I felt better—as if we were in good hands," Bat-Galim Shaar told Israel's Channel 10. "I was naïve. I told everyone Gilad would be home before Shabbat."

Not only had Netanyahu and the investigators hidden key facts from the mothers of the teens, they concealed the details of the case from the entire Israeli public, setting themselves up for a catastrophic reaction when the truth was finally revealed. The Israeli military had imposed a gag order on the investigation, threatening journalists with legal repercussions if they reported a single detail of it. According to the text of the gag order, the military had forbidden Israeli reporters from publicizing "all the details of the investigation" and "all details that might identify the suspect."

London-based Arabic-language news site Rai Al Youm (which was not subject to the gag order) reported that Israeli police and Shin Bet agents had raided the homes of Qawasmeh and Abu Aysha, the main suspects, near the southern West Bank city of Hebron as early as June 17. But the Israeli media did not report this crucial piece of information, which might have altered Jewish Israeli society's understanding of the crime.

Hamas leadership had no knowledge of the kidnapping when it took place and played no role in its orchestration. The family of the ringleader, Qawasmeh, was well known for going rogue, acting in direct contravention of Hamas ceasefires with Israel over the years. Though Israeli police spokesman Mickey Rosenfeld later admitted to the BBC's Jon Donnison that the killers represented a "lone cell," Netanyahu was not about to allow the facts of the case interfere with what seemed like a prime political opportunity.

The Prime Minister's target was not the teens' killers, but the new Palestinian unity government.

#BringBackOurBoys

On June 17, the Israeli army forcibly confiscated security cameras from a shopkeeper in Beitunia that captured footage of its soldiers killing two unarmed Palestinian boys during a Nakba Day protest a month before. That same day, Israeli Permanent Representative to the United Nations Ron Prosor appeared behind a lectern at the UN Mission in New York City.

"It has been five days since our boys went missing," Prosor thundered, "and I ask the international community—where are you? Where are you?!"

Referring to the Fatah–Hamas unity government, Prosor added: "All those in the international community who rushed to bless this marriage should look into the eyes of the heartbroken parents and have the courage to take responsibility by condemning the kidnapping. The international community bought into a bad deal and Israel is paying for it."

Beside Prosor stood a large placard displaying the smiling faces of the three missing teens beneath a Twitter hashtag that read: #BringBackOurBoys. Israel's propaganda blitz was in full swing.

For days, leaders of Israel's trained online propaganda brigades, from the Israeli army spokesperson's unit to the Jewish Agency, located in the Prime Minister's Office, flooded social media with the #BringBackOurBoys hashtag. Mimicking Michelle Obama's promotion of the #BringBackOurGirls hashtag launched to raise awareness of the kidnapping of Nigerian schoolgirls by Islamist militants, pro-Israel social media networks disseminated an image of Netanyahu's wife,

Sara, frowning and bearing a placard that read, #BringBack OurBoys.

The social media campaign reverberated throughout Jewish communities across the US, as synagogues around the country displayed yellow ribbons in a coordinated show of solidarity with the missing teens. In New York City, local politicians appeared at pro-Israel rallies, while American diplomats from Secretary of State John Kerry to US Ambassador to the UN Samantha Power to National Security Advisor Susan Rice competed with one another to deliver the most emotional tribute to the kidnapped teens.

Rachel Frenkel, the mother of the kidnapped student Naftali Frenkel, was junketed by the Israeli government to the UN Human Rights Council in Geneva, Switzerland to plead for help from the international community in rescuing her son. She was sent abroad in spite of the fact that Netanyahu and his inner circle knew that the teens were almost certainly dead. All this was made possible by the Israeli military's gag order, which even foreign correspondents honored.

Brother's Keeper

With the public in a frenzy over the missing teens, the military had all the political latitude it needed to rampage through West Bank cities and towns starting on June 15, even if they were far from the scene of the crime. As far as the Israeli public knew, the kidnappers could have been anywhere in the West Bank, in any schoolhouse or coffee house or henhouse where anyone remotely affiliated with Hamas congregated. So began Operation "Brother's Keeper," with thousands of Israeli troops storming into private homes and making mass arrests.

The army claimed to be engaged in a rescue operation, a desperate hunt for the missing teens. In reality, it was targeting the organization that Netanyahu had held collectively responsible for the crime—Hamas—rounding up hundreds of its members including scores of those released under the 2011 prisoner swap for the captive soldier Gilad Shalit. (Khader Adnan and Samer Issawi, two prisoners who had earned hero status in Palestinian society for their successful hunger strikes, were among those re-arrested.) In the process, Israel closed off the entire area around Hebron, trapping some 680,000 people inside the military cordon.

During a raid of Birzeit University near Ramallah on June 19, Israeli troops seized hundreds of Hamas flags, carting them away in a truck as though they had obtained valuable evidence in the kidnapping case. A poll released on July 2 revealed that 76 percent of Jewish Israelis approved of the army's actions, and expressed overwhelming support for the Shin Bet's efforts to recover the teens.

As the raids in the West Bank continued with overt cooperation from Palestinian Authority security forces trained and armed by the US to suppress native resistance to occupation—journalist Allison Deger reported Israeli soldiers and PA security officers "working in armed conjunction to suppress Palestinian protesters" on June 22—Hamas leadership watched with consternation. Their political cadres were being herded into prison cells without criminal charges, and all they could do was watch. For them, Operation Brother's Keeper was an act of war.

All along, the bodies of the three murdered Israeli teens lay in a shallow grave on the Qawasmeh property outside Halhoul, just over fifteen kilometers from the site of the kidnapping. They lay there for eighteen days, somehow eluding the advanced monitoring capabilities of Israeli satellites, surveillance cameras, police investigators, and the vast informant network the Shin Bet operated in the West Bank. The longer the teens' bodies decayed, the more rapidly Israeli society lost its composure. A spontaneously created Facebook page demanded the execution of one Palestinian prisoner for each hour the teens remained missing, while another called "The People of Israel Demand Revenge" garnered more than 35,000 members, most of whom were young Israelis, in just a few days.

When, at 6:00 p.m. on June 20, a team of soldiers and civilian volunteers happened upon the hitchhikers' bodies, the bloodlust seething just below the surface of Israeli society exploded into the open.

CHAPTER 2

Human Animals

Polls of Jewish Israeli opinion taken after the discovery of the bodies of the three teens that summer showed Israeli Prime Minister Benjamin Netanyahu under mounting pressure. Economics Minister Naftali Bennett, a youthful and politically savvy tech industry millionaire who had almost singlehandedly brought the hardline Jewish Home Party out of the margins and into the mainstream, was gaining in the polls. For his part, Foreign Minister Avigdor Lieberman had begun drumming up a full reoccupation of the Gaza Strip, a scenario the military-intelligence establishment considered a recipe for disaster. Having already set the stage for the crisis by blocking the release of Palestinian prisoners, the two would remain a thorn in Netanyahu's right side throughout June and the days of early July leading up to the 51 Day War, provoking him relentlessly towards inflammatory rhetoric and escalated violence.

When Netanyahu issued his first official statement on the discovery of the teens' bodies on June 30, he betrayed how much the far-right agitators had aroused his latent radicalism.

In remarks delivered to an emergency cabinet meeting and re-layed to the world through Twitter, Netanyahu declared that the teens had been "abducted and murdered by human animals."

He continued with a clear call for tribal revenge: "Vengeance for the blood of a small child, Satan has not yet created. Nei-ther has vengeance for the blood of three pure youths, who were on their way home to meet their parents, who will not see them anymore. Hamas is responsible and Hamas will pay."

Netanyahu's comments perplexed outsiders, but for those embedded inside the tight confines of Jewish Israeli life, they carried a familiar resonance. His statement alluded to the final stanza of a poem by the Hebrew writer Chaim Bialik titled "On The Slaughter."

In Bialik's verse, a searing lament anchored in biblical lan-guage, the poet dramatizes a brutal 1903 pogrom incited by Russian officials that left scores of Jews dead in the town of Kishinev.

Bialik followed his first account of the Kishinev massacre with "The City of Slaughter," an incendiary poem admonishing the victims of the pogrom for their supposed passivity in the face of armed marauders. (Reports of fierce resistance by the Jews there were overlooked.) This second poem helped radicalize thousands of young Jews across Eastern Europe, inspiring the formation of self-defense committees and winning waves of adherents to the militant wing of Zionism. Among those most influenced by Bialik was Vladimir Jabotinsky, the right-wing Zionist activist who would later become the political mentor to the Prime Minister's father, Benzion Netanyahu, who served him as his secretary.

In Netanyahu's demagogic appropriation of Bialik's verse, the "human animals" of Palestine had inherited the genocidal spirit of the Tsar's mobs and would repeat their crimes unless Jews were prepared to fight to the finish. Having manipulated the public into believing the teens were alive, he now spurred them to blood vengeance because they were dead.

Within hours, mobs of Jewish youths filled the squares of central Jerusalem chanting "Death to Arabs!" and searching for Palestinians to assault. The "ultras" who comprised the hardcore fan base of Jerusalem's Beitar soccer club provided experienced muscle to the demonstrations. As active duty Israeli soldiers took to Facebook to demand revenge, posting photos of themselves with the weapons they said they were aching to use, political upstarts rushed to issue calls for the "annihilation" of Hamas.

Ayelet Shaked, the telegenic, thirty-eight-year-old politician and poster girl of the right-wing Jewish Home party, earned thousands of Facebook "likes" from mostly young Israelis when she declared that Palestinians are "all enemy combatants" including "the mothers of the martyrs, who send them to hell with flowers and kisses. They should follow their sons, nothing would be more just," Shaked continued. "They should go, as should the physical homes in which they raised the snakes. Otherwise, more little snakes will be raised there." Though more restrained than Shaked, the grand old man of Israel's so-called "peace camp" and then the ninety-year-old President of Israel, Shimon Peres, used the funeral of the three teens as a platform to call for the Israeli army to "act with a heavy hand until terror is uprooted." Joining Peres on the dais was Netanyahu, who bellowed, "A broad moral gulf [that] separates us from our enemies. They sanctify death. We sanctify life. They sanctify cruelty. We sanctify compassion."

Rabbi Noam Perel, the secretary-general of World Bnei Akiva, the world's largest religious Zionist youth movement, upped the ante when he called for turning the Israeli military into an army of avengers "that will not stop at 300 Philistine foreskins." (Akiva's appeal alludes to the first book of Samuel, in which the biblical character David kills two hundred Philistines and brings back their foreskins as evidence that he had done so.)

As ultra-nationalist mobs gathered in cities across Israel, a small car entered the back streets of Shuafat, a Palestinian neighborhood in East Jerusalem. Behind its darkened windows rode three young men. They were on the hunt for Arab boys.

The Wrong Family

The stately stone homes of Shuafat line a four-lane boulevard that serves as the main artery between major bloc settlements like Pisgat Ze'ev and central Jerusalem. The steel tracks of Jerusalem's light rail system bisect the road, shepherding thousands of settlers through the Palestinian neighborhood each day, along with the private security guards hired to protect them. Shuafat's light rail stop bristles with security cameras installed by the Jerusalem municipality, another reminder of the endless occupation. To ease settlers' path through the neighborhood, the municipality has begun to build a new access road that slices directly through the olive groves lining the hillsides of Shuafat. Among the neighbors, there is talk that the road represents the first step towards the seizure of their land and perhaps their expulsion as well.

On a corner of Shuafat's main road, across a narrow lane from the local mosque, is the home of the Abu Khdeir family. Muhammad Abu Khdeir, a rail thin sixteen-year-old student at the Amal high school, wandered from inside his home and perched himself on a stone wall facing the road through the olive groves. It was early in the morning on July 2, just hours after the conclusion of the three Israeli teens' funeral. Three young men approached Abu Khdeir to ask for directions. As soon as he was within reach, they grabbed him and threw him in their car, then sped away. A group of locals attempted to give chase but failed to reach the vehicle or summon help quickly enough to stop it. Later that day, Abu Khdeir's charred body was found in the woods near Givat Shaul. He had been bludgeoned unconscious, doused with gasoline, and burned alive.

The crime contained all the signs of a Jewish nationalist revenge killing. Still, members of the Israeli media proceeded to insinuate otherwise, printing slanderous disinformation possibly leaked by the Israeli police that suggested Abu Khdeir was the victim of an honor crime—killed by a member of his own family for supposed homosexual activity. According to several members of the Abu Khdeir family I interviewed, Israeli police threatened to "ruin the lives" of the young men who attempted to chase down the killers' car, then sought interrogation sessions with members of Abu Khdeir's immediate family. While Netanyahu expressed shame over the murder, it was too late to contain the violence he had helped to incite.

The ringleader of Abu Khdeir's three killers, a thirty-year-old resident of the nearby Jewish settlement of Adam named Yosef Chaim Ben-David, had been arrested along with five other suspects on July 6, yet his name and the details of the crime he had confessed to remained concealed behind a gag order for eleven days. It was only on July 17 that the public received confirmation of the killers' motives, learning that they had been been riled to action after the anti-Arab revenge rallies that spilled out into the streets of Jerusalem when the teens' bodies were discovered; and that they had vandalized twenty cars in nearby Beit Hanina and attempted to kidnap a nine-year-old Palestinian boy before abducting Abu Khdeir. When Ben-David appeared in the courtroom for his arraignment, he was flanked by lawyers from Honenu, a radical settler outfit notorious for defending Jewish terror suspects. "I am the Messiah!" he bellowed, reinforcing the insanity plea his defense team had filed. (At the time of writing, no verdict has been issued in the case.)

Once again, the Israeli government's manipulations had accelerated the chaos. By the time Ben-David was finally brought to court, rioting had exploded in Shuafat, leaving the light rail station that served as a conduit for settlers in ruins. At Muhammad Abu Khdeir's funeral, a few weeks before the arraignment, gunshots rang out from rooftops as mourners chanted, "Intifada! Intifada!"

From then on, a nightly police detail would occupy the sidewalk outside the Abu Khdeir family's home. Among the twenty-five members of the extended family thrown in jail since the chaos began was Tariq Abu Khdeir, a fifteen-year-old Palestinian-American teen badly beaten by Israeli police. Tariq Abu Khdeir's case earned widespread attention when his neighbors in Shuafat provided media outlets with security camera footage they had recorded of the beating. The storm of press and international coverage prompted the US Department of State to intervene, eventually spurring Tariq Abu Khdeir's release on July 6. Days later, beneath the cover of darkness, Israeli police ransacked his cousins' home in Shuafat—an apparent act of revenge for publicizing the security camera video.

The authorities seemed determined to punish the pesky Abu Khdeir family at all costs.

In the Tent

That August, a month after Muhammad's murder, I spent a day with members of Abu Khdeir's family outside their stately stone home in Shuafat. We sat on plastic chairs beneath a tarp just a few feet from the ledge where the teen was kidnapped, and directly beside the family's mourning tent. Outside the home was a giant poster of a vulnerable-looking Muhammad that city authorities would later compel the family to remove. It was here that the family received a stream of visitors, from Palestinian dignitaries to random Jews from around the world, venturing to their home to express shame and sorrow for the murder of their son.

The Abu Khdeir family spans the Palestinian diaspora, with relatives across the United States, and in Venezuela and Bolivia, as well as around the Middle East. All of them are descendants of the same patriarch—they are his great, great grandchildren.

My American journalist colleague, Dan Cohen, had befriended Thawra Abu Khdeir, a college undergrad from Georgia who was spending the summer with her family in Shuafat. For his part, Dan was just starting out as a reporter for outlets like Vice and Mondoweiss. He had grown up in a conservative Jewish community in suburban Phoenix, Arizona and taken his first trip to Israel for his Bar Mitzvah. After returning to Israel on the Taglit-Birthright trip, a free vacation for college-aged diaspora Jews, he began to question the pro-Israel indoctrination that seemed to be *de rigeur* for Jews of his generation. His disaffection soon developed into a curiosity about the situation of Palestinians—the faceless people he had always heard described as either terrorists or a demographic threat. At age twenty-eight, he quit his job as a rope access repair technician on New York City buildings and industrial sites and bought a ticket to Israel-Palestine. Within a matter of months, he was making contacts across occupied Palestine while learning how to write breaking stories and edit video.

Thanks to Dan's friendship with Thawra, we were able to gain entry to the home of a family that felt deceived and smeared by the Israeli press, and which had sunk into a bunker mentality as a result. It also helped that Muhammad Abu Khdeir's twenty-eight-year-old cousin, a longtime resident of California who was also named Muhammad, recognized me from my articles and video documentaries.

While over time the Abu Khdeir family had grown wary of media, at that point it had formally rejected only one visitor: Shimon Peres, the then-President who had attempted to pay a condolence visit. (Even before Peres arrived at the tent, the Abu Khdeir family turned his security detail away.) Portrayed in the international media as one of Israel's last "doves" and presented by President Barack Obama with the Presidential Medal of Freedom, Peres is reviled across the Arab world for presiding over the 1996 massacre in Qana, Lebanon and assorted Israeli assassination campaigns in the Occupied Territories during the mid-1990s. When Peres arrived at the family's mourning tent, he was swiftly turned away. "We didn't want him," Muhammad Abu Khdeir's sixty-two-year-old father, Hussein, told me. "Peres says he's a man of peace but he's always making war. He doesn't really want peace."

The family was unable to dispatch the Labor Party stalwart and former army major Amir Peretz when he arrived at their mourning tent unannounced. "When Peretz came, he barged in without advance notice, surrounded by bodyguards," twenty-eight-year-old Muhammad Abu Khdeir, recalled. "We saw him sitting down next to Hussein [Abu Khdeir] out of nowhere. If it was a normal Israeli citizen, then fine, but this guy was in the government and supports the killing of Palestinians. So he wasn't very welcome. He took a couple pictures and then he left. He just wanted to show that he was here." For Peretz, the meeting had serious consequences, as he was bombarded with death threats and hate mail by right-wing Israeli Jews.

Like many of their neighbors in Shuafat, the Abu Khdeir family was no stranger to discrimination. After spending years of savings he had set aside as an electrician to expand his property on land he owned, Hussein Abu Khdeir told me he was fined 100,000 shekels (about $40,000) by a municipal court, ostensibly for building without a permit. Unfortunately for Palestinians in East Jerusalem, obtaining a permit from the municipal government is next to impossible, forcing them to build under circumstances the authorities consider illegal. In many cases, their homes are demolished as punishment. "I'm not allowed to build on my own land just because it's not included in their plan," he remarked. "If it was a Jew who did what I did it would have been maybe a 3,000 [shekel] fine." Hussein said that the land behind his home had been expropriated by the city to build a public school, and that the city had begun uprooting the family's orchards in order to build new access roads for settlers living on land taken from their neighbors. "Forty percent of my family's land is going to be taken just to build settlers a short cut!" twenty-eight-year-old Muhammad exclaimed.

Near the grave of Muhammad Abu Khdeir was that of another murdered family member. In 2009, a Jewish Israeli murdered Amjad Abu Khdeir in a random racist attack. According to family members, the killer was also allowed to file an insanity plea that let him off with the lightest possible sentence. "It's not just our family that's at risk. Every family here in the occupied areas has lost someone," Hussein Abu Khdeir said.

Just days before I met the Abu Khdeirs, two of their friends from nearby Beit Hanina, twenty-year-olds Amir Shweiki and Samer Mahfouz, were beaten by a mob of pipe and baseball bat–wielding settlers in central Jerusalem. Ten young Jewish nationalists were said to have beaten the young men nearly to death, but none have been sentenced at the time of this writing. "Everyone's scared to let their kids out because at any moment a settler can take your kids and just keep going," Thawra Abu Khdeir said.

Among the young men I spoke to in the neighborhood, particularly within Muhammad Abu Khdeir's teenage clique, the fear of entering Jewish areas of Jerusalem was universal. And in the neighborhood, the teens made a point of traveling in groups to avoid abductions. Whatever segregation the Israeli-run local government had failed to establish in the supposedly "united" Jerusalem, gangs of vigilante Jewish nationalists were enforcing. The regime of separation was radicalizing an entire generation and deepening a crisis for which the government seemed to have no solution.

The Other

Seated under the tarp with us was a young white American woman who had just enrolled in Islamic Studies at Hebrew University. She wore a keffiyeh around her neck, spoke with unrestrained resentment about the "jaysh" (a Palestinian Arabic term for the Israeli army) and identified as a member of the Abu Khdeir family. Yet she was a Mormon from Salt Lake City, Utah named Alyssa. I was confused. How in the world had she wound up here, in the midst of this roiling cauldron?

Like many Mormons, Alyssa had taken an interest in her genealogy. Through a DNA test she learned that she was related to an Arab-American family in Washington D.C. After contacting them, she learned that her great-grandfather was a Palestinian immigrant named Abu Khdeir who had married a white Christian woman in the 1930s. The couple was forced to give up their son for adoption to a Mormon family in Salt Lake City under harsh pressure from the wife's racist family.

Learning about her Palestinian roots prompted Alyssa to study Arabic, plunge into Islamic Studies, and make contact with her extended family to "bring some closure," as she explained. Before long, Alyssa was on a flight to Jerusalem with her cousin, Thawra, from Georgia. On her way to spend the

summer with their family in Shuafat, Alyssa had no idea what she was in for when she landed at Ben Gurion International Airport.

As soon as Alyssa arrived with her veiled Palestinian cousin, she was taken aside by airport security and seated in what Palestinians call "the Arab room."

"I grew up white and middle class in America," Alyssa reflected. "I'm privileged over there and other than the fact that I'm a woman, I have a full deck of cards. I come here and all of the sudden, I'm the other. My cousin's a hijabi and when they see her they take me aside at the airport and detain me for five hours and feel me up while I'm topless. Why? As the airport person said, 'To find the Muslim connection.'"

Alyssa emerged from her airport nightmare to experience the daily discrimination that pervades life in Shuafat. "When I'm with her," she said, pointing to Thawra, "the soldiers will be calling her profanities and beating her up and then in the next breath, they turn to me and ask me about my emotional well-being. Then when I tell them I'm her cousin I suddenly become the wrong race."

It has been a deeply radicalizing experience for Alyssa, and unlike most of the youth who grew up under the regime of discrimination she has another frame of reference. "It's really hard coming here," she said as tears welled up in her hazel eyes. "I find myself crying here and it's frustrating because there's nothing I can do. Gaza's sixty miles away and there isn't a damn thing I can do about it."

An hour after my first visit with Abu Khdeir's parents, I received a call from members of the family informing me that police had burst onto the property to arrest a nineteen-year-old cousin of theirs on the grounds that he had participated in illegal demonstrations.

Over the Cliff

The killing of Abu Khdeir and the subsequent rebellion in East Jerusalem was a trigger point in the events leading up to war in Gaza. On July 6, two days after Abu Khdeir's funeral, armed factions in the Gaza Strip launched a heavy barrage of rockets into southern Israel. Though rockets had battered southern Israel from Gaza for days, Hamas took no credit for the attacks up until this point. When Israel responded with airstrikes that killed seven Hamas members the following day, Hamas finally took credit for a rocket salvo into southern Israel. On July 8, the Izz Ad-Din Al-Qassam Brigades—Hamas's military wing—launched long-range M-75 rockets toward Jerusalem and Tel Aviv.

As Shuafat residents poured out of their homes at the sound of rocket warning sirens, cheers erupted and cries of "Allahu Akhbar!" erupted from the streets. Allison Deger, a correspondent from Mondoweiss, was at the Abu Khdeirs' home at the time. Outside the house, she told me she watched a young woman squeeze the hand of another as they watched the bright glow of an M-75 sail overhead.

"That rocket's for Muhammad," the woman said, staring at the sky with astonishment.

The Israeli Army had been planning a major ground and aerial assault against the Gaza Strip since late 2013. On December 31 of that year, Defense Minister Moshe Ya'alon had announced: "The operation that the [Israeli Army] would be required to undertake would have to deal a harsh blow to Gaza and to the organizations operating there, in a way that would damage their capabilities and exact a heavy toll." On July 8, Netanyahu gathered his entire cabinet to announce the beginning of Operation Protective Edge. The operation's Hebrew name, Miv'tza Tzuk Eitan translates literally to English as "Strong Cliff."

CHAPTER 3

The Resistance

By July 16, after eight days of relentless aerial bombardment of the Gaza Strip, and on day 9 of the 51 Day War, the Palestinian death toll stood around 200. Among the dead were eight members of the Kaware family, who were killed in the southern city of Khan Yunis by a guided Israeli missile. They had reentered their home after momentarily evacuating, only to have the house collapse on their bodies. The Israeli military initially claimed the bombing was a mistake, yet they ultimately justified it on the basis of the family's alleged affiliation with Hamas. Another Israeli missile struck the beachside Fun Time Beach Cafe south of the city, where nine young men—who had gathered during an electricity outage in Khan Younis to watch the World Cup—were blasted to pieces. "And the result from this match here? The Jews won 9–0," one of the survivors, Ahmad al-Aqad, remarked to Agence France Press afterwards.

On July 16, Israeli naval gunboats lobbed a shell towards a group of young boys playing on the beach. Journalists assembled at the Al-Deira hotel restaurant watched in astonishment from two hundred meters away. As the boys ran from the explosion for the safety of the hotel, they waved for help from the journalists. The Israeli gunners readjusted their sights to lob another shell at the boys, all members of the Fatah-aligned Bakr family that earned its keep in Gaza's fishing industry. "They are only children!" a group of reporters shouted. "In the space of forty seconds, four boys who had been playing hide-and-seek among fishermen's shacks on the wall were dead," wrote Peter Beaumont, a correspondent for the *Guardian* who witnessed the incident. Footage of the shelling captured by the dozens of photographers and camera people on the scene made it one of the war's iconic moments, transforming the four Bakr boys and their failed flight to safety into a symbol of young lives cut short by Israeli violence.

To date, one Israeli had died in the rocket salvos launched by the Izz Ad-Din Al-Qassam Brigades, the guerrilla group that functioned as the military arm of Hamas. The Al-Qassam Brigades operated cells within the West Bank and in Jerusalem, where affiliates could be activated at a moment's notice to carry out deadly attacks on Israeli civilian targets. But the organization's strategy had changed since it fell under the control of a new breed of leaders intent on developing its military capacity to compete in the field with the best of Israel's special forces. The bus bombings and random shootings of the past were no longer a priority. Al-Qassam now focused its most lethal force on military targets, aiming to humiliate Israel's ground forces in face-to-face confrontations.

The Al-Qassam Brigades drew its ideological inspiration from the days of the Arab Revolt of 1936–39 in the British Mandate for Palestine, naming itself after Izz ad-Din al-Qassam. Al-Qassam was a militant Islamic preacher and veteran of anti-colonial agitation in Libya and Syria, and was based in

Haifa in northern Palestine. There he served as a functionary in the local *shariah* court and helped lead the Young Men's Muslim Association, offering him direct access to the masses of dispossessed peasants pouring into the city. Many of the impoverished farmers had been run off the land they rented from absentee landlords by the Jewish National Fund. So Al-Qassam found no shortage of eager recruits among them for the Black Hand cells he organized to carry out armed attacks on British and Zionist targets. Killed in a dramatic shoot-out with British forces in 1935, where he was said to have exhorted his men to fight to the last bullet and accept their martyrdom with zeal, Al-Qassam became a symbol of defiance for Islamist and secular Palestinians alike. For Hamas, his legacy represented the cultivation of grassroots support through a blend of social welfare programs, religious ardor, and anti-colonial resistance.

Al-Qassam began organizing its original nucleus of fighters in the mid-1980s, recruiting on university campuses and cultivating young members in the growing network of Hamas-affiliated mosques. It drew its most enthusiastic cadres from impoverished youth orphaned or otherwise scarred by Israeli violence, promising them a chance at retribution and an honored place in society. By 1991, Al-Qassam Brigades had just a single rifle, a 1960s-era 9mm Carl Gustav M45 submachine gun that barely functioned—bullets fell from its barrel to the ground once the weapon heated up. Without the capacity to confront Israeli soldiers directly or to attack the settlements in Northern Gaza, most Al-Qassam attacks were aimed at collaborators, the Palestinians who had been compromised or induced into spying on fellow Palestinians. As Al-Qassam's offensive capacity progressed with the development of homemade rockets and the ability to shell settlements with mortars, those collaborators enabled Israel's Shin Bet intelligence service to pick off its leaders, one by one.

Imad Aqel, an early commander of the Al-Qassam Brigades' original cell, spent two years as a fugitive after an audacious and lethal attack in 1992 on Israeli settlers in Hebron. After slipping back into Gaza from the West Bank disguised as a Jewish settler, he hid out in a tunnel under his home before a collaborator gave up his location, leading to his death at age twenty-two. Aqel's successor, Yahya Ayyash, was an explosives expert known as "The Engineer" who was also a master of disguise—he attended the funeral of a comrade dressed as a woman. When the American-born Jewish fanatic Baruch Goldstein massacred twenty-nine Palestinian worshippers at the Ibrahimi Mosque in Hebron, on February 25, 1994, Ayyash stepped up Al-Qassam's campaign of revenge, initiating a wave of suicide bombings that tormented Israeli society. After a frenzied search by the Shin Bet, Israel's intelligence services finally caught up with the elusive Engineer in 1996. He was killed at a safe house when one of his best friends passed him a mobile phone that turned out to be packed with explosives by a collaborator—his friend's uncle. The charge was detonated by an Apache helicopter hovering in the area. Ayyash was succeeded by Salah Shehadeh, a skilled guerrilla organizer who died in 2002 when an Israeli F-16 dropped a 2,000-pound bomb on the apartment compound where his family resided, killing him and fourteen others, including seven children. As in the past, a collaborator had given up Shehadeh's location.

Both Ayyash and Shehadeh's assassinations occurred during periods of truce between Hamas and Israel, and led to severe interruptions of the peace process. For two months, Ayyash had abided by an agreement to cease attacks on Israeli targets when then-Prime Minister Shimon Peres—a figure widely identified with Israel's so-called "peace camp"—authorized his killing. "The act disillusioned many moderate Hamas members in the territories who were willing to give the peace a chance," international relations professor Alon Ben-Meir wrote at the time. "It has embarrassed the Palestinian Authority and undermined Chairman Yasser Arafat's credibility." During the height of the Second Intifada six years later, Israel made the decision to kill Shehadeh as Palestinian factions introduced a proposal for a unilateral ceasefire aimed at returning to negotiations. The killing reinforced the perception among Hamas's political leadership that negotiations with Israel were fruitless.

It was under the leadership of Mohammed al-Deif, who took over after Shehadeh's assassination in 2002, that the Al-Qassam Brigades began to transition away from the kind of suicide operations on civilian targets overseen by Ayyash. Deif took extreme measures to cover his life in a veil of secrecy. He did not use a cellphone, preferring instead to relay verbal messages through a handful of close associates. He never appeared in public, not even to attend his own mother's funeral. Born as Mohammed Diab Ibrahim al-Masri, he was nicknamed Deif, or "guest" in Arabic, because he was constantly on the run from Israeli assassination plots, making him a perpetual guest in homes across Gaza.

Israeli intelligence was at least as obsessed with eliminating Deif as it was with his forerunners, attempting to kill him at least five times. The closest it came to assassinating Deif before Operation Protective Edge was in 2002, when an Apache helicopter found him driving through the Sheikh Radwan neighborhood of Gaza City. Deif's driver was killed but Deif managed to emerge from the burning wreck. The cumulative attempts on Deif's life have left him blind in one eye and partly immobilized, only able to walk for short distances.

When Deif escaped to Egypt to receive medical care for his injuries, his role was filled by another veteran Hamas cadre named Ahmad Jaabari. Jaabari had proven indispensable in Deif's absence, continuing the transformation of Al-Qassam into a professional guerrilla force along the same lines as Hezbollah, a goal he shared with Deif. Jaabari masterminded the daring tunnel operation that brought the Israeli soldier Gilad Shalit into captivity on June 25, 2006, prompting the deal five years later with Israel that led to the release of more than 1,000 Palestinian prisoners. The swap was arguably the most substantial concession any Palestinian faction had extracted from Israel since the Camp David negotiations collapsed in 2000. Despite his widely reported role in negotiating several ceasefire agreements and in overseeing the safe release of Shalit, Jaabari wound up at the top of the Shin Bet's target bank. During the November 2012 military escalation in Gaza known as Operation Pillar of Defense, a military stalemate that saw Israel attack Gaza exclusively by air, Israel assassinated Jaabari in a targeted airstrike. Deif, who had returned to Gaza through a tunnel from Egypt, was now in full command of Al-Qassam—and at the top of the Shin Bet's hit list.

Thanks to the ingenuity of Deif's late comrade, Adnan al-Ghoul, Al-Qassam was able to initiate the local production of the short-range rockets and the Yasin RPG-7 rocket launcher that remains at the forefront of the organization's arsenal. (Al-Ghoul was assassinated by the Israeli military in 2004.) Under al-Ghoul's watch, Al-Qassam even began exploring plans to develop weaponized drones, an effort that was finally realized during Operation Protective Edge when the group flew its first drone over Israeli territory. By 2012, Al-Qassam boasted that locally made long-range rockets like the M-75 and R-160 could reach centrally located Israeli cities. During the military escalation that took place in Gaza that year, rockets struck Tel Aviv, marking the first missile attack on the city in twenty years.

Though the rockets did little structural damage, they shook the psyche of Israeli society and fostered a sense of redress to Palestinians withstanding the brunt of the Middle East's most powerful military. During the 2012 escalation, a fast-paced pop song with a taunting tone thumped from shops and cars from Ramallah to Gaza City. Conceived by a popular wedding singer from the West Bank, Qasem El-Najjar, the song was called "Bomb, Bomb, Tel Aviv."

Psy-ops

Songs like these were almost as useful to Al-Qassam as its arsenal of long-range rockets. As long as Israel remained the favored client of the West, Palestinian armed factions had little chance of defeating its military in a head-to-head confrontation. Through psychological warfare, however, it could at least disrupt Israel's sense of inviolability and the control it enjoyed over daily Palestinian life. Catchy pop songs trumpeting armed resistance to occupation proliferated as the assaults on Gaza increased. When the 51 Day War began, a new resistance anthem called "Zalzil Amna Israel," or "Shake the peace of Israel," exploded in popularity across Palestine. It was promptly re-recorded in native level Hebrew to ensure that its mocking lyrics entered the Israeli consciousness:

Indeed, they are weak and doubtful
with no spirit to fight
They are like the spider web
When facing strong people
Shake the peace of Israel
Burn down that state with fire

During the war, few songs resonated with the youthful masses of Gaza as much as "Here, We Prepare," a macho battle anthem delivered over a driving, hip-hop inspired beat. It was sung by Ramzi al-'Ak, a former prisoner in Israeli jails who hailed from the Deheisha Refugee Camp in the West Bank and was deported to Gaza in the swap that led to Gilad Shalit's release. Performed with a band of fellow ex-prisoners who had also been deported to Gaza after the Shalit deal and indefinitely confined there, the *basso profundo* al-'Ak lionized the fighters who confronted Israeli forces in the border areas of Gaza:

> *Here! We've prepared for you*
> *Here! We've returned for revenge*
> *Here! There are resisting men on the borderlines*
> *Here! There are men in the tunnels, hiding out*
> *Come forward and wait for your grave*
> *You'll see us torment you*
> *Here! Here! Gaza defeated you*

As the 51 Day War took hold and leaders of Hamas's political wing disappeared into shelters and safe houses, a charismatic figure known as Abu Obeida was left as the voice and masked face of Gaza's guerrilla operations. Obeida was the main channel of psychological warfare against Israeli society and became one of the most identifiable symbols of Palestinian armed resistance, inspiring a popular song that proclaimed, "Oh Obeida, your words are gunpowder!" As the spokesman for Al-Qassam, he was a ubiquitous figure during the war, launching verbal broadsides at the Israeli military during regular press conferences and appearances on the Hamas-controlled Al-Aqsa TV, which were regularly translated and relayed to the Israeli public through Israel's Hebrew language media. In a 2009 interview with a British reporter, one of his few engagements with Western media (Al-Qassam generally spurned the Western press during wartime for security concerns), Obeida demonstrated a keen ability to cater to his audience. When he discussed Hamas's political goals, for instance, he did so in terms of rights guaranteed under international law and referred to Palestinians as a whole: "They're not...asking to invade or ethnically cleanse another people; they're not asking to commit a holocaust against another nation. They just want their rights," Obeida declared in near-native English.

In the interview, Obeida denied any intention of imposing Islamic law on Israeli Jews, referring to a future regime of "co-existence between Jews and Palestinians," and insisting that Al-Qassam intended to target members of the Israeli military and armed settlers: "We are fully committed to keeping civilians on both sides out of the conflict," Obeida said. "Civilian loss, whether on this side or that side, is something that is not good and is not something that one can be happy about. But the picture has to be viewed wholly and not from one small angle."

Despite Obeida's prolific image, little was known about the masked man Palestinians had taken to calling "The Ghost." Nicknamed after Abu Obeida al-Jarrah, a companion of Prophet Muhammad, he was a PhD student at Islamic University who had earned his master's degree in comparative religion, according to the London-based *Alsharq Al-Awsat* newspaper. When Israel's intelligence agency, Mossad, briefly hacked the Hamas-controlled Al-Aqsa TV Channel in July, it broadcast what it believed to be the face and real name of Obeida: Hozaifa Samir Abdullah al-Kahlout. (Al-Qassam never confirmed the veracity of the claim.)

When, on July 17, Israeli Minister of Defense Moshe Ya'alon announced the launch of the ground invasion in Gaza, Obeida took to the airwaves with a bloodcurdling statement: "Are you threatening us with what we expect you to do, you son of a

Jewess?" he railed at Ya'alon, breaking from his usual protocol of referring to Israeli Jews as "Zionists." "The bodies of your soldiers will litter the streets of Gaza and the children of Palestine will step on your skulls."

A dramatic clash was on the way that would test the advancement of Al-Qassam against an Israeli army willing to act without restraint. But the violence might have been avoided had the US and the Egyptian regime been willing to entertain Hamas's ceasefire demands.

The Road to the Status Quo Runs Through Cairo

On July 16, the day before Israel announced its ground invasion of Gaza, Hamas and the Palestinian political faction known as Islamic Jihad released a list of demands for a ten-year truce, outlining details of their cause. The demands were entirely humanitarian in nature, relating to the lifting of the Israeli and Egyptian siege. Most notably, the factions called for international forces to guard Palestinians in Gaza from Israeli violence along the border areas. The demands were as follows:

- *Withdrawal of Israeli tanks from the Gaza border.*
- *Freeing all the prisoners arrested after the killing of the three youths.*
- *Lifting of the siege and opening the border crossings to commerce and people.*
- *Establishing an international seaport and airport, which would be under U.N. supervision.*
- *Increasing the permitted fishing zone to ten kilometers.*
- *Internationalizing the Rafah Crossing [administered by the Egyptian regime] and placing it under the supervision of the U.N. and some Arab nations.*

- *Placement of international forces on the borders.*
- *Easing conditions for permits to pray at the Al Aqsa Mosque.*
- *Prohibition of Israeli interference in the reconciliation agreement [with Fatah].*
- *Reestablishment of an industrial zone and improvements in further economic development in the Gaza Strip.*

Days later, US Secretary of State John Kerry thrust himself into negotiations led by the regime of Egyptian President Abdel Fattah El-Sisi. Sisi was the military strongman who had led a bloody coup against the democratically elected, Muslim Brotherhood–affiliated President Mohammad Morsi, and had only recently "won" an election widely considered by international observers as undemocratic. While Sisi's regime jailed Muslim Brotherhood supporters by the thousands either summarily or after convictions in kangaroo courts, it incited against Palestinian refugees from Gaza, scapegoating them, and by extension, Hamas, for the instability that gripped the country after the coup. Indeed, the Egyptian junta made little distinction between the Brotherhood and Hamas, aiming to put both out of business through all means available to it.

When Sisi seized power in July 2013, he initiated close co-ordination with the Israeli military to tighten the siege on Gaza, prompting the Israel lobby in Washington to pressure Congress not to cut off arms shipments to his regime. So zealous was Sisi in enforcing the siege that Israeli military administrators began to worry about overkill. "They actually were suffocating Gaza too much," an Israeli official told the *Wall Street Journal*.

Throughout the 51 Day War, Cairo served as the site of negotiations between the Palestinian factions and representatives of Prime Minister Benjamin Netanyahu's inner circle over the cessation of hostilities. At every stage of the wrangling, Sisi and the Egyptian junta reinforced and even hardened Israel's position, demanding that the Hamas governors of Gaza accept an immediate ceasefire without any preconditions or guarantees of relief from the siege, while refusing to push Israel to halt its assassinations of Hamas leadership. Palestinian Authority President Mahmoud Abbas did little to counter the Egyptian position, and seemed convinced that undermining Hamas could bring his Fatah-controlled PA the foothold it could not find in Gaza through popular election. Behind the main parties were the US, EU, the Saudis and the United Arab Emirates, the funders of Sisi's regime and guarantors of his legitimacy. Together, these forces contrived to produce a deal that sent Gaza back into the suffocating grip of siege.

When presented with the Hamas/Islamic Jihad proposal for an extended truce, Sisi and Kerry produced a document of their own that offered residents of the Gaza Strip a temporary cessation of hostilities without any of the humanitarian concessions Hamas demanded.

"Hamas has a fundamental choice to make, and it is a choice that will have a profound impact for the people of Gaza," Kerry declared. Kerry's proposal did not really present a choice; rather, it offered the option of returning to the status quo of siege and occupation, or facing the full brunt of the Israeli military.

Soon after Israel and its international allies abruptly dismissed Hamas's demands, Israeli armored personnel carriers from the Golani Brigade rumbled towards Shujaiya, a population center located just east of Gaza City. Awaiting them were teams of fighters huddled in tunnels and poised for a defensive guerrilla battle on friendly terrain.

CHAPTER 4

The Battle of Shujaiya

On July 8, Al-Qassam offered a preview of the tactics it had cultivated under Jaabari and Deif's leadership. A frogman team swam from Gaza to the Israeli naval base at Zikim and then attempted to storm the outpost from the sea. Though all members of the raiding team were killed, the Israeli army covered up details of the incident, which were later revealed in leaked internal army video showing that one member of the unit was able to plant an explosive device on a passing Israeli bulldozer, though the explosive charge caused no injuries. The fear of infiltrations from Gaza and sustained mortar and rocket fire prompted thousands of residents of southern kibbutzim to evacuate in fear. "The kibbutz members said that as far as they are concerned, it is Hamas that is in control of the agenda and not Israel, and that situation does not allow routine life to continue," Haaretz reported.

Four days later, an Al-Qassam unit managed to intercept a late night landing by Israeli naval commandos at Sudaniya, a beachside city in northern Gaza. According to accounts from Hamas-related media, Al-Qassam fighters pinned down the commandos, forcing them to call in covering fire from navy ships and Apache helicopters as they withdrew. The Israeli military claimed that four of its soldiers had only been "lightly wounded" before being evacuated to Israeli hospitals.

When the Israelis poured ground troops into Shujaiya on July 20, the Israeli army Spokesperson's Unit published a series of online graphics asserting that its forces were aiming to eliminate a vast "terror fortress." The Spokesperson's Unit claimed that Hamas had commanded Shujaiya residents to ignore orders to evacuate, and therefore "ordered them directly in the line of fire." It appeared that the Israeli military's public relations arm was preparing for the fallout from the staggering amount of civilian casualties its combat units might be causing.

As Israeli soldiers took up positions in Shujaiya early that Sunday morning, Al-Qassam fighters in full battle dress uniform and balaclavas were stationed in tunnels in small teams. They were supplemented by fighters from an array of factions, of whom the Palestinian Islamic Jihad's Al Quds Brigades were most numerous and well armed thanks to help from their Iranian sponsors. Back in October 1988, when Hamas was still in quietist mode and avoiding direct confrontations with the Israeli occupation, an Al Quds unit staged a headlong attack on the Israeli military in Shujaiya, killing ten soldiers in a ferocious clash that became known as "The Battle of Shujaiya." With Israeli soldiers back in the Gaza City suburb twenty-six years later, Islamic Jihad's Al Quds Brigades were back on the front lines, but this time as a supplement to the better armed Al-Qassam, and alongside smaller factions like the Fatah-affiliated Al Aqsa Martyrs Brigade and Popular Resistance Committees, as well as the Abu Ali Mustafa Brigade of the leftist Popular Front for the Liberation of Palestine. On July 19, 2014, the Second Battle of Shujaiya began.

Dan Cohen in Shujaiya
after the Israeli Army
destroyed it.

The battle began after Israeli troops had situated themselves in the densely populated neighborhoods. Teams had
waited patiently before sallying forth from their tunnels, am-
bushing the Israeli soldiers with light weapons like AK-47s
and homemade rocket launchers like the Yasin. Sapper teams
from Al-Qassam attacked armored vehicles, sometimes with
nothing more than improvised explosive devices in their
hands. In the past, Gaza's fighters had staged brief hit-and-run
attacks, shrinking away when Israeli forces responded with
massive firepower, but this time they pressed the attack, re-
maining engaged at distances of less than 15 meters, neutral-
izing the Israeli army's ability to call in air and artillery
support and shocking young soldiers who had never seen such
intense combat.

Making its debut in the battle of Shujaiya was the Al-Ghoul, a homemade 14.5 mm sniper rifle named for Adnan al-Ghoul, the assassinated Al-Qassam weaponsmith. The gun measured about a meter and a half in length and was said to be able to hit long distance targets with devastating accuracy. Toted by masked snipers in swamp creature–style ghillie suits, the gun embodied Al-Qassam's heightened focus on engaging the Israeli military in head-to-head confrontations. A video produced by Al Aqsa TV showed snipers using the gun to hit several Israeli soldiers including an officer while he was giving an order to fire from the turret of a Merkava tank.

As the crackle of rifle fire reverberated through the streets of Shujaiya, an Al-Qassam team lured an M113 armored personnel carrier into a field laced with improvised explosive devices. That the Israelis had invaded using a thinly armored Vietnam-era American relic signaled their underestimation of Al-Qassam's capabilities. The vehicle went up in a ball of flames, killing six soldiers inside and badly wounding one, Sgt. Oron Shaul. Al-Qassam fighters grabbed Shaul and quickly spirited him away, hoping to use the live soldier as leverage in ceasefire negotiations.

In fear that Hamas would photograph the flaming wreck when daylight broke and broadcast the image around the world, the Israeli army command ordered an engineer unit into the neighborhood to remove the M113. The engineers panicked under the threat of fire from surrounding buildings and inadvertently drove over the bodies of their dead countrymen as they struggled to complete the operation. Oron would not survive the night, nor would as many as thirteen other Israeli soldiers. At least fifty-six more had been wounded in the battle, marking the greatest loss the Israeli army had suffered in Gaza in such a short period of time. "The casualties that the Qassam fighters caused since the eruption of this operation...are more than what we caused in all [the] PLO wars in southern Lebanon," an officer in the Palestinian Authority's security apparatus told *IHS Jane's 360*, a military magazine.

As dawn broke on July 21, the streets outside Gaza City's Al-Shifa Hospital, the city's main medical clinic in the relatively upscale neighborhood of Rimal, filled with ambulances carrying wounded civilians from Shujaiya, which lay just a few kilometers away. Crowds of refugees were beginning to pour in from the embattled neighborhood as the Israeli shelling intensified. Interspersed among the crowd of frenzied medics, reporters, and stunned onlookers were masked Al-Qassam fighters who had been engaged moments before in heavy combat.

A young woman from Gaza City rushed to join the crowds in Rimal. Her reaction typified the reception the fighters received. "I don't believe in God or religion, but when I caught the attention of one of the guys from the resistance, I wanted to give him support in a way he could understand," she recalled to me. "So I shouted to him, 'God bless you for what you did!' He looked over at me in this confident way and gave me a thumbs-up sign. I was overcome—my heart just melted."

The Al-Qassam Brigades had not vanquished the vaunted Israeli army. However, they delivered a bloody nose to its most elite units in the same way Hezbollah did during the battle of Bint Jbeil in 2006, when the Lebanese guerrilla force delivered what Israeli troops described as "an ambush from hell." In fact, Al-Qassam had applied lessons it learned through training with Hezbollah and its sponsors. As a senior commander of the group told *Jane's*, "We have benefited from all the Iranian, Syrian, [and] Hizbullah tactical combat schools, and finally formulated [an] independent one that matches our situation and [leaves us] capable to respond to our enemy's challenge."

Israeli Army Chief of Staff Benny Gantz and his senior staff assembled in the Ha'Kirya command center in north Tel Aviv were startled at reports of Sergeant Shaul's capture. In fact, Shaul likely died immediately after he was pulled from the burning vehicle, but this was unknown to the military high command. Having bombarded Shujaiya from all sides for hours in a ham-handed effort to dislodge Al-Qassam and its tunnel network, with negligible success, the army turned its attention to the civilian population.

Mowing the Lawn

The elite divisions of the Golani Brigade were quickly pinned down in the narrow lanes of Shujaiya and unable to withstand coordinated attacks by lightly armed fighters from the Al-Qassam Brigades and assorted Gazan armed factions. So the Israeli military's high command made an audacious decision. It ordered all infantry to take shelter in heavily protected Namer armored personnel carriers, then let loose an artillery barrage that engulfed the entire area in a storm of explosive rain. "We gave them half an hour to get into the vehicles and we laid down fire, after which there was no more shooting from there, not even light weapons," an Israeli army officer told Haaretz. Were it not for the dangerous step, which threatened to expose Israeli troops to friendly fire, "we would be returning dozens of [soldiers'] bodies from the field," the officer remarked.

In the end, the desperate maneuver wound up obliterating most of Shujaiya, killing over 120 of its residents and badly wounding hundreds more. A senior US military officer with access to a July 21 Pentagon briefing of the battle in Shujaiya told Mark Perry of Al Jazeera America that the Israeli military had deployed eleven battalions of heavy artillery against Shujaiya.

This meant that at least 258 artillery pieces blasted the neighborhood with some 7,000 high explosive shells, including 4,800 during a seven-hour period. Details of the operation shocked US officials, prompting Secretary of State John Kerry to sarcastically remark on a hot mic before a Fox News appearance, "It's a hell of a pinpoint operation." It might not have occurred to Kerry that he could have prevented the destruction by negotiating on some of Hamas's humanitarian demands the week before.

"Eleven battalions of IDF artillery is equivalent to the artillery we deploy to support two divisions of US infantry," the US Department of Defense officer told Perry. "That's a massive amount of firepower, and it's absolutely deadly."

A report broadcast on Israel's Channel 2 news profiled one of the artillery crews posted on the border of Gaza. (A comment attached to the video dates the footage as taken on August 3, 2014.) The report is an eight-minute broadcast portrait of an all-female unit with a few male trainers and soldiers assigned to help them carry the 15-kg artillery shells they lob into Gaza neighborhoods with regularity. "Every two minutes we fire a shell [into Gaza]," Corporal Noam Casman, a young female conscript, told Channel 2. Throughout the broadcast, the soldiers are seen signing each 120 and 155 mm artillery shell they launch with messages like, "To Adi, Good luck with the new job!"

The shelling depicted in the news piece appeared to be so random that the soldiers must have had little idea where the munitions were falling. And the atmosphere was so casual they had time to play backgammon and eat delivered sushi in the shade. "This one's because I haven't showered in a week!" one of the troops exclaimed as a smiling member of her unit launched another mortar.

"How long have you been firing?" the Channel 2 reporter asked Corporal Noy Dayan.

"Wow, I can't keep count, but I think we've been at it since morning."

The Dahiya Doctrine

Israel's response to the humiliation it received at the hands of local fighters from the Al-Qassam Brigades and other armed factions in Shujaiya was entirely characteristic of the military policies it had enacted over the last decade, and especially since its disengagement from Gaza. Rather than target its guerrilla foes, the Israeli military unleashed massive force against the civilian population in the theater of engagement. By the time the army was done, entire neighborhoods in and around Shujaiya like al-Shaaf and al-Tuffah had been reduced to apocalyptic moonscapes, with stately, four-story homes transformed to blackened concrete shells.

Nearly every building I came across when I visited Shujaiya weeks later was damaged to the point of being uninhabitable. Many had been reduced to rubble by 2,000-pound missiles fired by US-made F-16s; others featured gaping holes from shells fired from the barrel of Israeli Merkava tanks, while many more were filled with spent mortar and 155 mm artillery shells and littered with empty bullet casings left by the Israeli soldiers who occupied them during the four days of the ground invasion. In some of the houses the soldiers occupied, I found Stars of David scrawled on furniture or etched into walls.

The strategy Israel employed in Shujaiya after the attempted capture of Sgt. Oron Shaul was developed during its attack on Lebanon in 2006. Against stiff resistance on the ground from well-trained fighters from Hezbollah in the rocky terrain of Southern Lebanon, the Israeli military resolved to obliterate Dahiya, the heavily Shi'ite southern Beirut suburb that served as Hezbollah's base of political support. "What happened in the Dahiya quarter of Beirut in 2006 will happen in every village from which Israel is fired on," Maj. Gen. Gadi Eizenkot, then the commander of the Israeli Northern Command attacking Lebanon, told the Israeli newspaper *Yedioth Ahronoth* at the time. "We will apply disproportionate force on it and cause great damage and destruction there. From our standpoint, these are not civilian villages, they are military bases. . . . This is not a recommendation. This is a plan. And it has been approved."

The Dahiya Doctrine reflected the thinking of a new generation of Israeli military strategists poised to confront the nation's enemies through a policy of collective punishment, preferably delivered by air, where Israeli pilots were impervious to death and injury. In 2008, two years after the doctrine was introduced, an Israeli military-academic training center called the Institute for National Security Studies issued a remarkably similar blueprint entitled, "Disproportionate Force." The paper's author, Col. Gabi Siboni, wrote, "With an outbreak of hostilities, the [Israeli army] will need to act immediately, decisively, and with force that is disproportionate to the enemy's actions and the threat it poses. Such a response aims at inflicting damage and meting out punishment to an extent that will demand long and expensive reconstruction processes."

The Dahiya Doctrine guided Israel through its first two major assaults on the Gaza Strip, first in 2008–09 with Operation Cast Lead, and then in 2012, during the military escalation known as Operation Pillar of Defense. When the Israeli military assassinated a few leaders of Gazan armed factions months before the latter operation, *Jerusalem Post* military correspondent Yaakov Katz wrote, "The IDF is using this as an opportunity to do some 'maintenance work' in Gaza and to mow the lawn, so to speak…"

Katz had let slip a phrase—"mowing the lawn"—that was becoming code among Israeli military strategists for the policy it would employ towards Gaza. Two years later, as Israel prepared for another assault on Gaza, Efraim Inbar, an Israeli political scientist and director of the Begin-Sadat Center for Strategic Studies, outlined the political roots of the strategy. According to Inbar and a research associate, Eitan Shamir, a two-state solution with the Palestinians had become virtually unthinkable, leaving no other option but perpetual occupation maintenance. In Gaza, he explained, Hamas had become intractable and had little intention of abandoning its armed resistance to the occupation. Unlike many other Israeli rightists who cast Hamas as an ISIS-like organization that ruled over Gaza against the consent of its population, Inbar recognized Hamas as a popular organization "well-rooted in Palestinian society" that could not be destroyed through military force. At the same time, Inbar derided thinking emerging from Washington and Israeli liberals as "solution-oriented," instead suggesting that there was no peaceful solution whatsoever to Israel's Palestinian problem.

Gaza had become a warehouse for surplus humanity—a mostly young population of refugees caged in what British Prime Minister David Cameron called in July 2010 "an open air prison or even concentration camp." Whenever Gaza's inhabitants rattled their cage, as they would inevitably do, the Israeli military would have to teach them a harsh lesson. "Against an implacable, well-entrenched, non-state enemy like the Hamas," Inbar wrote, "Israel simply needs to 'mow the grass' once in a while to degrade the enemy's capabilities. A war of attrition against Hamas is probably Israel's fate for the long term."

In the summer of 2014, as the Israeli military embarked on another exercise in "mowing the lawn" in Gaza, its senior staff offered units in the field more latitude than ever before. When it published its findings on the 51 Day War, the Israeli human rights group B'Tselem found that the Israeli military had embraced an "open-fire policy…in which residential buildings were attacked from the air or ground, causing them to collapse on entire families." In other words, the Israeli air force was given authorization to target multi-family homes in precision airstrikes without proving their military value or their relation to any faction involved in the fighting. The policy resulted in a chilling statistic: According to the Palestinian Ministry of Health in Gaza, ninety families were removed from the civil record after the Israeli military exterminated most or all members. "B'Tselem has no knowledge of who is responsible for formulating this policy under which such strikes on homes were permitted, nor who ordered it," the organization noted.

With unprecedented freedom to attack civilian targets, the Israeli army enacted the most robust fulfillment of the Dahiya Doctrine in its history, obliterating Shujaiya in the course of about forty-eight hours on July 19 and 20. The US Defense Department official who had received internal Pentagon briefings on Israel's assault on Shujaiya reacted with shock at Israel's use of US-made 155 mm howitzers with a kill radius of 164 feet. "The only possible reason for doing that is to kill a lot of people in as short a period of time as possible," the senior US military officer told Perry of Al Jazeera America. "It's not mowing the lawn. It's removing the topsoil."

Surviving Shujaiya

When I arrived in the Gaza Strip on August 14, the war was into its thirty-eighth day. By this point, Al-Qassam fighters were still huddled in tunnels and completely out of view. The Israeli

Khalil Atash of Shujaiya in the remnants of his son's bedroom. Photo by Dan Cohen.

military had pulled back and was preparing to prosecute the rest of the war by air—from F-16s and drones. Hundreds of thousands of residents of Gaza from obliterated border areas like Shujaiya had been left homeless and were forced to languish in United Nations Relief Works Agency (UNRWA) schools, where they were still vulnerable to targeted Israeli airstrikes. With the announcement of a five-day humanitarian ceasefire on the fourteenth, however, Shujaiya's residents were able to return to the ruins of their homes and pitch tents outside. On the first day of the brief ceasefire, neighbors greeted one another with joyous hugs, celebrating their survival and asking after those who had gone missing.

I entered Gaza with my colleague, Dan Cohen, who was living in the occupied West Bank at the time. When we entered

Gaza in mid-August, we were among only a handful of Western reporters working in the Gaza Strip. The pack of correspondents who had flooded Gaza City to cover the Israeli ground invasion had mostly left, with many heading immediately off to Kurdistan to follow the US campaign against ISIS. Though we received credentials from Israel's Government Press Office (GPO) without any trouble—the GPO was freely issuing press cards to foreign reporters, enabling their entry into Gaza after having banned them during Operation Cast Lead in 2008–09—Israeli authorities had just denied Amnesty International and Human Rights Watch entry to Gaza. With residents flooding back into Shujaiya for the first time, Dan and I were able to gather firsthand accounts of what happened on the fateful night when Israeli forces invaded.

During the August ceasefire, we were accompanied through Gaza by Ebaa Rezeq, a twenty-four-year-old translator and researcher from Gaza City's middle class Al-Nasr neighborhood, whom I had corresponded with via social media well before I arrived in Gaza. Ebaa and I had many friends in common, though she had only met most of them through Skype and social media, as she was unable to visit the West Bank and could rarely obtain a visa to travel to the Western world at all. Like many of her friends, she was secular, went around Gaza without a *hijab*, was unaffiliated with any political faction, and prone to savage criticism of both Hamas and the Fatah-run Palestinian Authority—but especially the PA, which she viewed as a corrupt occupation subcontractor.

When Ebaa appeared on an Israeli news program with a hostile anchor who demanded to know if she would condemn Hamas during the 2012 military escalation, Ebaa shot back that despite whatever internal criticisms she might have, "In times of war, Gaza is Hamas and Hamas is Gaza." Some of the educated,

English-speaking youth in Gaza referred to her comeback as "the Ebaa moment"—the point when a young Palestinian woman told Israel that she understood what Israel wanted and that she would never give it to them. Ebaa's name was inspired by a distinctively Palestinian term that meant stubbornness in the face of power, and she seemed determined to live up to it.

Almost as soon as Dan, Ebaa, and I arrived in Shujaiya, a group of men reclining on mats beside a makeshift stove summoned us inside what was left of their home, a four-level, multi-family structure that was barely distinguishable from the other mangled wrecks lining the dusty roads of the neighborhood. Khalil Atash, a tall, sixty-three-year-old grandfather, implored us to sit down with his family and hear about the attack that destroyed everything he had. As we entered an exposed area that used to serve as the family's salon, Atash motioned to his son heating a teapot above a few logs. "They've set us back a hundred years. Look at us, we're now burning wood to survive," he muttered.

After handing us coffee in small plastic cups, Atash led us up a still-intact staircase and into the home to see what was left of it. On the second floor, tank shells had blown off the walls of what was supposed to have provided boudoirs for two of his newly married children. All that was left of the bathroom were the hot and cold knobs on the shower. On the next floor up, four small children scampered barefoot across shattered glass and jagged shards of concrete. A bunk bed and crib were badly singed in the attack. Gigantic holes opened walls to a panoramic view of the destroyed neighborhood. Everything Atash had worked for was gone. But the damage could have been far worse.

According to Atash, as the attack on Shujaiya began, the Israeli army attempted to evacuate the family. They had received a phone call in which they were ordered to leave, in Arabic. But the family was sure the call was a prank. When they answered the phone again, a soldier exclaimed, "You think this is a joke? You have five minutes." Three minutes later, an F-16 sent a missile through the roof. In an incredible stroke of luck, the missile did not explode. It remained lodged in the ceiling until a day prior to my visit, when a bomb detonation crew dismantled it.

I asked why the family remained in the ruins of their home when the army could attack again at any time.

"We have nowhere else to go now," Khalil Atash explained. "You only die once and we're not afraid after what we've been through. So we just decided to live in our house."

As with Shujaiya, during the ground invasion, the Israeli military comprehensively flattened other border areas from Beit Hanoun in the north to Khuza'a to Rafah in the south. By flooding border areas with explosives until nearly all of their residents were forced to head west for shelter, Israel was tightening the cage on the entire population. No matter where the refugees fled, there was no safe space.

In an empty chamber upstairs where the mothers and children of the Atash family slept—the only inhabitable room in the house—the family gathered to recount their story of survival.

Khalil Atash's son, thirty-year-old Tamer, described to me how the night unfolded:

"The missiles started getting closer and began to hit everywhere so randomly," he said, detailing how the strikes on Shujaiya gradually intensified after the first hour. "So I just lost it. I was watching my neighbors die and I was so close to them, I felt like I was dead, too. I had two choices: Either I die doing nothing at that house or do something about it. So I chose to do something."

Tamer called an ambulance crew and begged the driver to help rescue his trapped family. "All I can do is pray for you," the driver

Children of the Atash family in the remains of their bedroom.

told him, refusing to come to their aid. But other first responders rushed headlong into the maelstrom, risking their lives to save as many of the fleeing residents as they could. By this time, the neighborhood was engulfed in flames and shrouded in darkness—Israeli forces had bombed all of its electrical towers. He and his family decided to make a run for it in the street. Neighbors followed closely behind them, embarking on a desperate sprint for survival as homes went up in flames around them.

Relying on cell phone flashlights to illuminate their path, the fleeing residents rushed ahead under withering shelling. Tens of people fell every few hundred meters, Tamer told me. But they continued anyway, sprinting for a full kilometer until they reached safety close to Gaza City.

As soon as he reached what seemed to be a sanctuary from the fury of explosions and collapsing buildings, Tamer said he was overcome with guilt. Friends and neighbors were stuck in the neighborhood with no one to evacuate them. He decided to return to help anyone he could. "I'm from Shujaiyia, I have no other place to go, and we don't own land," he explained. "This is our only home. So of course I came back."

It was well past midnight, Shujaiya was in flames, and fighters from the Al-Qassam Brigades were beginning to mobilize for a counterattack. "The situation outside was literally hell," Tamer recalled.

Tamer Atash noticed the violent frenzy intensify around the time that news of the alleged capture of Sgt. Oron Shaul by Qassam fighters reached Israeli army commanders. He had no idea that a soldier might have been taken, but he sensed that something dramatic had just taken place. "The F-16s were no longer up in the sky bombing us, they were flying just above the houses," Tamer recalled. "It felt like an atomic bomb with four F-16s coming one way and another four from the opposite direction, weaving between the houses. At this point, we decided we were not going to make it. We said our last prayers, and that was it. Because we know that when the Israelis lose one of their soldiers they become lunatics. We just knew they had suffered something, we could sense it."

Tamer watched some of his neighbors jump from fourth-floor windows as their homes burst into flames. Others rushed out in their night clothes, prompting him and other men to hand over their shirts and even their trousers to women scurrying half exposed through the darkened streets. After giving the shirt off his back to one woman, he gave his sandals to another who had sliced her feet open on rubble.

"Sure, I was crazy and stupid, but I just wanted for them to survive," he said. "If I had to die, then fine, but someone had to make a sacrifice."

By dawn, waves of survivors poured from Shujaiya into Gaza City. Sons had carried their fathers on their backs; mothers had hoisted children into trucks and ambulances; others searched frantically for missing family members when they arrived, only to learn that they had fallen under the shelling. For many, it seemed to be a continuation of the Nakba, the fateful days of 1948 when Zionist militias forcibly expelled hundreds of thousands of Palestinians from their land. This time, however, there was almost nowhere for the refugees to flee.

Back in Shujaiya, the shelling momentarily subsided for a two-hour truce. But the International Committee of the Red Cross (ICRC) proved generally unable to evacuate those trapped in the area, possibly because of the Israeli army's refusal to coordinate with its first responders. Thus the stragglers and wounded were at the mercy of Israel's Golani Brigade, whose soldiers had taken up positions at the edge of Shujaiya, occupying homes just east of the area's main mosque. Anyone bold enough to return to the besieged neighborhood to search for lost family members had entered a death trap.

CHAPTER 5

A Thin Red Line

As the day of August 14 wore on in the ruins of eastern Shujaiya, I began to sense that I was inside a vast crime scene. Dan Cohen, Ebaa Rezeq, and I visited almost a dozen homes occupied by Israeli soldiers in Shujaiya, wading through rubble and piles of shattered furniture in search of clues into the Israeli plan of operation. I found floors littered with bullet casings, sandbags used as foundations for heavy machine guns, sniper holes punched into walls just inches above floors, and piles of empty Israeli snack food containers.

In the stairwell at the entrance to one home we visited, soldiers had engraved yet another Star of David—we would find these in vandalized Palestinian homes across Gaza's border areas. In a nearby house, soldiers used markers to scrawl in mangled Arabic, "We did not want to enter Gaza but terrorist Hamas made us enter. Damn terrorist Hamas and their supporters."

A wall in another home had been vandalized with the symbol of Beitar Jerusalem, the Jerusalem-based football club popular among the hardcore cadres of Israel's right-wing. Below the Beitar logo was the slogan, "Price Tag." The phrase refers to the price settlers seek to exact on the native population of the occupied West Bank each time one of their illegal outposts is demolished or a settler is attacked by Palestinians. Over the past decade, the attacks have grown in frequency and spread into Arab neighborhoods in core Israeli cities, with racist graffiti appearing on Palestinian Christian churches and businesses. The appearance of price tag–style vandalism during the war in Gaza coincided with a 45-percent plunge in price tag attacks against Palestinians in the West Bank, leading an Israeli army official to speculate that "solidarity with the [army]" had provided an outlet for the violent impulses of Jewish fanatics.

In each home the soldiers had occupied, we found crude maps of the immediate vicinity etched on the walls. Each house was assigned a number, possibly to enable commanders to call in air and artillery strikes ahead of their forward positions. Names of soldiers were listed on several walls, but were mostly covered with spray-paint upon the troops' departure. I learned later through several Israeli friends who had served in combat units that these were shooting schedules that determined who would be on sniper duty and when.

In the ruins of a second-floor bedroom, in an empty ammo box under a tattered bed, a group of young local men had discovered two laminated maps of Shujaiya. They eagerly handed them over to me, hoping that I would be able to make sense of them. I was immediately able to determine that the maps were photographed by satellite at 10:32 a.m. on July 17, just days before the neighborhood was flattened. The date in the upper-right-hand corner of one map was written American-style, with the month before the day, raising the question of whether it was a US or Israeli satellite that had captured the image. (The US National Security Agency has routinely shared information

The Israeli army map I retrieved from a home in Shujaiya occupied by Israeli soldiers.

with Israel's Unit 8200, a cyberwarfare and surveillance division embedded within military intelligence, according to journalist James Bamford writing for the *New York Times*.) Outlined in orange was a row of homes numbered between 16 and 29; the homes immediately to their west were labeled with arrows indicating forward troop movements.

A local man who had accompanied us into the house pointed at the homes on the map outlined in orange, then motioned out the window to where they once stood. Every single house in that row had been obliterated by airstrikes. I looked back at the map and noticed that the dusty field we faced was labeled in Hebrew, "Soccer Field." Devised at least two days before the assault as an apparent guide for invading soldiers, the map sectioned Shujaiya into various areas of operation, with color-coded delineations that were difficult to decipher.

After the war, Eran Efrati, a former Israeli combat soldier turned anti-occupation activist, interviewed several soldiers who participated in the assault on Shujaiya. "I can report that the official command that was handed down to the soldiers in Shujaiya was to capture Palestinian homes as outposts," Efrati wrote on his Facebook page. "From these posts, the soldiers drew an imaginary red line, and amongst themselves decided to shoot to death anyone who crosses it. Anyone crossing the line was defined as a threat to their outposts, and was thus deemed a legitimate target. This was the official reasoning inside the units."

Months later, when we met in Brussels to present testimony on Israeli war crimes in Gaza at the Russell Tribunal, Efrati helped me decipher the map I found. He pointed me to a red line drawn on the map that bisected Shujaiya from east to west. It was labeled in Hebrew as "Hardufim," or "Dead People." Efrati explained that while the term "Hardufim" was often called out through Israeli army radios when a soldier was killed and required transport from the theater of battle, the word was also used to mark free-fire zones in the Gaza Strip where soldiers could kill people regardless of their involvement in battle. Efrati was a veteran of Operation Cast Lead in Gaza in 2008–09 and had personally witnessed the delivery of this order.

In the area occupied by Israeli soldiers around the red "Hardufim" line, the killing that had previously taken place by air and distant artillery assaults took on a gruesomely intimate quality. It was there, in the ruins of their homes, that I met with returning locals who survived what they described as a spree of coldblooded executions by Israeli soldiers.

The Killing Fields

That day in mid-August, at the eastern edge of the "Soccer Field" now occupied by tents and surrounded by demolished five-story apartment complexes, I encountered a middle-aged man wearing an eye-patch. Introducing himself as Mohammed Fathi Al Areer, he led Dan, Ebaa, and me through the first floor of his home, which was now little more than a cave furnished with a single sofa, then into what used to be his backyard, where the interior of his bedroom had been exposed by a tank shell. It was here, Al Areer told me, that four of his brothers were executed. One of them, Hassan Al Areer, was mentally disabled and likely had little idea he was about to be killed. Mohammed Al Areer said he found bullet casings next to the victims' heads when he discovered their decomposing bodies days later.

Just next door lived the Shamaly family, one of the hardest hit clans from Shujaiya. Hesham Shamaly, twenty-five, described to me what happened when five members of his family decided to stay in their home to guard the thousands of dollars of clothing and linens they planned to sell through their family business. When soldiers approached the home with weapons drawn, Shamaly said his father, Nasser, emerged with his hands up and attempted to address them in Hebrew.

"He couldn't even finish a sentence before they shot him," Shamaly told me. "He was only injured and fainted, but they thought he was dead so they left him there and moved on to the others. They shot the rest—my uncle, my uncle's wife, and my two cousins—they shot them dead."

Miraculously, Shamaly's father, Nasser, managed to revive himself after laying bleeding for several hours. He walked on his own strength toward Gaza City and found medical help.

"Someone called me to tell me he was alive," Shamaly said, "and I thought it was a joke." In December 2014, Dan Cohen located Nasser Shamaly, who recalled for him how he managed to escape the shooting gallery of Shujaiya by navigating through his neighbors' destroyed homes, flagging a taxi, and finding medical treatment at Al-Shifa Hospital in Gaza City. He confirmed that he had been shot in the left arm while addressing the Israeli soldiers in Hebrew, and added that his family had no idea he was alive until he phoned them from the hospital.

On July 20, Hesham's twenty-three-year-old cousin Salem Shamaly returned to his neighborhood at 3:30 p.m. during the temporary ceasefire to search for missing family members alongside members of the International Solidarity Movement (ISM). At the time, Salem's parents had no idea he was in the neighborhood. As Salem waded into a pile of rubble wearing jeans and a green t-shirt with the ISM volunteers just meters away, who were clad in neon-green vests identifying them as rescue personnel, a single shot rang out from a nearby sniper, causing his body to crumple to the ground. As Salem attempted to get up, another shot struck him in the chest. A third shot left his body completely limp. Apparently, he had crossed the red free-fire line.

The incident was captured on camera by a staffer at Gaza's media ministry named Mohammed Abdullah. As international broadcast news outlets reported on the startling execution, Israeli military spokespeople were strangely silent. Back in Gaza City, where survivors of the Shamaly family had taken shelter in a relative's apartment, Salem Shamaly's sister and cousin received the link to the video in an email from a friend. In the course of three minutes, they watched Salem die. They knew it was him because they recognized the sound of his voice as he cried out for help.

Amina Shamaly sobs after watching video of her son Salem's execution by an Israeli soldier.

Missing Salem

In an apartment in the central Gaza City neighborhood of Rimal, I met the parents, siblings, and cousins of Salem Shamaly. They had been forced to relocate here after their home was completely obliterated by Israeli tank shells and drone strikes in Shujaiya. The apartment was crowded but impeccably clean, a far better arrangement than one of the squalid UN schools where most of their neighbors lodged with little to no privacy.

Salem Shamaly's father, sixty-two-year-old Khalil, said the family had evacuated Shujaiya at 8 a.m. As soon as they reached safety, they realized Salem was missing. "It's impossible to put into words how difficult it was," Khalil Shamaly said. "We waited for two or three days not knowing and when we found out, it was too difficult to handle. I have had to call on God and he helped me."

The attacks on Shujaiya continued for days, making it impossible for the Shamaly family to retrieve Salem's body. They beseeched the ICRC for help, but after so many attacks on their vehicles from the Israeli army, which had declared all of Shujaiya a "closed military zone," they were unwilling to approach the area. Salem's father, Khalil, still believes his son might have been saved if he had been evacuated right away.

When Salem's family finally retrieved his body, they found it badly burned, almost unrecognizable, and tossed dozens of meters from the location where he had been killed by subsequent bombardments. The death toll had reached such unbearable levels he could not be buried in Shujaiya, where the cemetery was overfull. When the Shamalys finally found a place to bury him, they had to open a grave that was already occupied because that cemetery was also full.

During my visit with the family, Salem's cousin, Hind Al Qattawi, whipped out a laptop and played for me a clip of a report on the killing by NBC's Ayman Mohyeldin. Al Qattawi had wanted to demonstrate for me the international impact the incident had made, but instead, by playing the video, she summoned barely submerged emotions back to the surface. As soon as the clip of Salem's killing began to play, his mother, Amina, sobbed openly.

"The real problem is not just losing your home in the bombardment," Muhammad Al Qattawi, Hind's brother, told me as Amina Shamaly brought a wad of tissues to her eyes. "The problem is you have lost your future, you lose your hope, and you can even lose your mind. Two million people here are on the verge of losing their minds."

He handed me a packet of pills that had been prescribed by local doctors to family members diagnosed with varying degrees of depression. Deprived of justice, they had been given antidepressants to numb their despair.

Among those suffering most was Salem's younger brother, Waseem. The slightly built, sad-eyed fourteen-year-old recalled his brother as a bright accounting student who paid for his education by working in his father's corner store. He was one of his best friends.

"We used to go out with him whenever we were bored and he used to take us places," Waseem said. "Now, he's gone, and there's no one else to fill his place."

Tears suddenly came streaming from Waseem's eyes. He covered his face with his hands and shook with sorrow. While his mother, Amina, and grandmother cried, the rest of the family sat in uncomfortable silence. After our interview, I approached Waseem again and asked him what he wanted to be when he came of age. He replied without pause that he planned to join the resistance. A look of intent had replaced his desolation.

Waseem told me he had not considered becoming a fighter until the war came down on Shujaiya.

CHAPTER 6

Bloodlands

The ruins of Khuza'a's main water tower and Ebad Al-Rahman mosque, both destroyed with high explosives by Israeli soldiers.

Once a bucolic farming town of about 14,000, Khuza'a is situated just a short walk from the kibbutzim that lay in Israeli territory. The only thing that separates the two populations

are kilometers of concrete walls studded with remote controlled machine guns and a buffer zone that makes the surrounding farmland inaccessible. For two decades, the farmers
of Khuza'a have been subjected to relentless violence from the
Israeli army stationed around the kibbutzim, first with the razing of their citrus and olive trees, and then with sniper fire
when they attempted to harvest their land. The buffer zone
imposed on them had been used as a pretext to destroy the
farming that served as the town's single productive industry.
But even after years of continuous violence, nothing could
have prepared them for the horrors visited on them during the
51 Day War.

As the Israeli army's Golani Brigade wrapped up its assault
on Shujaiya on July 22, the Israeli army rolled waves of troops
from the Givati Brigade into Khuza'a and declared the town a
closed military zone. This meant that thousands of terrified
residents were prevented from escaping, media was forbidden
from entering the town and the International Committee of the
Red Cross (ICRC)—which insisted on coordinating with an
obstinate Israeli military—was not able to get its ambulances
inside the cordon. For ten days, the pastoral town became the
setting for the worst atrocities of the war as the Gazan border-
lands were transformed into bloodlands.

At the helm of the Givati Brigade was Col. Ofer Winter, a
religious nationalist officer who was emerging as one of the
most revered military figures in Israeli society. Days before the
invasion of Gaza, Winter distributed a motivational letter to his
troops later published in the Israeli paper *Ma'ariv*. It perfectly
reflected the apocalyptic messianism coursing through the
ranks of the new generation of the Israeli military's officer
corps: "History has chosen us to be the sharp edge of the bay-
onet of fighting the terrorist enemy 'from Gaza' which curses,

defames and abuses the God of Israel's battles," Winter wrote to his troops.

The letter continued: "I turn my eyes to the sky and call with you 'Hear, O Israel: The Lord our God is one Lord.' God, the Lord of Israel, make our path successful, as we are about to fight for Your People, Israel, against an enemy who defames your name."

Impelled by their commander's call to punish the infidels of Gaza, the soldiers of the Givati Brigade rolled into Khuza'a on July 22. The brigade was accompanied by an engineering company that used Giant Viper mine clearing devices in Khuza'a's outlying neighborhoods. The Viper consists of a towed mobile launching pad that propels a two-meter-long barrel filled with C4 explosives into open fields, triggering the detonation of mines planted across a wide swath. In Khuza'a, however, the explosive-laden barrels were fired into the center of densely populated neighborhoods with devastating effects—multiple residents complained to me of "barrel bombs" that left the interior of their homes charred while plastic furniture and ceiling fans were left looking melted.

The Givati special forces were aided by a tank unit that barreled around Khuza'a's perimeter, indiscriminately firing into the town center and pinning residents down as they tried to flee to the west. Shelling from tank positions was rampant, flooding the town with 120-mm shells while the air force bombarded civilian homes with missiles. Under cover from heavy fire, the special forces troops took up positions on rooftops, sometimes with bound and blindfolded Palestinian men as human shields against possible guerrilla raids.

On July 22—the day now known in Khuza'a as Black Tuesday—the Israeli special forces accosted Khalil al-Najjar, the fifty-five-year-old imam of the local Kuuza Mosque and one of the most respected members of his community. Al-Najjar was in his home with fifteen members of his family after a night of heavy bombardment when a tank shell hit their house. With the house surrounded by Israeli soldiers, al-Najjar beseeched the troops in Hebrew to allow him and his family to leave. Instead of permitting them to seek refuge elsewhere, the troops seized al-Najjar, forced him to strip and paraded him through the streets to the Kuuza Mosque to be interrogated.

"Making me, a well-respected man, stand completely naked, in front of everyone, was the most humiliating thing of my life," Khalil al-Najjar told Mohammed Omer, the Gaza-based journalist who broke the news of the imam's humiliation.

At the mosque, an Israeli soldier summoned a bulldozer after discovering graffiti on one of its walls celebrating the guerrilla activities of Islamic Jihad. After the bulldozer sent the walls crashing down, a unit commander badgered al-Najjar for information on the tunnels. "You are Israeli intelligence with all your technology, drones, F16s, and you don't know where the tunnels are?" he told Omer he had replied. "Do you think those who are building tunnels are going to come and tell me where they are?"

Having failed to provide the soldiers with the intelligence they sought, the frustrated troops demanded Khalil al-Najjar put his clothes back on. He was then paraded back down the center of Khuza'a's main street and ordered to call all the young men to assemble outside. According to Omer, the soldiers had warned al-Najjar that they would shoot him and his brother if he violated their orders. Eventually, since not all of the military-aged males had emerged from their homes, the troops took al-Najjar back to the mosque along with a power generator and then ordered him to use the loudspeaker system normally used for the call to prayer to order all the young men in the town to assemble.

As droves of confused young men appeared in the streets, heeding the call from one of the most trusted figures in town, they were separated from women and children and abducted en masse, then taken to Israeli prisons for interrogation. According to Omer, a soldier poured water down the front of one man's pants while another threatened to burn a prisoner alive. As the line-up and abductions concluded, Khalil al-Najjar was allowed to carry his elderly mother out of town, past columns of tanks and stunned locals who had just witnessed the respected clergyman stripped of everything, from his clothing to his dignity.

"I felt inside myself sorry for the imam, because he's done," Omer later testified at the Russell Tribunal on Palestine. "He's the most trusted [figure in town]. The Israeli military had used his voice to attract the young people . . . and then they were trapped from everywhere by the military."

After bulldozing the Kuuza Mosque, Israeli troops laid C4 explosives inside the main mosque in the town, Ebad Al-Rahman. From inside a tank, a group of Israeli soldiers filmed themselves awaiting the detonation of the mosque, which they claimed lay above the entrance to a tunnel. "This explosion is dedicated to the memory of the three people from the battalion who have fallen since the beginning of the operation—Amit Yeori of blessed memory, Guy Boylend of blessed memory, and Moshiko Dvino of blessed memory," one of the troops declared.

As the mosque and an adjacent water tower went up in a ball of flames, the soldiers erupted in rapturous celebration. "Long live the State of Israel!" one of them exclaimed. The Israeli army later claimed that the mosque contained a tunnel used by the Al-Qassam Brigades, though for some reason the soldiers had not filmed any evidence. "Soldiers are perfectly entitled to be happy about destroying a tunnel used to carry out attacks against Israel," an army spokesperson told *France 24*.

For around ten days, Khuza'a remained under siege, closed to the outside world with thousands of residents trapped inside. F-16 missiles and tank shelling had destroyed all the power lines and its main water tower had been detonated. It was not until a humanitarian ceasefire finally took hold on August 2 that the full extent of the horrors that unfolded behind the military cordon became known.

Among the first journalists to make it into the town was Tamer al-Meshal of Al Jazeera Arabic. Al-Meshal arrived in Khuza'a as hundreds of traumatized refugees fled in the other direction, many carrying decomposing bodies wrapped in blankets. The road was littered with the corpses of those cut down by Israeli tank fire as they tried to escape. Among the bodies was that of a teenage girl killed a few meters in front of her wheelchair. In a home at the eastern edge of town, al-Meshal found a pile of burned bodies in a bathroom spattered with dried blood and pieces of flesh.

The owner of the home, Hani Yusuf Najjar, stood at the entrance to the bathroom and shook with outrage. "These men were executed in cold blood because they fought for the honor of our town!" Najjar exclaimed on camera.

"The house has no signs of being bombed. Were the bodies brought here?" al-Meshal asked Najjar.

"They were brought here and executed in cold blood, as you can see," Najjar replied.

The Murder Room

Two weeks after the discovery of the bodies, Dan, Ebaa, and I met thirty-two-year-old Hani Najjar in front of his modest two-story home. Situated in the Al-Najjar neighborhood named for his vast extended family, his house was among a cluster of dwellings that surrounded a patio shaded with fruit trees and bougainvillea vines. It was one of the few structures in Khuza'a that had not been battered by tank shells or utterly destroyed by F-16 missiles. He led me inside and showed me the bathroom. "It smells one percent as bad as it did when I first found the bodies," al-Najjar remarked.

The bodies had been removed from the bathroom but the signs of a mass execution remained: Crimson blood and the blackened crust of charred flesh stained the white shower tile; the floor was drenched in pools of congealed blood and small piles of human hair. Embedded in the carrion were grenade pins and bullet shells that read, "IMI," or Israeli Military Industries. Najjar pointed to blood-caked knives on the floor and told me that the blades he used to slaughter his chickens were used by Israeli soldiers to kill the men they had dragged into his bathroom. It was also possible that the doomed men had taken the knives in a desperate, last-ditch bid to defend themselves.

"I spent fourteen years building this house," Hani Najjar remarked to me, "and now I want a bulldozer to demolish the entire house." I commented that the rest of the house was intact and asked why he didn't just rebuild the bathroom.

"If you were me, would you agree to come back to live here?" he responded, explaining that his top priority was shielding his young twin daughters from the trauma. "It's very hard to keep a strong mind. That's why I decided to never come back here until this whole house is bulldozed or burnt down. Then we are going to rebuild again."

Najjar worked as a nurse in the surgery department in Nasser Hospital in the nearby city of Khan Younis. Having evacuated his wife and daughters from Khuza'a two weeks before the ground invasion, he was uncertain about the identities of the men found slaughtered in his bathroom. But he thought they must have been resistance fighters who had been taken prisoner after fighting to the last bullet. A local who led Tamer al-Meshal to the site of the execution described witnessing local fighters harrying the Israelis around the town. The man remarked that they had exacted numerous casualties on the Israelis at the edge of the Al-Najjar neighborhood, suggesting that the executions might have been an act of revenge.

Later in August, the Canadian reporter Jesse Rosenfeld published an interview he conducted with a fighter from Islamic Jihad operating under the alias of Abu Mohammed who had participated in the battle in Khuza'a. The veteran guerrilla told him that the six men found in the house had intended to ambush invading Israeli troops but were caught in the open as they emerged from a tunnel. They retreated under heavy fire and barricaded themselves in Hani al-Najjar's home. One of the fighters who was badly wounded in the melee demanded to make his final stand by the door of the house, hoping that he could hold off the Israelis long enough to enable his comrades to escape.

When he and his unit ran out of ammunition, the Israelis "pulled him outside and shot him in front of the house," Abu Mohammed told Rosenfeld. "Then they went into the house with dogs. In situations like this there is no way for these guys to fight off the dogs. I heard their screaming and begging for mercy on the radio."

It was then that Abu Mohammed heard "a long burst of fire from an M16, and then silence."

Escaping Khuza'a

While Hani al-Najjar had managed to escape to the nearby city of Khan Younis during the assault on Khuza'a, much of his family remained trapped in the town along with some one thousand others who had taken shelter there. At first, his younger brother, Muhammad, who lived next door with his wife, Aman, had been unable to flee. The interior of their house had been incinerated and turned to rubble.

In the shady courtyard outside, Muhammad Najjar seated himself in a plastic chair and described the six days of terror he survived. Slender and taller than his older brother, with auburn hair and a closely cropped beard, he detailed the atrocities in a flat tone that belied the fresh trauma that seemed to be eating at him. "The experience I lived with [will] always be stuck in my head and I will never be able to get over it," he remarked with a distant stare.

Najjar said the nightmare began when hundreds of locals fled from downtown Khuza'a when Israeli special forces landed from helicopters on top of their homes. It was Ramadan and food was scarce. For days, the adults fasted and gave any food they could find to the small children among them. They called the ICRC again and again but to no avail—the Red Cross was unwilling to send its ambulances into the besieged town without Israeli approval. With the pangs of hunger gnawing at them and the tank shelling growing closer with each passing hour, the group resolved to make its escape.

At 5 a.m. on July 26, hundreds of besieged residents rushed from the neighborhood through the gauntlet of Israeli tanks and infantry that lay between them and the main road out. Along the way, Muhammad Najjar saw fleeing refugees fall under direct sniper fire and shrapnel from tank shells. He helped gather the wounded on stretchers and carry them towards the Hamza mosque at the western edge of town. But before the group could escape, it ran into a squadron of Givati special forces gathered around a tank for a cigarette break.

"That's where the humiliation started," recalled Muhammad Najjar. "They were shooting directly at us, so we had to lay on the ground. We put our hands on our heads and took off our clothes without being ordered to because that is what we used to witness on TV when you run into special forces. We kept screaming, 'Civilians! Civilians!' But they didn't respond."

From the tank, a soldier called out for an elderly man to step forward from the terrified group, which had huddled behind a large mound of dirt. Najjar said when the man emerged the soldier shot him to death without explanation. Next, the soldier ordered another man forward, demanding he strip and turn around. Finally, the group was allowed to march forward behind the naked man, continuing their escape along a road strewn with dead bodies of the elderly, the weak, and those not able to escape the shells that were still landing all around. At the gates of Khuza'a, Najjar phoned the ICRC one final time. Once again, they refused to dispatch an ambulance. And so the march continued west until the refugees found cars to take them to the main hospital in Khan Younis.

Ultimately, Najjar escaped with his immediate family, but not everyone was so lucky. He rattled off the names of more than ten members of his extended family who were kidnapped by the soldiers and taken to a prison on the Gaza border where they were beaten and interrogated. When we met, he said four were still in detention.

After returning to Khuza'a, Najjar's wife Amman used a jagged piece stone to inscribe a few messages on the charred walls of their ruined house, in her best English:

Khuza'a is a symbole [sic] of dignity
My small heart can't afford more
I'll be optimistic in spite of these disastrous things

Alone on the Road

Every member of the Rujeila family managed to survive the ten-day siege of Khuza'a—except one. Seated in a circle of plastic chairs in a barely furnished salon, twenty-eight-year-old Ghassan Rujeila told me how his sixteen-year-old sister, Ghadir, was left behind. As he spoke, his younger brother, Bilal, who wore a bandage around his right ankle, hopped to and from the kitchen on his left leg, bringing us trays filled with cups of sugared tea.

Ghassan Rujeila's story was almost identical to that of so many other residents of Khuza'a whom I spoke to: He and his family became trapped in their home when the Israelis invaded on July 22, were shot at each time they attempted to escape, and despite countless calls to the ICRC begging the organization to send ambulances, were ultimately left to fend for themselves. On the day of the invasion, the family gathered with hundreds of their neighbors at the home of the town doctor, Kamal Qudeh, who was treating more than a hundred wounded patients in his tiny clinic, and would continue to tend to the rising tide of injured in the besieged town even after shrapnel from a tank shell wounded his right arm.

Along with any of the wounded and elderly who could walk or be carried, the Rujeila family rushed to the edge of town, arriving at the dirt mound described by Muhammad al-Najjar as a de facto checkpoint guarded by Israeli soldiers. Bilal Rujeila was pushing his sister, Ghadir, in her wheelchair. Ghadir was capable of walking at a deliberate pace, however, she was severely mentally disabled. Ghassan Rujeila told me he called out to the soldiers and asked permission to pass towards Khan Younis, where ICRC ambulances were said to be waiting for them. The soldiers rejected their request, and then opened fire.

A tank shell exploded just a few meters away from the family, wounding Bilal in his leg and arm and sending them in flight for safety. As the tanks targeted the scattering crowds, the family realized they had left Ghadir behind in the street. "I saw the tank shoot at us, and in the face of death we all worry about ourselves," Ghassan explained. With their neighbors falling all around them, the family retreated back into town where they spent the next three days without food, under relentless bombardment and imploring the ICRC to retrieve Ghadir from the dusty road where she had been left.

After Israeli forces bombarded an adjacent neighborhood—"They burned the area," Ghassan Rujeila commented—the family made another break for safety. This time, they finally managed to reach the city of Khan Younis. Back in Khuza'a, Ghadir remained alone on the road in unknown condition. As before, the family's calls to ICRC begging them to retrieve Ghadir yielded nothing—the organization was unable to gain Israeli permission to approach the town.

On August 2, when a seventy-two-hour ceasefire finally took hold, Ghadir Rujeila was found by refugees who had been streaming out of the village. She lay dead six meters in front of her wheelchair, crumpled along the side of the road, filled with shrapnel and partly decomposed. The teenage girl had apparently attempted to chase after her fleeing family before Israeli tank fire cut her down. Left behind in the chaos, she bled to death alone.

Ghadir's family carried her body three kilometers to a cemetery and buried her in a hastily dug grave. While lowering his sister in the ground, Ghassan Rujeila said Israeli drones fired five rockets into the graveyard. No one was injured, he explained in an understated, chillingly clinical tone, "but it was very, very difficult. Especially after not being able to see her for eleven days."

Stars of David spray painted by Israeli soldiers on the walls inside a USAID-funded school in Khuza'a.

A Window into Hell

Spending the day of August 17 in Khuza'a was like peering through a window to Hell. But what we witnessed in the landscape of apocalyptic oblivion paled in comparison to the experience described to me by two Palestinian Red Crescent volunteers who had attempted to break through the Israeli military cordon during the siege of the town.

Twenty-five-year-old Ahmed Awad and twenty-four-year-old Ala'a Alkusofi arrived at the edge of Khuza'a at a time when ICRC ambulance crews refused to travel anywhere near the town. They said they had come to collect the body of a man whom soldiers had lashed to a tree by both arms and shot in the leg. When they arrived at the site, the soldiers ordered the driver of their ambulance, Mohammed Abadla, to exit the vehicle. When he obliged, they told him to walk five meters forward and switch on a flashlight. As soon as he flicked the light on, the soldiers shot him in the chest and killed him.

"It was something I'll never forget," Awad recalled, "seeing a colleague killed like that in front of me. I couldn't believe what I witnessed."

The two Red Crescent volunteers told me they later found a man in Khuza'a with rigor mortis, holding both hands over his head in surrender, his body filled with bullets. Deeper in the town, they discovered an entire family so badly decomposed they had to be shoveled with a bulldozer into a mass grave. In a field on the other side of town, Awad and Alkusofi found a shell-shocked woman at least eighty years of age hiding in a chicken coop. She had taken shelter there for nine days during the siege, living off of nothing but chicken feed and rain water. "She couldn't believe it when we found her," said Alkusofi. "She was sure she would die with the chickens."

In nearly every shattered home I entered in Khuza'a, on every bomb-cratered street, in destroyed mosques and vandalized schools, I heard horror stories like this. Every resident I met in this town was touched by the violence in one way or another.

While visiting the town, I wandered into the courtyard of a USAID funded rehabilitation clinic for women and children afflicted with Continuous Traumatic Stress Disorder—a condition that affects a solid majority of youth in Gaza. Located on a street lined with four-story apartments pockmarked with bullets and tank shells, the school was completely empty, but the signs of an Israeli presence were everywhere. As we entered, we found Stars of David spray painted by soldiers across the walls, right below colorful heart-shaped paper cut-outs bearing the names of students. In the closet of an administrative office that was neatly kept except for a few scattered papers, I found a spent M72 Light Anti-Tank Weapon. It was one of the shoulder-mounted launching tubes manufactured in Mesa, Arizona—just miles from Dan Cohen's hometown of Phoenix—by the Norwegian-owned Nammo arms corporation. The weapon had been used by the Israelis to rocket civilian homes across Gaza's border regions.

In a classroom across the courtyard, sunrays burst through a gaping hole in the wall about the size of a 120 mm tank shell. They shone light on a series of colorful posters decorated with matching ribbons that contained motivational messages. They read:

It always seems impossible until it's done

Stay alive

Look to the future

No negative thoughts allowed

We wandered around the corner, past a group of children filling a jug of water from a truck that replaced the water tower Israeli forces detonated, past the giant dome of the Ebad Al-Rahman mosque, which now sat on a pile of rubble next to the toppled water tower like the ancient ruins of some bygone empire. Nearby, we entered a small courtyard surrounded by a warren of shattered homes. At the edge of the yard, a small boy lay impassively in his bed in a room with no walls. A ceiling fan that looked as though it had been melted dangled above his head. In the center of the yard sat a gigantic olive green barrel. It was a spent Giant Viper round—one of the C4-packed mine clearing devices the Israelis fired into the center of Khuza'a during the assault on the town. A hen flapped its wings next to the barrel and chased after baby chicks bouncing through the rubble.

"Where are you from?" an old man called out to me from the road. He wore large spectacles and a morning robe, his front pocket stuffed with paper notepads, various cards and a glasses holder. He reminded me of my older Jewish relatives who came of age before the digital era and grew accustomed to carrying stacks of business cards, coupons and handwritten reminders in their shirt and coat pockets along with assorted mints and pens.

"I'm from America," I told the man, readying for an indignant response.

"Ahhhh, Amreeka," he grumbled. "I want to thank the American people," the man continued, advancing to within two feet of me. "They are nice people, they give us food and bread and they give the Israelis weapons to kill us. They have different standards. It would be nice if they treated us all as humans."

He introduced himself as Ali Ahmed Qudeh, the father of Kamal Qudeh, the doctor who treated the town's wounded under heavy bombardment and in spite of being injured himself. Like his son, Ali Ahmed was a supporter of Fatah, the rivals of Hamas. And like virtually everyone I met in Gaza, he was an ardent supporter of Al-Qassam's armed resistance. "Our weapons are not terrorist weapons, our weapons are [for] self defense," he insisted. "Our weapons are to free our land. We are dignified people, we love life. We don't hate life like they say. But we'll die for our land."

As a group of small children gathered in the courtyard, Ali Ahmed detailed to me how many family members each child lost in the assault on Khuza'a. Pointing at the little boy lying in bed, he suggested that the most devastating consequence of the war was not the death toll, but the psychological impact on the youngest members of his community.

"That kid wants to make an atomic bomb and obliterate Israel!" he roared. "Why? Because he saw his family members die in front of him! How can you raise kids who want to make bombs?"

When I made my way back into the road, I heard Ali Ahmed call after me again. He was rushing forward through the rubble with a tray of sweets. "I don't mean to say that all Americans are bad," he said, urging me to take a freshly baked cookie. "It's the government that's the problem, not the people."

Just then, an Israeli squadron of American-made F-16s roared through the sky. A small girl standing beside me ducked reflexively at the sound of the jets, bracing for another missile strike. The war was far from over.

CHAPTER 7

Human Shields

To enter the Gaza Strip from Israel, a visitor must first pass through the eerily empty Erez terminal. The border is managed by members of the army's COGAT (Coordination of Government Activities in the Territories) division: young female conscripts with tightly pulled back hair seated behind flat computer screens inside small kiosks thickly shielded with bulletproof glass. A visitor with a Jewish-sounding last name will receive greater scrutiny from COGAT administrators seeking to prevent any Jewish Israeli from slipping into Gaza for fear they might be kidnapped. Down a fenced-in corridor, the visitor arrives at a concrete blast wall; a female COGAT administrator's voice blares through a loudspeaker, then an iron door slides open. Beyond is another long fenced-in corridor extending through the buffer zone, and beyond that, Gaza.

Walking the corridor through the buffer zone, the only sound a visitor is likely to hear is the single note, lawnmower-like buzzing of an Elbit Hermes 450 drone hovering overhead. A few hundred meters to the right, a remote controlled machine gun is visible atop a sentry tower along the walls of the Gaza ghetto. It is a component of Israel's "Spot and Strike" system, an automated weapon apparatus controlled by female soldiers in air conditioned offices tens of kilometers away at a Negev Desert army base. When one of the young desk jockeys notices a figure approaching the buffer zone whose gait matches that of a "terrorist," they aim remotely, press a button on a joystick, and kill the target. As with the Israeli air force's drone pilots, those managing the "Spot and Strike" system view residents of Gaza as little figures on a black and white television monitor whose lives can be turned off with the flick of a switch.

At the end of the fenced-in corridor is the makeshift trailer Hamas erected in place of the newly constructed border terminal Israel forces destroyed on their way into Gaza. Beside bombed-out structures on a road chewed up by Israeli Merkava tank tracks, sweaty men in tattered uniforms hastily examine passports, scribble down identification numbers, and wave in foreign aid workers and journalists. Though the border sentries sometimes check visitors' bags for contraband like alcohol, which is banned in the Gaza Strip, outsiders often manage to smuggle bottles of liquor past the exhausted guards. ICRC staff routinely truck SUVs full of liquor into Gaza to furnish a de facto bar the organization maintains at its compound in Gaza City, according to several friends who have patronized the "bar."

Beyond the Hamas border terminal is Beit Hanoun, a border city of more than thirty thousand that lies in the northeastern Gaza Strip. After a taxi ride through the neatly tended southern Israeli kibbutzim on the way to the border, it is a startling sight to behold. Nearly everything in Beit Hanoun seems to have been flattened. Even the UNRWA school in the center of town bears the marks of an Israeli attack that killed seventeen and wounded two hundred among the hundreds of local residents sheltering there during the ground invasion.

The ruination of Beit Hanoun was merely the peak of years of continuous Israeli violence against the impoverished city. It was a frequent site of rocket launches towards southern Israeli cities like Sderot and the nearby Erez crossing and had experienced routine Israeli bombardments since 2006. When I arrived in Beit Hanoun with Dan and Ebaa during the five-day ceasefire that began on August 14, the sound of gunshots marking the discovery of new bodies sounded in the distance. Thousands of residents had returned for the first time to the ruins of their homes to survey the damage. Among them was a fifty-year-old farmer who introduced himself to me as Abu Rahman.

Like his neighbors who had eked out a living in the rich soil lining Gaza's borders, Abu Rahman had lost virtually everything at the hands of the Israelis. In 2005, Israeli bulldozers razed his citrus grove to extend the buffer zone, wiping out trees that provided oranges throughout the Gaza Strip. They then destroyed the wells he used to irrigate his land. And when they returned that summer, they leveled his four-story home, killed his flock of eighty goats and incinerated the five tons of wheat he had stored there. Bees buzzed from out of the first floor, which lay below three layers of concrete floor like a destruction sandwich, the only survivors of his apiary.

"In the blink of an eye, everything my father worked for, for seventy years, was gone," Rahman said. "During the past month, I feel like I aged two years."

Unlike Shujaiya, where residents in the local market were bombarded without warning, or in Khuza'a, where thousands of civilians remained in town under the assumption that they would not be directly targeted, most of Beit Hanoun's population was able to escape ahead of the Israeli onslaught. When Rahman returned to his home during the first temporary cease-fire on August 2, however, he found rubble of his neighbors' home littered with human flesh and dismembered limbs. Some had not been able to escape after all.

According to Rahman and several of his neighbors, Israeli troops from the Givati Brigade ordered the Wahadan family who lived next door to him to remain in their home when they invaded on July 17, warning them that if they attempted to evacuate they would be shot. Seven military-aged males among the family were blindfolded and abducted to Israeli prisons, where they were subjected to days of interrogations about Hamas, tunnels, and guerrilla operations they had no involvement in. The rest of the family—women, children, and an older man—were then kept on the ground floor of the house for six days.

During that time, while the Israeli army engaged in periodic clashes with fighters from the Al-Qassam Brigades and other armed factions operating around Beit Hanoun, it held the Wahadan family in the ground floor of the house, refusing to allow them to leave as the soldiers maintained the home as a base of operations. When it appeared that a brief ceasefire would take hold on July 25, the soldiers retreated from the home, but ordered the family to stay inside. The following day, with the Wahadans still inside their home under direct army orders, the Israeli military called in strikes on the area, killing every trapped member of the family. In the course of an hour on July 26, much of Beit Hanoun was destroyed under a storm of Israeli artillery shells.

Thirty-year-old Rami Hatem Zaki Wahadan was one of the few members of the family to survive, but only because Israeli forces abducted him at the onset of the ground invasion. When the ceasefire began on August 2, Rami returned to his home to search for his family. In the rubble, he found severed and badly seared limbs and torsos belonging to his grandmother, Su'ad Wahadan, sixty-seven, her grandchildren, Zeinab, twenty-seven, Sumoud, twenty-two, Ahmad, fourteen, and ten-year-old Hussein. Two-year-old Ghena and fifty-one-year-old Baghdad Wahadan still lay somewhere under the rubble when I arrived two weeks later—their relatives were unable to locate any of their body parts.

Around this time, Rami learned that his own father, his niece, and two other members of his family had taken shelter from the Israeli assault on Beit Hanoun in the northern city of Jabalia on July 20. Rami went to Beit Hanoun on August 2 but could not reach his grandparents' house as Israeli forces briefly returned to the area. There he learned that his father and three other family members had been killed in an Israeli drone strike on their home in Jabalia on July 20.

On a street lined with the ruins of what used to be a vibrant neighborhood, friends and neighbors of the Wahadan family patiently helped me piece together the gut-wrenching details of what happened, jotting down the names and ages of each dead family member in my reporter's notebook. As they described the massacre, a friend of Abu Rahman's rushed out of a house with a bunch of grapes and handed it to me along with a bottle of ice-cold water. Although it was happening again and again during the days I spent in the rubble among homeless and grief stricken survivors, it was difficult to take this level of hospitality for granted.

A few weeks after I reported news of the massacre of the Wahadan family, Defense for Children International (DCI), a London-based human rights NGO with an office in the occupied West Bank, managed to track down Rami Wahadan.

"I cry a thousand times a day," Rami told DCI-Palestine. "I cannot and will not forget what Israel did to us in this war and how they executed my family in two different incidents. They murdered my little brothers, my two sisters, my mother and my grandparents in Beit Hanoun. And they murdered my father, my niece, my brother's wife and my uncle's wife in the Jabalia refugee camp."

The Survivor

When Israel's Givati Brigade began to withdraw from Beit Hanoun on August 1, it was still operating in Rafah, the Gaza Strip's southernmost city, which lies hard against the border with Egypt and serves as the source of the tunnel economy that has brought everything from vital food and medicines to zoo animals into the Gaza Strip. From the summary execution of more than one hundred local men by Israeli forces during their temporary occupation of Gaza in 1956 to the campaign of home razing the Israeli military oversaw in 2004, the one hundred fifty thousand residents of this city have been exposed to decades of disproportionate violence. At Rafah's eastern edge are the ruins of Yasser Arafat International Airport, a relic of the era of the defunct and discredited Oslo Accords—the basis of the so-called peace process—that had served a minuscule elite in Gaza before Israeli airstrikes and bulldozers blasted it to smithereens. After Operation Cast Lead concluded in 2009, scavengers set in on the airport, digging concrete from its runway to rebuild their destroyed homes. Its reconstruction was one of the terms Hamas offered in exchange for a ten-year truce—an offer the US, Israel, and the Egyptian military junta rejected.

One of the most violent assaults in Rafah's bloodstained history began on July 14, 2014, when Givati special forces under

Mahmoud Abu Said beside the window in his home where he said Israeli soldiers used him as a human shield, sniping at his neighbors from over his shoulders.

the command of Col. Ofer Winter staged a limited incursion through the fallow fields around the airport and took up positions in the city's eastern suburbs. I visited the area during the five-day ceasefire that began on August 16, arriving via a dusty lane littered with the shards of spent Israeli munitions, which had been dumped indiscriminately on residents on August 1 and 2. Lying in a pile in front of a bombed-out home were shards of artillery shells, US-made Mark-82 dumb bombs, drone missiles, and spent bullet casings—the calling cards Israel's military left across Gaza.

In front of a warren of shattered houses whose facades appeared to have been ripped down by bulldozers, we met members of the Abu Said family. They took us to the porch of their home to talk in the shade of a red tile roof punctured with gaping holes from Israeli shrapnel. The interior of the house had been trashed by the soldiers who transformed it into a base of operations. As they introduced themselves, a drone buzzed incessantly overhead while squadrons of F-16s roared by.

After several minutes of conversation about the Israeli attacks, a friend of the family rushed to another house to summon his cousin. He returned with an unkempt teenager in baggy sweatpants, a sweat-stained t-shirt, bloodshot eyes and an almost catatonic expression on his face.

"Traumatized!" his friend exclaimed. "He's completely traumatized."

Nineteen-year-old Mahmoud Abu Said could hardly speak about what happened to him when the soldiers first arrived to his neighborhood. When I asked him about the incident, his eyes filled with tears, the muscles in his face began to twitch, and his voice faltered. As the baby-faced teenager attempted to recount how Israeli soldiers used him as a human shield, torturing and then kidnapping him, he collapsed into a plastic chair.

"I feel so afraid," he muttered. "It's not normal. I feel weak and I'm not myself."

After a drink of water, Mahmoud managed to pull himself together. He then explained what happened when the soldiers arrived on July 14 during the first stage of Israel's ground invasion of the Gaza Strip. The entire Abu Said family had gathered at his spacious home, including thirty cousins. When a platoon of Israeli troops appeared on the dirt road outside the house, the terror began.

The soldiers ordered the family to evacuate the house under the shelling their army had just initiated. Then they summoned Mahmoud's father, Abdul Hadi El Said. As soon as he appeared at his doorstep, they asked him if he spoke Hebrew. When he answered in the affirmative, the soldiers shot him in the chest, leaving him to die. This was one of several cases I documented in which Gaza residents described to me the shooting of older male relatives who had revealed their ability to speak Hebrew. Were the men shot because the soldiers feared Hebrew-speaking Palestinians might be able to decipher their orders? Were orders issued to kill them? I found no answers among the survivors of the shootings, only harrowing testimony that formed a clear and chilling pattern. The Israeli military has offered no explanation either.

Left for dead, Abdul Hadi El Said managed to get medical help that allowed him miraculously to survive. While the other members of the family fled to safety in the urban center of Rafah, the soldiers grabbed Mahmoud and didn't allow him to leave.

Mahmoud said the Israeli troops dragged him back into his house, blindfolded him, and wrapped him in a blanket on the floor. They began to blow holes in the walls to use as makeshift sniper slits—what US troops in Afghanistan called "murder holes," according to journalist Dan Lamothe. The soldiers then stripped Mahmoud to his underwear, handcuffed him, slammed him against a wall and began to beat him. With an M16 at his back, they forced him to stand in front of open windows as they hunted his fleeing neighbors, sniping directly beside him and over his shoulders at virtually anything that moved. When they were not using him as a human shield, Mahmoud said, the soldiers left him alone in the room with a muzzled army dog who was off the leash.

It was on the top floor of Mahmoud's home, in a darkened crawl space, that an Israeli sniper killed two of his neighbors through a murder hole. Saleh Israibi and Ala Abu Shabab, two young men who had attempted to flee under the intensifying Israeli shelling, were killed in front of their own homes. By the ruins of his house, I met Saleh Israibi's father, Suleiman, who told me his twenty-two-year-old son was shot to death while attempting to rescue Abu Shabab, who he found bleeding in the street.

Israeli forces had destroyed virtually everything Suleiman Israibi owned with a combined salvo of missiles and artillery shells. Behind him was the car his son once drove for a living as a taxi driver. It, too, had been destroyed by Israeli shells, reduced to a pile of gnarled metal.

"We've been suffering for more than sixty years, so this didn't start yesterday," Suleiman Israibi exclaimed. "When I build a house, the Israelis bomb it. When I try to make a living, they destroy my business. When I try to raise a child, they kill him."

Israibi had managed to escape to a squalid, overcrowded UNRWA school where he had been living for the past forty days ("The life there is shitty," he remarked). Meanwhile, Mahmoud Abu Said was removed from his wrecked home where he had been held and taken by soldiers to a prison cell in southern Israel.

In the Israeli jail, Mahmoud said he was blindfolded and taken to questioning sessions every three hours. Interrogators routinely beat and slapped him as they demanded information about tunnel networks and armed resistance activity. After six days and in coordination with the ICRC, which arranges for prisoners to be dumped from Israeli jails back into Gaza, usually at the Erez crossing, Mahmoud said he was released back into the Gaza Strip. He returned just in time for the unrelenting forty-eight-hour-long Israeli assault his neighbors now refer to as Black Friday.

CHAPTER 8

Hannibal

On July 31, with morgues across the Gaza Strip overflowing and large swaths of the besieged enclave reduced to rubble, diplomats from Israel and Hamas agreed to a seventy-two-hour ceasefire that was to begin at 8 a.m. the following day. But the US, which as a matter of longstanding policy has refused to negotiate directly with Hamas, had apparently allowed Israeli troops to remain inside Gaza and be able to maneuver freely. In a vaguely worded statement, US Secretary of State John Kerry declared that the terms of the ceasefire authorized Israeli forces to "continue its defensive operations for those tunnels that are behind its lines." Hamas had never agreed to the unusual stipulation.

On the morning of Friday, August 1, at 6:22 a.m.—an hour and a half before the ceasefire was to take hold—the Qassam Brigades published a report on the organization's Twitter account about a clash near Rafah: "At 6:30 a.m. a group of Al-Qassam infiltrated behind enemy lines at east Rafah and bombed a house that the enemy had taken as a stronghold with a Tandem missile after the enemies bombed the whole area."

Al-Qassam tweeted an update on the battle at 7:34 a.m., apparently with real-time information from its fighters: "At 7 a.m. a group [of Hamas fighters] clashed with [Israeli] forces east of Rafah and caused many injuries and death to them."

The clashes began when a small deployment of Israeli soldiers from the Givati Brigade's elite Palsar reconnaissance unit that included twenty-three-year-old Lt. Hadar Goldin attempted an incursion east of Rafah, in the Abu Rous area, occupying a local home with armored vehicle accompaniment. Launched just minutes before the ceasefire, the raid was a provocative maneuver. A group of Al-Qassam fighters emerged from a tunnel to attack the Israeli soldiers. With AK-47 rifles and a tandem-charge anti-armor explosive device launched from a RPG-7, they killed two soldiers, Maj. Benaya Sarel and Staff Sgt. Liel Gidoni, and badly wounded Goldin, whom they then attempted to spirit away through a tunnel as a captive.

Givati Brigade commander Col. Ofer Winter immediately ordered soldiers in the area to give hot pursuit to the Al-Qassam ambush team. Lieutenant Eitan (his last name was withheld by the Israeli army for unspecified reasons) lobbed a grenade into the tunnel shaft, and then led two other soldiers inside. On the way through the tunnel, he found pieces of Goldin's uniform, suggesting that Goldin had been mortally wounded. The physical evidence Eitan retrieved allowed the Israeli army to declare thirty-six hours later that Goldin was a casualty of war.

Goldin's personal background gave the incident special gravity: He was the second cousin once removed of Israeli Defense Minister Moshe Ya'alon. The family tie was withheld from the Israeli public by an official gag order while the Israeli military deployed another deception to establish political space for a major escalation in violence.

Hours after the seventy-two-hour humanitarian ceasefire was to go into effect, a tired-looking President Barack Obama appeared before the press corps in Washington DC to accuse Hamas of violating the terms of the deal. "I have unequivocally condemned Hamas and the Palestinian factions that were responsible for killing two Israeli soldiers and abducting a third almost minutes after a ceasefire was announced," Obama said.

In fact, Obama was acting on dubious information supplied to him by the Israeli military, which claimed that the clash east of Rafah took place at 9:30 a.m.—an hour and a half after the ceasefire was in place and several hours after the clashes in eastern Rafah began. Besides the information published at 6:30 a.m. on Al-Qassam's Twitter feed about the fighting, more than a dozen civilian residents of eastern Rafah who witnessed the clashes and the subsequent Israeli bombardment told me in separate accounts that the battle began at 7 a.m. or minutes before.

Echoing the disinformation that had been fed to President Obama, Kerry declared that Hamas had committed an "outrageous" violation of the ceasefire. White House Press Secretary Joshua Earnest reinforced Kerry's denunciation by saying it "would be a rather barbaric violation of the ceasefire agreement."

Having falsely accused Hamas leadership of orchestrating the kidnapping of the three Israeli teens in June, and then assailing the group for "purposely playing politics" when it rejected the Egyptian ceasefire proposal that offered it nothing beyond a return to the status quo of siege, Kerry and the Obama administration once again provided the Israeli military with the diplomatic cover it needed to escalate the violence.

While the White House harrumphed condemnation of the impudent Hamas, the Israeli military bombarded eastern Rafah with almost every mode of destruction available to it, from F-16 missiles to naval shelling to drone strikes, mortars and tanks. In a matter of hours, at least five hundred artillery shells and hundreds of missiles were dumped on the city, almost entirely in civilian areas.

The Israeli army had activated the Hannibal Directive.

Forced to Pay with Their Lives

The Hannibal Directive was established in 1986 following the Jibril Agreement, a prisoner exchange in which Israel traded 1,150 Palestinian prisoners for three Israeli soldiers. Amidst the political backlash, the Israeli military drafted a secret field procedure to prevent future kidnappings. The proposed operation was named after the Carthaginian general who chose to poison himself rather than be held captive by the enemy. Among those who drafted the doctrine were Asa Kasher, a Tel Aviv University philosophy professor who serves as a house "ethicist" for the Israeli military and developed the army's so-called "purity of arms" doctrine, which governs its policies on attacking civilian targets. Kasher denied knowledge of the policy in a 2003 exchange with one of his students but now admits its existence and has even defended Ofer Winter's decision to implement it. (Maj. Gen. Yaakov Amidror, a former National Security Advisor for Prime Minister Benjamin Netanyahu, and former Israeli army Chief of Staff Gabi Ashkenazi also participated in devising the Hannibal Directive.)

Kasher has fervently denied that the official policy is aimed at killing captured Israeli soldiers, however, claiming that "you cannot throw a grenade towards the three of them, two abductors and the soldier, in order to abort the abduction." Yet, Amidror conceded to Israeli reporter Mitch Ginsburg:

"It's a military operation to return a hostage soldier. Soldiers' [lives] can be risked."

In 2009, the Israeli military killed Yakir Ben-Melech, an Israeli citizen and patient at a mental health clinic in the southern city of Ashkelon. He had escaped and was scaling a fence to the Gaza Strip. The former deputy chief of the Israeli army's Southern Command, Zvika Fogel, later admitted that the military had enacted the Hannibal Directive to prevent Ben-Melech from being taken captive by Hamas. "The Hannibal procedure is definitely the right procedure. We cannot afford now some cellmate next to Gilad Shalit," Fogel said, referring to the captured Israeli soldier whose freedom cost Israel the release of more than a thousand Palestinian prisoners.

Within minutes of Goldin's capture near Rafah, Israeli military correspondent Attila Somfalvi reported that the words, "Hannibal! Hannibal!" began blaring across Israeli army communications systems. Lieutenant Eitan, one of the soldiers assigned with pursuing and killing Goldin, later declared, "I didn't give an order to shoot, I told [a fellow soldier] you identify [anyone] you shoot. Even if this means killing Hadar [Goldin], even it means wounding Hadar—this is what you do. Painful as it is, it's better this way."

Heavily edited audio recordings released in December by army sources that were cleared by the military censor offered new details on the spree of destruction around Rafah. The possible capture of Goldin had sent Lt. Col. Eli Gino into a state of extreme agitation. Having not witnessed the incident, Gino can be heard in the audio frantically ordering his troops: "Go, go, go! Give him another shell."

"Bring [a weapon whose name is excised from the recording] into that darn [refugee] camp and send it up into the air," an unidentified officer can be heard exclaiming.

"The entire mosque is full of holes. There's nothing of it left," another declares.

As members of the Givati reconnaissance unit opened fire with reckless abandon, as though they were re-enacting an American Western gunplay, the gung-ho Gino eventually realized that the main threat to their lives was not from Al-Qassam fighters, but from each other. "You're shooting like retards. You'll kill one another. Enough!" Gino shouted. "I already have dead, retards. Wait a minute..."

The application of the Hannibal Directive in Gaza should have provoked widespread controversy in Israel, regardless of whether Jewish Israelis cared about the lives of Palestinian civilians. After all, it was designed to kill Israeli soldiers to spare their government the political cost of securing their release in a prisoner swap. The parents of active duty soldiers would undoubtedly prefer to have their children released at any cost, so long as they were returned alive. Yet there was little public protest of the policy's application in the Israeli media or from the parents of soldiers.

The right-wing governing coalition that had rebuffed a US demand to release a batch of Palestinian prisoners in the final stages of framework negotiations earlier in the year had even approved a law that effectively banned future prisoner releases. In a political landscape dominated by hardliners like Economics Minister Naftali Bennett and Foreign Minister Avigdor Lieberman, who were vocally against prisoner swaps, the Hannibal Directive was the military's only option for dealing with the possible capture of Goldin. It was not just an order that the military could choose to exercise, but had become a political imperative.

One of the few Israeli public figures to protest the policy's application in Rafah was Uri Arad, a veteran of the 1973 war who had been held captive by the Egyptian army, a member of the medical faculty at Tel Aviv University, and a political opponent of Netanyahu. According to Arad, the Hannibal Directive represented "a radical change from this way of thinking that propped up the value of human life." It was a disturbing sign of the dominance of a ruthlessly authoritarian right wing, he argued. "Now, in place of the government serving its citizens," Arad wrote in the Israeli daily newspaper, *Yedioth Ahronoth*, "it is the citizens who are forced to pay with their lives in order to serve the interests of government. This is simply called fascism."

Col. Ofer Winter, the religious nationalist commander of the Givati Brigade who vowed to wage a "holy war" to punish Gaza for the crime of blasphemy, claimed his forces implemented the Hannibal Directive for the sole purpose of battering Goldin's captors, not to kill him. "That's why we used all this force," Winter insisted in an interview with the newspaper *Yedioth Ahronoth*. "Those who kidnap need to know they will pay a price. This was not revenge. They simply messed with the wrong brigade."

"My soldiers killed five terrorists out of the tunnel shaft," he claimed, referring to Lieutenant Eitan rushing into the tunnel where Goldin was taken. Raising his hands to the heavens before his Israeli interviewer, Winter exclaimed, "Thank God, thank you God!"

However, the attack on Rafah extended well beyond the fighters who attacked Goldin's unit and captured him. By sundown on August 1—the day known in southern Gaza as Black Friday—much of Rafah lay in ruins, and as many as 121 lay dead, including 55 children, 36 women, and five men over the age of 60. Indeed, the overwhelming majority of those killed during the two days of hellish bombardment had no role in the fighting.

Children of the Qadan family display spent Israeli munitions they found in and around their house after Black Friday. Photo by Dan Cohen.

No Sanctuary

On August 18, day three of the ceasefire, I returned with Dan Cohen and Ebaa Rezeq to the easternmost area of Rafah where Goldin was allegedly captured and where Israel's rampage began. It was where Mahmoud Abu Said had been taken hostage and used as a human shield two weeks before, and where Israeli snipers occupying the top floor of his house had picked off his neighbors.

On the dusty lane where I had first met the shell-shocked Mahmoud, next to the crater of an exploded missile, his cousin, thirty-three-year-old Nidal Abu Said remarked to me, "I've been married for five years and thank God we don't have a child. I wouldn't want them to witness what we went through here. We lived through a real-life horror movie."

Nidal Abu Said and over a dozen of his family members and neighbors told me that the violence began on August 1 at around 7:30 a.m. with the sound of loud explosions from Abu Rous, an area just east of their neighborhood, near the ruins of the airport. This contradicts US and Israeli claims that the Al-Qassam Brigades attacked Israeli soldiers after the seventy-two-hour ceasefire was in place.

Like the Abu Said family and residents across Rafah, Abu Said had left the UNRWA shelter when the ceasefire was announced and returned to his home. When the Hannibal Directive was declared in response to Goldin's capture, these civilians were like sitting ducks. "We saw every kind of weaponry directed at us," Abu Said told me, pointing to the shards of Israeli munitions scattered across the road where we stood.

Abu Said told us his cousin witnessed a missile strike in the middle of a crowd attempting to flee from the Israeli bombardment engulfing the neighborhood. "There was a huge number of martyrs there," he said, claiming Israeli forces deliberately concentrated their shelling on the crossroads to prevent anyone from escaping. "They trapped us," he said.

From the Abu Said home at the eastern edge of Rafah, we traveled closer to the city center to meet more survivors of Black Friday. We arrived at the home of fifty-six-year-old Kamal Qadan, who gathered about twenty members of his extended family in a long salon. While we sat on cushions on the floor, listening to Qadan's story of escape, his grandchildren played in a corner of the room with pieces of the Israeli mortars and flares that had exploded nearby.

Qadan said he and thirty members of his family had watched from their windows as their neighbors attempted to flee, only to fall under the intensifying shelling. For the next three hours, they remained inside until the bombardment grew even stronger, shaking the walls of the house.

"They fired every kind of weapon at us and bombed us indiscriminately," he said. "Finally we decided to go out and prayed to God we would arrive safely to a hospital."

The ICRC and Palestinian Red Crescent had been barred from entering eastern Rafah by the Israeli military, so the Qadans were left to find their own way to sanctuary. Kamal Qadan said he ordered his family into the road and instructed them to walk in a straight line towards Youssef Al-Najjar Hospital in central Rafah—the only major medical facility in town. However, the shelling on the main road grew so intense the family had to change course.

"We could see tall buildings totally leveled," Qadan said. "People were being shelled, their bodies flying into pieces right in front of our eyes. We survived because God watched over us. We were running blindly, we just wanted to survive. We were running like insane people—we weren't thinking about anything."

Miraculously, the Qadan family arrived at Al-Najjar Hospital without losing a single member. But they were not safe yet. "The moment we got to the hospital and could catch our breath," Kamal Qadan said, "Israel called the hospital and said they were going to bomb it."

"The condition in the hospital was disastrous," he continued. "It was full of wounded patients and martyrs. The Israelis insisted on bombing the hospital, so we evacuated and left the dead bodies. It was such a hideous scene I cannot even put it into words. It was insane, we were waiting and the hospital was begging the Israelis to delay and give us some time to evacuate and get the wounded out. The whole time, ambulances were rushing to the hospital with large numbers of injured people. Some of the ambulances arriving at that time had been attacked."

With the sound of exploding bombs growing closer, Qadan and his family escaped again, to his brother's house in western Rafah, where they remained for the next three days. Qadan told me he did not seek shelter in an UNRWA school because Israel had begun shelling those, too. There was no sanctuary anywhere in the Gaza Strip, not in UN-operated schools, nor in hospitals.

According to the UNRWA, by Saturday, August 2, the Israeli military had attacked a full third of Gaza's hospitals, along with fourteen primary healthcare clinics and twenty-nine ambulances belonging to either the Red Crescent or the Ministry of Health.

The Cooler

As the dead and wounded descended on tiny Kuwaiti Hospital, the duty of imposing order on an impossibly chaotic situation fell to Samir Homs, the hospital's sixty-seven-year-old director. He was no stranger to violence. The Israeli army killed his father when he was six months old and his first son during the Second Intifada. Still, he told me Black Friday was like nothing he had ever witnessed.

"Out of the twenty hours we were treating patients, I was running for fifteen hours—not walking," he told me in his office on the second floor, speaking in the passable English he honed during a medical stint in the United States. "Every floor was covered with wounded patients. We were treating the injured in dental chairs, doing surgery on the ground, doing anything we could to save people."

In normal times, Kuwaiti Hospital serves two or three cases a day, usually older women. "Our colleagues weren't used to seeing bodies that were 70 percent burned or decapitated heads," Homs explained. When one of the hospital's nurses,

Dr. Samir Homs of Kuwaiti Hospital in Rafah, beside the ice cream cooler where dead children were stored on Black Friday.

Karam Dhair, arrived among the dead, torn in half by a drone missile, Homs said several of her female co-workers fell to the ground in grief.

As the dead bodies continued to be piled up throughout the day, Homs was forced to send for ice cream coolers and vegetable refrigerators from local shops. It was in coolers normally used to preserve food that Gaza-based journalist Mohamed Omer reported that he saw "the corpses of children, young men and women lying on top of one another, soaked in blood. Many were impossible to identify and only a few have been placed in white burial shrouds."

In one ice cream cooler laid the corpses of several infant children tightly wrapped in white sheets.

While shrapnel caused most of the wounds Homs treated, he described treating patients for unusual injuries that suggested that Israel was using experimental weaponry. They consisted of one-millimeter entry wounds that did negligible damage to the skin or skeleton, but left widespread burns on the internal organs of the patients, usually leading to their deaths within two or three days. The wounds Homs described were telltale signs of Dense Inert Metal Explosives (DIME), an experimental munition that generates high intensity explosions in a concentrated area. Since 2006, doctors in Gaza have documented unusual injuries suggesting the weapon's use by the Israeli military against civilians.

Though the worst was over by the time we met him, Homs said all supply lines to his overwhelmed hospital remained blocked.

"They are just hunting us and everyone is a target no matter who they are," Homs sighed. "We love peace and we want dignity but the Israelis won't allow us to practice these things."

The Fog of Holy War

Having reduced Khuza'a, Beit Hanoun, and eastern Rafah to ash and rubble, Colonel Winter was back in Israel on August 10 for a concert arranged to honor his Givati Brigade. When Winter learned that a female singer, Sarit Haddad, would perform before his troops, however, he announced his objection on religious grounds, prompting her replacement by a male singer. Yet when religious soldiers in the Givati Brigade followed suit, attempting a protest walkout over the presence of female musicians in the army band backing the male singer, Winter was compelled to issue orders forbidding them from leaving the auditorium.

A graduate of the Bnei David yeshiva in the religious nationalist settlement of Eli, which has sent at least fifty commissioned officers into the Israeli army, the Givati Brigade's Winter channeled the attitudes of the young citizen-soldiers rising through the ranks of the military. The hero of a generation, Winter returned from the battlefield to bask in the adulation of his countrymen. On August 15, *Yedioth Ahronoth*, the country's most influential paper, published a lengthy interview with the commander, noting, "Winter cannot walk around today without being stopped [by passersby on the street], hugged, asked for a photo opportunity." According to the paper, "there is no officer currently in the [army] who is as admired" as Winter.

The interview highlighted Winter's unabashed Jewish fundamentalism. Recalling a mission to destroy several rows of civilian homes in Khuza'a where Palestinian fighters had supposedly taken shelter, Winter conjured a hallucinatory vision of godly intervention. "We were protected by clouds, clouds of divine honor," he claimed. "We—all the warriors—were suddenly covered by a heavy fog, which came with us throughout the attack."

Asked about the orders he gave after Goldin's capture, Winter freely admitted to invoking the Hannibal Directive. "I announced on the communication system the word that no one wants to say—'Hannibal,'" Winter told his interviewer. "In other words, there had been an abduction. I instructed all the forces to move forward, to occupy space, so the abductors would not be able to move."

Winter then boasted of the violence he ordered, declaring: "We shredded them. We can do it much worse, and it's best for them that we not do it. We gave them a much stronger beating than in Cast Lead [in 2008–09]."

The Givati commander held the civilian population of Gaza— those whom he had cast as blasphemers against God—responsible for their suffering: "In almost every home there is a son or other relative that is a partner in terror," Winter remarked. "How do you raise children in a home with explosives? In the end, everyone gets what they choose." They were all, every last one, even the children, enemies deserving to die.

The 51 Day War elevated the status of fundamentalist warriors like Winter and electrified militant nationalist elements on the homefront. Back in Israel, in cities from Tel Aviv to Haifa to Jerusalem, the right wing pressed its attack against those they identified as enemies within.

Banner in Israel: "Winning is possible—Shut off Gaza's electricity—Electricity, gas, food—Yes, it is moral." Photo by David Sheen.

CHAPTER 9

Good Night, Left Side

The invasion of Gaza served as a bonanza for right-wing political mobilization, catalyzing an ultra-nationalist march through the institutions of the Jewish state. The right-wing's wartime success represented the culmination of the process the Israeli sociologist Baruch Kimmerling of Hebrew University called "politicide," or the calculated destruction of part or an entire community of people in order to deny them self-determination.

"Murders, localized massacres, the elimination of leadership and elite groups, the physical destruction of public institutions and infrastructure, land colonization, starvation, social and political isolation, re-education, and partial ethnic cleansing are the major tools used to achieve this goal," Kimmerling wrote in his classic 2003 biography of Ariel Sharon, the rightist warrior-politician and then-Prime Minister he cast as the architect of the practice.

Kimmerling concluded that the application of politicide against the Palestinian people had transformed Israel into "a

Thatcherist and semi-fascist regime" hostile to dissident expressions, resentful of the "other," and limiting democracy. Since his book's publication, the draconian trends he outlined have intensified dramatically, elevating into positions of power figures who have made the famously belligerent Sharon seem like a cautious moderate. Calls for ethnic cleansing and even incitement to genocide have become a routine feature of mainstream Israeli discourse while a majority of Jewish Israelis favor a broad array of policies aimed at forcible segregation, discriminatory laws and population transfer.

Once one of the Likud party's radical Young Turks, by the time the 51 Day War began, Prime Minister Benjamin Netanyahu found himself at the hollow center of Israeli politics, reacting to unrelenting pressure from incipient rightist forces—Economics Minister Naftali Bennett was a constant source of political coercion—to pursue the most drastic measures at his disposal against the Palestinians, particularly in Gaza. While Israeli parties across the spectrum traditionally closed ranks behind the military during periods of escalated violence, political opposition to disproportionate violence on civilians had never been more marginal and marginalized. The muted domestic response to the actions of Col. Ofer Winter's Givati Brigade in Rafah, Beit Hanoun, and Khuza'a, and to his apocalyptic rhetoric offered an illustration of the quelling of dissent in Israeli society.

Death tolls inside the Gaza Strip have risen dramatically since Israel withdrew its settlers in 2005, laid siege, and introduced its "mowing the lawn" strategy. With the steady escalation in violence, the Israeli government has advanced the process of politicide internally as well, cracking down on the isolated voices of dissent by cultivating a climate of intimidation and incitement. The near deafening silence was among the greatest political achievements of the right wing.

When the rocket warning sirens blared out across Israeli cities during the 51 Day War as the army moved in on the towns and cities of Gaza, hyper-nationalist elements in Israeli civil society emerged with a bellicose show of muscle, the fruits of years of mobilization. Throughout the summer, leading cultural figures, soccer hooligans, and settlers teamed up as if on command, to clear the streets of dissent, threatening and punishing the enemies within.

The Shadow

Yoav Eliasi is not only one of Israel's most prominent rap artists, he was a key organizer of the far right during Operation Protective Edge. A former low-level discipline officer in the Israeli army, Eliasi gained popularity during the Second Intifada as a rapper called The Shadow. He appeared on stage alongside his childhood friend, Kobi Shimoni, aka Subliminal, aping the sound and aesthetic of American hip-hop, but with a uniquely Israeli spin. Over the sound of gritty break-beats and stirring string samples, The Shadow and Subliminal defended cops and lionized army service, upending the anti-authority sensibility that defines traditional rap culture. When the two self-styled Zionist rappers performed during the bloodiest days of the intifada, their audiences often erupted with chants of "Death to Arabs!"

In June, following the abduction of the three Israeli teens, Subliminal took to Facebook to lash out at a Palestinian-Israeli member of the Knesset, Haneen Zoabi, who had objected to her interviewer's characterization of the kidnappers as terrorists. "I'm not ashamed to say that I hope she'll be run down [in an auto accident] and die, or slip in the bath and rip her head off, or eat a rotten egg and die of food poisoning, or anything the IDF can 'arrange'; for her, the quicker the better," Subliminal wrote on Facebook, earning thousands of "likes" from his fans. When Operation Protective Edge began, The Shadow took a more proactive approach, issuing an online call for his Facebook followers to confront a July 12 anti-war demonstration in Tel Aviv—"Looking for Traitors," it was titled. The response was so overwhelming, the rapper promptly transformed his Facebook page into an organizing hub for anti-leftist activity, inaugurating a nationwide movement named for the order issued to summon reservists to battle: Order Number 8.

Throughout the 51 Day War, The Shadow organized alongside Michael Ben-Ari, a ringleader of some of the settlement movement's most extreme elements. Ben-Ari was a former lieutenant of Rabbi Meir Kahane, the patron saint of Israel's ultra-nationalist right who immigrated from Brooklyn to Israel in 1971 to organize militant cells among fanatical Jewish youth. Though he was banned from the Knesset, where he served during the mid-1980s, for his open calls for violence, and his Kach party was outlawed, Kahane's influence has lived on in the discriminatory laws introduced by mainstream parties and through acolytes like Ben-Ari, who held a seat in the Knesset from 2009 to 2013. While in the Knesset, Ben-Ari turned his parliamentary field offices into organizing hubs for the anti-African movement, which organized vigilante patrols that harassed and incited violence against the sixty thousand non-Jewish African refugees living in Israel. Through Lehava, a radical hate group dedicated to preventing romantic relationships between Jews and Arabs, Ben-Ari and fellow Kahanists held rallies in mixed Jewish-Arab cities across Israel to spread fear and hatred of supposedly predatory Arab males. In June, Lehava had helped organize the "Death to Arabs" rallies in Jerusalem that inspired the killing of Muhammad Abu Khdeir.

Among the crowds were young people sporting stickers that read, "Kahane Tzedek," or "Kahane was right."

The Shadow and Ben-Ari's forces stormed the July 12 anti-war demonstration in Tel Aviv with reinforcement from the "Ultra" hooligans of the soccer teams Beitar Jerusalem and Maccabi Tel Aviv. When the police fled the area during a rocket warning siren, the rightists promptly set in on the protesters, attacking anyone they could find with chairs, sticks, rocks, eggs, and their bare fists. Among the mobs that assaulted demonstrators were a group of Maccabi Ultras sporting t-shirts emblazoned with the phrase, "Good Night Left Side"—a slogan first popularized by European neo-Nazis seeking to assault anti-fascist protesters.

A week later, a mob of assorted right-wing nationalists assaulted an anti-war rally in Haifa, bombarding the gathering of Palestinians and leftists with a hailstorm of stones while police stood by and watched. After burning a Palestinian flag while chanting "Death to Arabs," a group of right-wing activists went looking for Arabs to assault. They found Suhail Assad, the deputy mayor of the city, beating him and his son so severely that they had to be hospitalized. When police passed by, the assailants simply walked away, and the police made no arrests.

The next day, the Palestinian member of the Knesset, Haneen Zoabi was momentarily handcuffed during a protest, and then accused of insulting a police officer. Soon after, she was suspended from the Knesset for six months for her comments on the three kidnapped teens. Since Zoabi traveled on the Free Gaza Flotilla, where Israeli commandoes killed nine activists in a brazen high seas raid, she has become the most hated woman in Israel. Every election cycle since she has served in the Knesset, a coalition of major Zionist parties has introduced successful motions to ban her from running for office, not only because of her involvement in the flotilla, but because of her advocacy of transforming Israel into a state with no racial or religious preferences—a "state of all its citizens." Supreme Court decisions overriding the elections ban are all that has separated Zoabi from a permanent ban from the Knesset.

When the beleaguered anti-war forces regrouped in Tel Aviv on July 26, the right-wing mobs were ready. Photos of key radical left organizers—many taken by right-wing thugs during the previous rally—had been circulating on the Order Number 8 Facebook page. As soon as the protest concluded, small groups of rightists followed those they recognized as anti-war activists to their homes and attacked them at their doorsteps.

After attacking the anti-war demonstrations, Order 8 followers proceeded to supply the names of so-called traitors to their employers, pressuring companies and government agencies to fire the anti-war elements burrowing within the system. Dozens lost their jobs, most of them Palestinian citizens of Israel who had taken to Facebook to protest the army's actions in Gaza. When a postal employee posted a call for sending leftists to gas chambers, however, her government employer defended the statement on the grounds of free speech.

The violent onslaught of these right-wing groups startled even the most experienced Israeli leftists. "One of the effects of this war is the loss of Tel Aviv. We used to think of Tel Aviv as this liberal bubble, but that's gone," Kobi Snitz, a math professor, filmmaker, and veteran activist from Anarchists Against the Wall, remarked to me at an anti-war rally on August 8 in the Jewish-Arab city of Lod. "There is simply no space left for us to organize in, and it's because there is official approval and even encouragement for the people beating us in the streets."

Two days later, I watched riot police break up an anti-war demonstration of about five hundred protesters in north Tel

GOOD NIGHT, LEFT SIDE

Aviv on the grounds that gathering in large groups placed them in danger from rocket fire. The police proceeded to push the demonstrators from the vast concrete park in front of the Habima Theater towards Rotschild Boulevard, where they began tackling demonstrators and hauling them away to jail. I followed the demonstrators to a small park where they gathered momentarily to display photos and names of the dead in Gaza before suddenly dispersing. I asked a veteran activist why the march had ended so abruptly.

"Because we heard that fascists are on their way," he told me. "They are coming to hunt us."

I stood around for about twenty minutes waiting for the onslaught of angry nationalists, but it never came. A young woman in a tight-fitting pink tank top and toting a Hello Kitty purse arrived to heckle the few protesters, calling them traitors who deserved to be murdered by Hamas, but that was it. The fear spreading peripatetically throughout Israeli society had finally reached the normally undaunted forces of the radical left.

Bewildered by the well-choreographed assaults on their demonstrations by right-wing nationalists, ragtag bands of radical leftists regrouped under the banner of "Antifa," or anti-fascist action, gathering in semi-underground fashion to plan protests and train in Krav Maga, an Israeli hand-to-hand combat style taught to frontline soldiers that emphasized exceptionally aggressive attacks on the most vulnerable parts of the opponent's body. For the military draft refusers who formed the hardcore of Israel's radical left, the desire to defy the violent mentality and practices of a militaristic society had been supervened by the need to protect their bodies from it.

"The radical left didn't have the experience or the militant spirit to deal with the fascists' violence," Yigal Levin, an anarchist organizer of the self-defense groups, told left-wing Israeli journalist Haggai Matar. "That is why we brought people who know martial arts and offered free weekly lessons for any leftists who were interested. It wasn't only the anarchists or communists who attended—even liberals feel like anyone who is seen as a 'leftist' can be hurt now."

Many Israeli leftists I know confided to me that they were making plans to leave Israel for good. Some said the only thing preventing their immediate exodus from the violent pressure cooker was the lack of a second passport or adequate finances.

As Israeli Minister of Internal Security Yitzhak Aharonovitz issued a ban on all public demonstrations against the war— "There is no left and right here—we need to unite as a country and support the IDF soldiers who are fighting," he declared— the pro-war nationalists centered in on the media. Gideon Levy, one of only a handful of major Israeli columnists to have publicly protested the assaults on Gaza, faced an overwhelming deluge of death threats and attacks from fellow media figures for a column in Haaretz in which he cast pilots in the Israeli Air Force as the elites of Israeli society "perpetrating the worst, the cruelest, the most despicable deeds" by bombing civilian homes in Gaza. Eventually, his employers at Haaretz were compelled to hire him a bodyguard. According to Israeli reporter Orli Santo, several major news personalities were harassed, but only for perceived expressions of opposition to the war—some of those threatened had actually supported the attack on Gaza.

With paranoia spreading throughout the country, calls for genocide by Israeli public figures grew more frequent and forceful. Moshe Feiglin, a Deputy Speaker of Knesset so extreme Likud employed legal tricks to keep him off its 2009 electoral list, issued a detailed proposal on his Facebook page on August 1 to "designate certain open areas on the Sinai border, adjacent to the sea, in which the civilian population will be concentrated" and after shelling "formerly populated areas", "exterminate nests of resistance, in the event that any should remain." Dov Lior, the chief rabbi of the religious nationalist settlement Kiryat Arba, published a religious edict in July 2014 declaring that Jewish law supported "exterminating the enemy." Mordechai Kedar, a lecturer on Arabic literature at Bar-Ilan University, suggested on Israeli Radio that same month that raping the sisters and mothers of "terrorists" might deter militant activity. "This is the culture of the Middle East," Kedar explained. "I didn't create it, but this is the situation."

The incitement from the top emboldened Israeli teens flooding social media with genocidal fantasies of their own. David Sheen, an independent, Canadian-born Israeli journalist, published a collection of dozens of startling Twitter posts by adolescent Jewish Israeli women alternating between revealing selfies and annihilationist rants. "Kill Arab children so there won't be a next generation," wrote a user called @ashlisade. Another teenage female Twitter user, @shirzarfaty, declared, "Not just on summer vacation we hate stinking ugly Arabs, but for the rest of our lives." On a mortar shell that was to be launched into a civilian area in Gaza, a young Israeli soldier complained about a boy-band concert that was scrapped because of the fighting: "That's for canceling the Backstreet Boys, you scum!" he wrote.

Foreign Minister Avigdor Lieberman did his best to answer the teenagers' summertime blues, proclaiming during a visit to Ashkelon where he had to scurry into a shelter when rocket sirens sounded, "To the best of my understanding, it is not possible to ensure summer vacation, a normal summer for our kids, without a ground operation in Gaza."

Lieberman was struggling to keep his finger on the pulse of the Jewish Israeli public that, in late July 2014, told pollsters from the Israel Democracy Institute that they supported the war in Gaza at levels of 95 percent, with at least 45 percent complaining that the army had not used enough force. When he was not demanding an intensification of violence against Gaza, Lieberman was urging a boycott of Palestinian businesses in Israel that were striking in protest of the war on Gaza, or clamoring for the revocation of Qatari news organization Al Jazeera's broadcast license. But he could not keep up with the Jewish Home Party's Bennett, the hardline Economics Minister, whose party mates lambasted even Lieberman as a "leftist." The wartime frenzy of hyper-nationalism had pushed Bennett's party into second place in opinion polls, eating into support for centrist parties like Yesh Atid.

In cabinet meetings with Netanyahu and Defense Minister Moshe Ya'alon, an old guard Likudnik who supported the Prime Minister's strategy against Hamas, which hinged on weakening the group without aiming to remove it from power altogether, the upstart Bennett pressed for a total war that would see Hamas forcibly dismantled, once and for all.

CHAPTER 10

The Attrition Factor

As Israel's Givati Brigade concluded its decimation of Khuza'a and made plans to advance on Rafah, the Qassam Brigades initiated a new wave of surprise attacks. On July 28, Qassam fighters launched a mortar strike at a rallying point of Israeli soldiers across the Gaza boundary. The following day, Qassam's media arm posted one of the most stunning videos of the 51 Day War.

In footage apparently captured with a GoPro camera affixed to a Qassam fighter's helmet the day before, nine guerrillas are seen emerging from a tunnel at Israel's Nahal Oz crossing and rushing through a thicket of brush towards a military base. The group bursts into the heavily fortified base and easily overpowers Israeli soldiers, who appear to be hapless in close quarters combat. One Israeli soldier who attempts to resist is quickly overpowered and shot at close range by fighters who sprint from the base with his Tavor standard issue rifle in hand. They then retreat back to Gaza through the same tunnel shaft with only one dead. Five Israeli soldiers were killed in the incident, according to the Israeli military, but the number may have been higher than the army revealed.

The following day, the Israeli army spokesperson's unit attempted to cover up the embarrassment on the battlefield. It claimed in a statement to the media that the soldiers had been killed in a single RPG strike, then insisted that the soldiers had successfully stopped a planned Qassam Brigade attack on civilians living in the adjacent Nahal Oz kibbutz. Both claims were proven false, and the veracity of the video confirmed.

As *Haaretz* correspondents Chaim Levinson and Amos Harel wrote: "The Hamas men did not kill the soldiers from a distance but entered the compound and shot them at close range; no firing of a rocket-propelled grenade can be seen at all. It's also clear that the militants had planned to storm the position from the start and were not en route to the nearby kibbutz to massacre civilians."

The casualty count at this point in the war gave new urgency to the strategy Qassam Brigades commander Muhammad al-Deif had overseen. By August 3, just after the Israeli army enacted the Hannibal Directive in Rafah, the Israeli death toll stood at just over sixty-seven—almost exclusively soldiers and military personnel. Meanwhile, the Israeli army had killed more than eighteen hundred residents of Gaza, among whom 80 percent were civilians, according to estimates by the United Nations Office for the Coordination of Humanitarian Affairs and the Al Mezan Center for Human Rights. While Al-Qassam aimed to kill soldiers in close quarters engagements, the Israeli army had resorted to the Dahiya Doctrine, employing disproportionate force to batter Gaza's civilian population in vain hopes that they would turn on Hamas.

On July 30, former President Shimon Peres visited troops wounded in Gaza at an Israeli hospital. He was moved to concede that the ground invasion had "exhausted itself" and "now we have to find a way to stop it." Nahum Barnea, a widely read liberal Israeli columnist for *Yedioth Ahronoth* and winner of the nationally esteemed Israel Prize for cultural accomplishment, noted the scowling and grief-stricken expressions that washed across the faces of Netanyahu and Army Chief of Staff Benny Gantz during their press conference about the attack on Nahal Oz. "From the first day of the operation, we have been dragged and we are still being dragged," Barnea wrote. "Hamas is dictating the extent and length of the conflict, and our forces have not found a move, an initiative or a patent to break this dictation."

The Nahal Oz raid reinforced long-standing criticism that the Israeli army had badly atrophied after decades of policing an occupied, largely defenseless population. Just as the army was routed during its ground invasion of southern Lebanon in 2006, it had proven incapable of defeating armed factions in Gaza whose firepower was only a shadow of Hezbollah's. "We have been to a number of rallying points, and were amazed to discover that the lessons of the Second Lebanon War and [the military escalation in 2012] had not been implemented," a soldier complained to the Israeli paper *Yedioth Ahronoth* about the deadly mortar attack on July 28. Another soldier remarked that the army had been "punched hard in the gut" by the Qassam Brigades.

As the war entered its fourth week, Netanyahu, Defense Minister Moshe Ya'alon, and their kitchen cabinet of military and political advisors seemed determined to resist calls from right-wing members of Likud and Foreign Minister Lieberman to expand the ground invasion and move towards a full occupation of the Gaza Strip.

On July 31, Netanyahu, Ya'alon, and Army Chief of Staff Benny Gantz gathered cabinet ministers representing mostly right-wing parties from the governing coalition for what one

minister described as an "intimidation meeting." In the closed
briefing, army officials warned the ministers that reoccupying
Gaza would cost Israel a devastating price in blood and treasure, conjuring memories of the German siege of Stalingrad.
"At that meeting, they described to us scenarios that seemed
like they were taken from World War II," one minister who
attended the meeting recalled.

Though the Israeli army's ground war had exhausted itself,
the fighting was far from over. Not only was Netanyahu determined to deprive Hamas of claiming significant wartime ac-
complishments, but the US and Israel's chosen intermediaries
in all negotiations with Hamas, the Egyptian military junta,
was determined to keep Gaza in a vise for as long as Hamas
remained in power. Nothing but a retrenchment of the status
quo and a tightening of the siege would satisfy Egyptian President Abdel Fattah El-Sisi and his generals, who viewed Hamas
as the devious cousin of their internal nemesis, the Muslim
Brotherhood. It was unthinkable that any deal the regime put
forward would offer Hamas the humanitarian concessions it
had demanded at the onset of hostilities.

On July 29, the day Qassam released video of the Nahal Oz
raid, Al-Qassam Brigades General Commander Mohammed al-
Deif addressed the public. The faceless figure known around
Gaza as "The Phantom" had not been heard from since Operation Cast Lead in January 2009. With his refusal to engage in
politics and unswerving belief in armed resistance as a means
to dislodge Israel's occupation, Deif's street credibility was in-
disputable. As a seasoned tactician and war veteran, he was as
influential as anyone among the political leadership of Hamas,
with enough power to veto a ceasefire deal.

Speaking for four minutes in a subdued, almost atonal voice,
Deif set out to affirm the justice of Qassam's tactics—targeting

military personnel and bases—against those of the Israelis, who had aimed the brunt of their force against Gaza's civilians. He declared: "We have prioritized confronting and killing the military and the soldiers at the checkpoints over attacking civilians at a time when the criminal enemy wades in civilian blood and commits massacres and brings down the roofs of homes on top of the heads of their inhabitants. The more they [attack civilians] the more justified it becomes [for us] to kill their soldiers."

Deif rejected out of hand any deal that failed to satisfy the demands first outlined by Hamas at the onset of the war. "The usurping entity will not enjoy security as long as our people do not enjoy it and do not live with freedom and dignity," he stated. "And there will be no ceasefire unless the aggression stops and the siege is lifted. And we will not accept any compromises that come at the expense of the dignity and freedom of our people." The guerrilla commander seemed to have aimed this part of his message as much at the Israelis as at the Palestinian negotiators in Cairo, cautioning them against accepting a bargain that wasted the achievements he believed his forces had made on the battlefield.

Though he did not say so explicitly, Deif seemed to sense that the war was entering a new phase. He described the ground invasion as a boondoggle "where Israel seems to be sending in its soldiers to die," suggesting that Al-Qassam was ready for a long war against an enemy with every mode of destruction at its disposal. "We confirm our preparedness [for a long war] and are working based on previously planned-out strategies," he said.

Deif's confidence irked Yair Lapid, the Finance Minister and center-right Yesh Atid Party leader. "For years, Mohammed Deif has been hiding in the tunnels underneath Gaza, and that is where he will remain because he's a dead man," Lapid, a veteran broadcast personality and former Hollywood studio executive, rumbled.

By the first week of August, Israeli military morale was at a low ebb, but it maintained a decisive edge in diplomatic support and sheer firepower. In his public statements, President Barack Obama expressed compassion for the devastated population of Gaza, stating in an August 1 press conference that the images of children torn to pieces by Israeli shrapnel were "heartbreaking." However, the president placed blame entirely on Hamas for the civilian casualties, claiming that Hamas was "hous[ing] these rocket launchers right in the middle of civilian neighborhoods." Obama went on to declare that "Israel has a right to defend itself and it's got to be able to get at those rockets and those tunnel networks." He seemed to have heeded the warning from Netanyahu, who after the collapse of the August 1 ceasefire had told US Ambassador to Israel Dan Shapiro that the Obama administration was "not to ever second-guess me again [on Hamas]."

The Al-Qassam Brigades had, in fact, launched rockets within the close proximity of civilian areas, but not necessarily because it sought cover among civilians. The Gaza Strip is one of the most densely populated places on Earth, packed with refugees and devoid of open space, leaving guerrilla groups with little choice but to operate from within an urban maze. Al-Qassam was an underground operation in the most literal sense of the term. Its fighters spent much of the war in tunnels, separated from the civilian population, and often launched mortars and rockets from tunnel shafts. Few civilians I interviewed in Gaza had seen any fighters operating openly in their neighborhoods during the war. However, several residents of Shujaiya described to me having witnessed Al-Qassam fighters help evacuate residents during a ceasefire. Their accounts contradicted those of the Israeli military, which claimed Hamas had ordered residents to stay in their homes ahead of the ground invasion.

On July 29, UNRWA inspectors found a cache of rockets in an empty school that had been closed for the summer. It was the third documented incident of rockets found in empty schools during the month of July. In most cases when the Israeli military claimed to be targeting civilian sites housing weapons, however, independent investigators like Amnesty International could not find any confirmation—even as Amnesty prepared a report accusing Palestinian armed factions of "war crimes" for firing rockets indiscriminately into Israel.

While Obama chastised Palestinian armed groups, he helped replenish Israel's supply of munitions after it exhausted them on civilian areas in Gaza. The most critical delivery of US weapons to Israel took place on July 20, just a day before the battle of Shujaiya that saw eleven Israeli artillery divisions reduce the eastern Gaza neighborhood to rubble, when the Pentagon to allow Israel to dip into the stockpile of more than a billion dollars of arms the US maintained in the country. The weapons transfer included all the 40 mm grenade launchers and 155 howitzer rounds the Israeli military needed to continue its assault without interruption.

Back in Jerusalem, Economics Minister Naftali Bennett of the far right Jewish Home Party leveraged the war in Gaza to make a power play against Netanyahu. He revealed to the Israeli media that he had made direct contact with commanders in the field to help them coordinate its campaign against Gaza's tunnel network. Rumors circulated that Bennett's liaison to frontline troops was Avichai Rontzki, the former Chief Military Rabbi of the Israeli army who served as a spiritual guide of Bennett's party and maintained close ties to religious nationalist soldiers. Bennett also disclosed that he had pressed

Netanyahu for a ground invasion of Gaza immediately after the discovery of the bodies of the three kidnapped Israeli teens in the West Bank in early July. (Rontzki, who had reportedly donned Israeli army garb and insinuated himself among combat units in Gaza despite not having been called up for duty, was promptly dismissed from the army reserves. He denied any wrongdoing.)

Defense Minister Ya'alon—one of Netanyahu's closest allies in the government—was furious that a junior minister from a competing party had circumvented his authority and publicly undercut him. "That's unacceptable," the Defense Minister raged two months later. "Is it legitimate for a politician to form direct ties with army officers, and based on that, try to manipulate the chief of staff in the cabinet and say that he's a lazy horse compared to the galloping horses, the officers in the field?"

Taking credit for supposed actions against Gaza's tunnel network, Bennett hammered Netanyahu and his allies for their refusal to march on Gaza City. His behavior recalled the part played by Ariel Sharon in the early 1980s when the gung-ho right-wing Minister of Defense drummed up pressure on Likud Prime Minister Menachem Begin to take Beirut from the PLO. Without outlining a plausible strategy to reoccupy Gaza, Bennett bellowed out populist bluster: "Hit Hamas without mercy. Day and night. On weekdays and holidays. Without respite and without rest. Until they are defeated."

No matter how long the war lasted, Bennett demanded its prosecution until Hamas was finished. "If it takes a month, we'll take it. If we need a year to work in the border areas, we will ask for it and get it. If we need freedom for IDF operations in the Gaza Strip indefinitely, then we will ask for it and get it," Bennett declared.

With his incessant calls for total war, Bennett successfully enhanced his political standing before the rightward trending

Israeli youth who identified with him as "Brother Naftali." But it was Netanyahu and his inner circle who would bear responsibility for the outcome of the fighting. With control of the skies, the Israeli military pressed ahead with the bombing campaign that targeted civilian homes, factories, and infrastructure. It aimed to fulfill the "Disproportionate Force" doctrine drawn up by military advisors in 2008 that called for "inflicting damage and meting out punishment to an extent that will demand long and expensive reconstruction processes." As ground troops were pulled from Gaza, the lawn mowing continued.

CHAPTER 11

Three Million Bullets

In early August, as right wingers in the Knesset and cabinet remonstrated, Netanyahu scaled back ground operations, pulling troops away from the devastated border regions. Meanwhile, armed factions in Gaza were fully focused on rocket and mortar launches. Even as the Israeli army spokesperson's unit hyped the threat Gaza's homemade rockets posed to Israeli civilians during Operation Protective Edge, they were hard-pressed to highlight any substantial damage they did. However, the strikes managed to make life unbearable for many residents in southern Israel. As the mayors of cities like Sderot hammered Netanyahu for pulling back the ground troops, Hamas was demonstrating its ability to sustain an extended war. "Israel cannot afford a war of attrition," Foreign Minister Avigdor Lieberman warned, demanding that the military somehow finish off Gaza's governing faction fast.

Most Israeli citizens were firmly protected from rocket fire by fortified bomb shelters, an advanced early warning system that included cellphone alerts, and the Iron Dome anti-rocket system whose US taxpayer subsidy had just been reauthorized by President Barack Obama and the US Congress. Funding for the Iron Dome system was subsidized by US taxpayers to the tune of $200 million, beginning in 2011. In mid-July, at the onset of the 51 Day War, the US Senate authorized another $351 million subsidy to support the Israeli government request for more Iron Dome systems. While Prime Minister Netanyahu claimed the system intercepted the overwhelming majority of rockets fired into Israel from Gaza during Operation Protective Edge, military experts have questioned the claims. Theodore Postol, professor of International Security at the Massachusetts Institute of Technology, who published one of the most thorough critical surveys of Iron Dome's performance, attributes Israel's low wartime casualty counts to the country's advanced sheltering and early warning system.

Another factor in the low Israeli civilian casualty toll was the rudimentary nature of the rockets fired by armed factions in Gaza. The combined payload of the four thousand or so rockets launched into Israel during the war equaled approximately a dozen missiles of the kind the Israeli air force launched on Gaza from their F-16s. And the further the rockets traveled from Gaza, the lower their explosive payload was. In southern Israel, the only communities that lay fully exposed to rocket strikes were those of Bedouin citizens of Israel who lived in "unrecognized communities"—towns and villages the state refused to provide with the Iron Dome, rocket warning sirens, bomb shelters, or basic public services like electricity and water. While Jewish communities adjacent to the Bedouins' unrecognized villages were fully protected and publicly subsidized, the Israeli government advised Bedouin citizens to "protect themselves by lying on the ground," according to the Association for Civil Rights in Israel.

With the Israeli army estimating just over three thousand rocket launches from Gaza between the onset of hostilities and early August, and the Israeli civilian death toll below five, the *Times of Israel* published a story on a long-eared owl injured by a mortar fired from Gaza towards Kibbutz Nirim. "The bird is undergoing treatment at the animal hospital," Lazar Berman reported, "and vets hope he will be able to return to the wild."

Bombing the Dead

Back in Gaza, the Israeli air force continued its policy of bombing civilian homes. On August 4th, an Israeli drone strike killed seven members of the Najam family in the Jabalia refugee camp. The family was found as so many others were: buried beneath piles of cement and shattered furniture that had been sent crashing down on them. Earlier in the week, residents of the beachside refugee camp of Shati had to form a human chain to exhume pieces of dismembered bodies from the rubble of another family's home destroyed by an Israeli airstrike. "They passed to one another bits of debris," journalist Hamza Hendawi reported, "which the last member of the chain on the street end dropped onto a growing heap."

All over Gaza, residents experienced the intimate encounter with horror described in a wartime diary by Atef Abu Saif, a political scientist living in the Jabalia refugee camp: "To see death—to touch it with still-living flesh, to smell its saliva, to feel it in your hands, around you, on every corner of the street. To witness its brutality, its vulgarity, its mercilessness. To watch as bodes are scattered about in piles in front of you, like discarded exam papers at the end of a school term. One leg here, one arm there, an eye, a severed head, fingers, hair, intestines."

Cemeteries were routinely attacked by Israeli jets so bereaved families started attending funerals in small groups. In Khuza'a, on October 2, while burying sixteen-year-old Ghadir—the

The yard of UNRWA school in Beit Hanoun shelled by the Israeli military.

severely disabled girl who was left to die on the street as she attempted to escape the shelling in her wheelchair—the Rujeila family had to take shelter from an Israeli airstrike. I was reminded of their experience when I visited a cemetery in Beit Hanoun during the extended ceasefire in mid-August, where graves had been blasted to pieces by Israeli artillery shells.

All around the cemetery were destroyed homes and groups of homeless residents standing around in a daze. In a nearby UNRWA school that had served as a shelter earlier in the war, I found a classroom pierced and scorched by an Israeli airstrike and dried blood in the courtyard where a mortar strike had killed fifteen civilians on July 24. It was the fourth Israeli attack on UN schools in four days. And as the ground invasion wound down, the strikes on UN schools persisted. On August 3, the Israeli military targeted a crowded UN-run school in Rafah, killing at least ten civilians who had taken refuge there after their homes were destroyed.

On August 3, in Washington, State Department Spokesperson Jen Psaki issued one of the most strongly worded statements of the war from the Obama administration. "The United States is appalled by today's disgraceful shelling," Psaki declared. She added, "The coordinates of the school, like all UN facilities in Gaza, have been repeatedly communicated to the Israeli Defense Forces. We once again stress that Israel must do more to meet its own standards and avoid civilian casualties."

By the end of that first week of August, the number of children killed in Gaza stood at 408. According to an Associated Press (AP) investigation of Israeli airstrikes targeting civilian homes during the 51 Day War, in 83 Israeli airstrikes targeting civilian homes, three or more members of a family were killed. Among the dead were 108 preschoolers and 19 infants. In all, Israeli attacks on civilian houses killed at least 844 Palestinians during the war, with 89 percent of the dead confirmed by the AP to be non-combatants.

The head of UNICEF's field operations, Pernille Ironside, observed that in addition to the staggering death toll among children, some four hundred thousand had been badly traumatized by the assault. "It is an extraordinary thing to live through, and especially to survive and witness the use of incredibly damaging weapons that tend to slice people with terrible amputations and maimings, shredding people apart in front of children's eyes and in front of their parents as well," she remarked.

Hazem Abu Murad, the chief of Gaza's bomb disposal teams, had estimated on August 10 that Israel had dropped somewhere between eighteen and twenty thousand tons of explosives on Gaza since the war began. (Murad was killed while attempting to defuse an unexploded munition on August 13.) The Palestinian-American author and analyst Ali Abunimah wrote on his blog that if Murad's estimate was anywhere close to accurate, Israeli forces had used almost more explosives on Gaza than the US did when it bombed Hiroshima with a nuclear weapon that contained the equivalent of 13,000 tons of TNT. Unexploded munitions were so pervasive in the rubble and back-streets of Gaza's border areas that I learned to ask locals if any live bombs were lying around before I wandered too far.

"The cost of the total ammunition used in Gaza fighting is estimated at about 1.3 billion shekels [$370 million]," *Haaretz* reported on August 14. "According to the army's figures, 39,000 tank shells, 34,000 artillery shells, and 4.8 million bullets were supplied during the fighting. Senior military figures estimate that land forces alone used at least 60 percent of the 5,000 tons of ammunition given to them, but the IDF [Israeli army] cannot yet evaluate it accurately."

By the army's own count, it had fired around 3 million bullets—almost two bullets for every one of Gaza's 1.8 million residents.

Spent Israeli 155 mm artillery rounds were omnipresent in the homes I visited in Gaza: The cylinder shaped shells that weirdly resembled ancient Mesopotamian pottery could be found standing upright in a corner of a badly damaged room or lying somewhere in the yard. Some residents had decorated the used shells and transformed them into flower vases, while others repurposed spent mortar shells into ashtrays.

The shocking level of firepower Israeli forces exerted against Gaza's civilian infrastructure told the story of a frustrated Goliath unable to punish its vastly underarmed foe into submission. As right wingers in the governing coalition brayed for a thrust of ground troops that would cut into Gaza's soft heart, Zehava Gal-On, the chairwoman of the liberal Meretz Party and de facto leader of Israel's faded peace camp, taunted Netanyahu for supposedly allowing Hamas to score points on the battlefield instead of enabling Palestinian Authority President Mahmoud Abbas to score points in the diplomatic realm. Growing desperate for a major wartime achievement, Netanyahu searched for battlefield scalps he could brandish before an increasingly frustrated Israeli public.

No Deal in Cairo

When representatives of Palestinian factions including Fatah, Hamas, and Islamic Jihad arrived in Cairo on August 5 to negotiate terms of a possible final deal that might bring the war to a close, the Palestinians could not have been more divided.

Earlier in the war, Palestinian Authority President Mahmoud Abbas had lectured Hamas on the need to accept a ceasefire without fulfilling any of its preconditions. "What are you trying to achieve by sending rockets?" Abbas told Palestine TV. "We prefer to fight with wisdom and politics."

Hamas's popularity was soaring, prompting the *Washington Post* to declare Abbas the "big loser" of the war. Al-Qassam's refusal to back down before Israel's tanks and fighter jets had won Hamas credibility even in the streets of Ramallah, the gilded canton Abbas controlled with the iron hand of his US-trained security forces, and under the careful watch of Israel's military administration.

"It's not important who wins or loses," Abbas declared in the same interview, "What's important is to end this bloodshed."

Throughout the ceasefire negotiations in Cairo, while Palestinian Authority negotiators lined up behind the Egyptian regime, the Israeli delegation remained intransigent, refusing to acknowledge the humanitarian conditions the Palestinians placed on the table. "The delegation did not sense a true seriousness from Israel in the negotiations, since it is still stalling to answer to the Palestinian demands," Mousa Abu Marzouk, a leader of Hamas's delegation in Cairo, complained. Meanwhile, Israel's allies among the Egyptian junta presented the Palestinian factions with a memorandum of understanding that contained no guarantee that any of the key demands introduced by Hamas at the onset of hostilities in July would be met. "This document did not respond to any of our requests—the airport, the sea port, the buffer zone, the expansion of the fishing area, etc. There was also no explicit mention of the lifting of the siege," Hamas spokesman Sami Abu Zuhri declared.

Another Palestinian negotiator grumbled to the Egyptian news agency, Mena, that Israeli negotiators had suddenly rejected "what had been already achieved"—a possible reference to an agreement on the Palestinian Authority taking control of Gaza's border crossings—"and discussions had returned to square one."

A Day in Gaza City

Back in Gaza, a shell-shocked population took advantage of the extended ceasefire to shop, greet neighbors and ask after friends. As the sun set over the Mediterranean on the evening of August 18, I rode north on the main coastal highway from Rafah, coasting past beaches filled with people seeking a brief respite from the war. The lights of two Israeli gunboats shined in the distance. When I arrived in Gaza City, I found the main shopping district bustling with families and lines out the door of the famed local ice cream shop. "People really missed the street," Ebaa Rezeq explained to me. "Once the ceasefire was on, I watched my neighbors come out of their houses and hug each other and just celebrate that they'd survived that long."

The next afternoon, I set out in the streets of downtown Gaza City to experience the atmosphere of the city without the fear of Israeli missile strikes. As I walked towards the Rimal district, the annoying hum of the Hermes 450 drone that constantly patrolled the skies blended into the din of traffic, the banter of young men chatting about the war, and the pulse of Arabic pop music blaring from local stores. Walking just ten blocks through the suddenly vibrant streets of Gaza City after spending all week in the rubble of the devastated border communities was such an exhilarating experience I nearly forgot that the ceasefire was due to expire at sundown.

I stopped for a late lunch with Belal Dabour, a graduate from the Islamic University school of medicine interning at Al-Shifa Hospital with whom I had been corresponding through social media. Belal explained what happened when a group of four killed in a car by an Israeli drone strike arrived at Al-Shifa on July 7. They were not only among the first casualties of the war, they were the first Belal had seen up close in his medical career. "I wanted to conquer my fear," Belal recalled, "so I forced myself to look at their bodies and I remember everything from that day." Weeks later, he treated scores of casualties from Shujaiya when the market there was shelled on July 21. It was such a chaotic scene, with hundreds of family members crowding the intensive care unit, screaming and remonstrating, that some of his overwhelmed colleagues collapsed. By the time we met, however, Belal had become so inured to the daily confrontations with death and trauma that he was virtually numb.

"I'm like a whole new person," he reflected. "Two or three injured come in [to Al-Shifa] and later they die. Then you go have lunch with your friends. I've gotten so used to the smell of burning flesh I don't notice it any more."

After lunch, Dabour walked me to a cafe on a leafy side street in Rimal called Marna House. On the way, we passed a concrete block home collapsed by Israeli naval shells. It was a reminder that this middle class enclave had been targeted with more force than in any previous military assault. At the cafe entrance, Belal offered his prediction that the ceasefire would be extended, echoing an increasingly common view that the war had exhausted itself. But he added with a resigned shrug, "We never know what to expect any more."

In the breezy courtyard, beneath a tarpaulin canopy, I settled down at a table with my colleague Dan Cohen, who had taken a taxi over from Abu Ghalion, the seaside apartment we were renting. In our immediate vicinity, we heard the sound of American-accented English. At a table across the cafe, I spied a slender older man with leathery skin sharing sheesha with a local friend of his. I immediately recognized the man as Denny Cormier, a sixty-eight-year-old anti-war activist from Santa Fe, New Mexico whom I knew as one of the few Americans who had been living in Gaza for a long term period. After I introduced myself, Cormier explained how he arrived in Gaza earlier in the year and became instantly enchanted. Having left one of America's top retirement destinations, Cormier said he intended to spend his twilight years in the seaside ghetto of Gaza. "Everywhere I go here," he remarked with a look of wonder, "I make new friends and people invite me into their homes for dinner. I've never met more beautiful, welcoming people."

Earlier in the day, I had made contact with Ahmed Alghraiz and Aboud Bsaiso, the founding members of a local breakdance troupe called Camp Breakerz. After a few minutes, they arrived at Marna House, joining us at our table to explain how they spread hip-hop culture to the Gaza Strip. With wool caps, baggy t-shirts and jeans, and high tops, they looked like they could have been b-boys from any urban metropolis in the US. Raised in a Nusseirat Refugee Camp, twenty-five-year-old Ahmed had introduced breakdancing to the millennial generation seared by the seven years of siege and periodic wars. For him, the rebellious, confrontational sensibility and flamboyant, combat-inspired dance styles spawned in the blighted ghettoes of American cities were a perfect fit for the youth of Gaza.

"We perform our issues in our breakdance shows. We mix our situation and our dancing," Ahmed said, whipping out his laptop to show me a video of a Camp Breakerz performance in which members of his group thrust themselves through a paper wall that symbolized the siege and occupation. "In the whole world, there is no crew that does what we do."

Ahmed said his attempts to evangelize Gaza youth on the gospel of hip-hop was initially received with hostility by the local functionaries of Hamas, who rejected the gritty music and flamboyant dance moves as an imported form of Western decadence. But as Camp Breakerz persisted, even the Islamist authorities were forced to respect the group's integrity. It was not the repressive government that runs the internal affairs of the Gaza ghetto that had interfered with their creativity, but the siege imposed on Gaza from the outside. "Every day I say that I need new breakdancers to battle with," Ahmed explained. "When I battle with my guys, I know how to win. It's the same thing every time. I wish we could go outside of the Gaza Strip to have more battles."

The restrictions of the siege prevented Ahmed from importing new equipment for the dance studio that, during the war, functioned as a shelter for his family. Graffiti art, breakdancing, and rapping were growing in popularity among Gaza youth, he explained, but the Israeli blockade had prevented access to proper DJ equipment. The imposed restrictions had even forced Aboud, an aspiring musician who was one of the original members of Camp Breakerz, to attempt to build a guitar from scratch. But his instrument was only half-done, as the tuning keys and fretboard he needed to finish it were unattainable in

Gaza. Ahmed and Aboud asked me if I could make a run to Tel Aviv for them to pick up turntables, a mixer, and possibly a whole guitar. For the rare visitor to Gaza, it was almost as common to get requests like these as it was to hear war stories.

As twilight set in on Gaza, our conversation returned to the last minutes of the ceasefire. Dan mentioned reports of scattered rocket launches from Gaza into southern Israel that Hamas had yet to take responsibility for. He said some locals he had spoken to earlier believed the launch was a false alarm, while others were convinced it was orchestrated by local collaborators with Israel's intelligence services to provide the Israeli military with a pretext for resuming its bombing campaign. Just then, I noticed a small orange light flicker against Ahmed's cheek. It was accompanied by a distant thud.

"What the hell was that?" I exclaimed.

Ahmed and Aboud turned to one another. "There goes the ceasefire," Aboud mumbled with a slight grimace.

Another thud followed, then another, this one louder than the first two. The Marna House wait staff continued to shuffle across the patio, freshening sheesha coals and dropping off clear mugs of black tea as if the noise outside was caused by fireworks or a tailpipe backfiring, and not missiles slamming into homes a few neighborhoods away. As Ahmed and Aboud showed us another video of Camp Breakerz performing, I struggled to contain my anxiety.

When Ahmed finally asked a waiter for the bill, he ordered us to head home right away and stay inside. "Just because you're Americans doesn't mean you won't be targeted," he said with a stern finger wag.

We were in for a long night of bombardment. What we didn't know was that Israel had just attempted its most ambitious operation of the war.

CHAPTER 12

Assassins

By the time Dan Cohen and I arrived back at our apartment, the Israeli Hermes 450 drone swooping low over Gaza City sounded like a weed whacker waving back and forth above our heads. The drone was hovering at low altitudes, probing for targets. Israeli F-16s roared by every few minutes, followed by the jarring crash of a missile exploding somewhere in the distance. I peered out the window of our kitchen and saw a rocket rise from what looked like a beach somewhere south of Gaza City. The forty-third day of war was underway.

Our apartment was located directly across from the Gaza seaport, on the fourth floor of a building called Abu Ghalion. Part of a cluster of high-rise hotels that surrounded the port, the neighborhood had been filled with Western journalists during the Israeli ground invasion, but now stood mostly vacant as the foreign press parachuted into Kurdistan to cover the gathering fight against ISIS. Thanks to the heavy presence of journalists and aid workers, this area was considered the safest in the entire Gaza Strip. But that did not mean it was off-limits to Israeli shelling.

From our window at Abu Ghalion, we could see the ruined shacks where the young Bakr boys were cut down in front of the foreign press. The sight reminded us that for all the effort and resources Israel's government channeled into public relations, its military was killing civilians with little concern for the opinion of outsiders. With missiles raining down again on Gaza, the thought troubled me, as did the explosions that were rattling the walls of our apartment. I felt weak and jittery, and found myself lurching suddenly when a group of kids playing in an adjacent alley slammed a metal gate over and over.

We later learned that the airstrike that took place while we were at Marna House had destroyed the home of a family called al-Dalou in the Sheikh Radwan neighborhood of Gaza City. Several children were badly wounded in the attack and an infant and woman were among the dead. During the November 2012 military escalation, the Israeli military had bombed the same home, killing ten family members. At first, the military claimed it had made a grave mistake before it declared that it had targeted a high-level "terror operative."

Now the news came in that the strike on the al-Dalou family home was, in fact, Israel's latest attempt on the life of Al-Qassam general commander Mohammed Deif, who was said to be hiding out in the house with his wife and infant son. Before the war it was not known that the resistance icon they called "The Phantom" had a wife or any children. With the strike on the al-Dalou family's home, all of Gaza learned that Deif was indeed a family man, and that the woman and infant killed by the missiles were, in fact, his wife, Widad Asfoura, his son, Ali and his daughter, Sara. Asfoura had been previously married to another Qassam commander named Bilal Kasaa'a. She lived in a state of constant suspicion, quitting her job at a charity when she feared that local spies were closing in, then vacating her rented apartment just days before it was bombed earlier in August.

It was a mystery still whether Deif had survived, or whether, after a sixth assassination attempt, he had fallen like his predecessors Emad Akel, Saleh Shahadeh, Yahya Ayyash, and Ahmad Jaabari. However, a letter by Asfoura's mother suggested he had made it out alive. Written with the help of a local writer, Hadeel Attallah, the letter addressed Deif through the voice of his dead wife. "You drove Israel crazy by allowing them to see your actions, but not your face," the missive read. "Their attempts to assassinate you have failed, and the entire nation wishes to see your shadow, my hero, even from afar, but only I know the color of your eyes, the etchings of your face, how tall you are, how much sugar you take in your tea, and what your toothbrush looks like."

Win or Die

As the bombings intensified, Dan and I went upstairs to visit with some other journalists in an apartment rented by an Italian NGO. Unlike our apartment, this one was well appointed with comfortable wicker furniture and outfitted with a covered deck that overlooked the port. It had been occupied since the onset of the ground invasion by a freelance photographer named Lazar Simeonov. Lazar was among the witnesses to the killing of the Bakr boys, sprinting from his apartment to the beach to capture the aftermath of the deadly shelling. His photos captured a harrowing look at the bloodied boys as journalists and hotel waiters carried their limp bodies to safety. When he filed the pictures with his regular clients, however, they were rejected on the grounds that the images were too graphic.

The scenes of carnage and destruction had been a radicalizing experience for Lazar and other reporters I met, including

journalistic veterans who had seen the worst of the Syrian conflict and Iraq. But after more than five weeks of fighting, Lazar
and the other photographers who sifted in and out of his apartment had fallen into a Gazan state of mind, weathering the
nightly Israeli bombardments with absolute stoicism.

Perched on a beanbag chair in the corner of the living room sat
a photographer with shoulder-length blonde locks who resembled
a war-ravaged Brad Pitt. Named Ted, he entertained himself with
YouTube clips of jihadi recruitment videos and complained about
running out of cigarettes as if he had suffered a medical emergency. Ted reached for his mobile and ordered a new pack, if only
to prove that even under heavy missile strikes, a man on a motor-
bike would deliver virtually anything for a nominal fee. Twenty
minutes later, to Ted's massive relief, he was chain smoking again.

In the meantime, while Lazar dragged slowly on a cigarette,
ashed into a spent artillery shell and stared at a Real Madrid
football match on his laptop, Ebaa Rezeq and a neatly dressed
graduate student named Sami carried on a steadily intensifying
argument over the war. "What are we always fighting the Israelis for when we're not improving ourselves internally and focus-
ing on educating ourselves?" Sami said. "If we don't build better
institutions and develop economically, we can never advance."

"It's like you're pretending we're not under siege and there's
no occupation," Ebaa responded with a contemptuous smirk.
"Are you saying I'm not educated? For fuck's sake, Gaza is one
of the most educated places on Earth. But I have no visa, I have
no way out through Rafah, I have nothing! What can I do with
my education? That's the issue."

"I just wish Hamas had told me before I got married and
had a kid that they were going to go into this fucking war,"
Sami complained, throwing his hands over his head. "There
isn't going to be anything left here when it's all over!"

Ebaa countered that Israel would never relinquish its control over Palestinian life without massive resistance. "Look, it's very simple," she said. "As long as Israel is there, we'll be occupied. So we have to resist Israel. Maybe we'll get a backwards, repressive Arab state in return, but at least I'll have a visa. As of right now, I have nothing."

While scrolling through her Twitter timeline on her smartphone, Ebaa learned that Al-Qassam spokesman Abu Obeida was due to deliver an address in a matter of seconds. Ted clicked over to Al-Aqsa TV's livestream and found Obeida on-screen in his trademark red keffiyeh balaclava and camouflage jacket with a statement on Mohammed Deif's condition.

"Forty-five days have passed since the offensive was launched but Israel has only dared to kill our women and children. You're not brave enough to kill Mohammed Deif!" Obeida proclaimed in his distinctively tinny voice. He insisted that Deif had survived Israel's sixth assassination attempt.

Denouncing the "sadistic missiles" that killed members of the al-Dalou family and Deif's wife and son, Obeida taunted Netanyahu and his ministers: "We inform you, Israelis, that you've lost the battle. Once again you proved that you are a pack of losers. After 45 days of fighting have elapsed...all that you've been able to do is to kill our women and children."

Obeida pledged a furious response from Al-Qassam, warning Israelis in southern communities not to travel in large groups and to stay clear from crowded events. This was more than another psy-ops ploy; it was Qassam's way of claiming it took measures to avoid civilian casualties. He then warned airlines against flying into Ben Gurion International Airport, pledging to disrupt flights at the airport for a second time with rocket strikes. The first time it launched a salvo of M-75s at the airport, on July 22, the US Federal Aviation Administration issued a blanket ban on flights to Tel Aviv, Israel that lasted just over a day, a move that infuriated American supporters of Israel.

Finally, Obeida took on the negotiations in Cairo, describing them as a pointless boondoggle that would only lead the Palestinian people back to the status quo of occupation, siege, and exclusion. "After long weeks of byzantine negotiations and a succession of Israeli crimes, we declare the Cairo truce a born-dead initiative buried in the tomb of [Mohammed Deif's son] Ali Deif," he proclaimed. Though it was bound to honor the imperatives of Hamas's political wing, Al-Qassam seemed to be asserting itself against anyone in the Palestinian delegation tempted to ink a deal behind the backs of those who had sacrificed their homes, businesses and lives for the promise of relief from the siege.

"Either we win or we die," Obeida declared.

As Obeida signed off, we heard a rocket roar into the sky. When I checked my Twitter feed a few seconds later, I noticed that Israeli journalist David Sheen had tweeted from Jaffa, just south of Tel Aviv: "BOOM!"

Over a hundred rockets sailed from Gaza into Israeli territory that night, doing no major damage but reinforcing the point that Israel's operations had done nothing to weaken Al-Qassam's capacity to respond. Though Ben Gurion International remained open, scores of flights into the airport were cancelled due to "security reasons."

Afternoon at Al-Shifa

The impact of Israeli missiles was so powerful that locals slept with their windows open for fear of being injured by shattering glass from explosions hundreds of meters away. The incessantly buzzing drone, the roaring of the F-16s and the deep reverberations of the munitions pouring into Gaza from fighter jets and

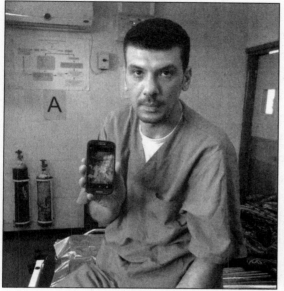

Dr. Hani Shaniti shows a photo he took of one of the Dalou children badly wounded in the Israeli assassination attempt on Mohammed Deif.

naval cruisers was so disconcerting, however, that I shut the windows in my room, cranked up an industrial size fan, and jammed foam plugs into my ear canals to deaden the noise of war.

I woke in the late morning to the thud of a naval shell and forced myself into the shower. With Gaza's desalination plants bombed to smithereens, showering had become an unpleasant experience. Warm, brackish water piped in from a Mediterranean coast saturated with fresh sewage—Israel had repeatedly attacked Gaza's ramshackle sewage infrastructure over the years—poured from the shower head, replacing my dried sweat with a soap-scented layer of grime. Some Gazans would purchase distilled water to wash off the dirty seawater that flowed from the shower. Hundreds of thousands of others in the strip had no running water at all, as the sanitation lines had been comprehensively destroyed across the decimated border areas. In the teeming UN schools where recently homeless refugees had taken shelter, doctors were battling an outbreak of scabies.

With my ability to travel around Gaza limited by the bombing, I spent the afternoon at Al-Shifa Hospital with Dan Cohen and Ebaa Rezeq. We wound up in an empty operating room with Dr. Hani Shaniti. A tall, slender surgeon in his early thirties, he described to us in a flat tone of having treated scores of unusual injuries characterized by tiny entry wounds that left extensive internal burns, possibly the result of DIME weapons like the kind Samir Homs had described at Kuwaiti Hospital in Rafah. The hospital was still running on short supply, with only three types of anesthetic and one size of needle, but highly professionalized staff like Shaniti had become experts at improvising with what little they had. He whipped out his phone to show us photos of some of the children delivered to the hospital by ambulance during the past day. Among them was a little girl from the al-Dalou family who had survived the five Israeli missiles sent crashing into her home, but who emerged from the rubble with her arms severed from her body. This child, who lay somewhere in Al-Shifa, sedated and behind a white sheet, had joined the more than 3,300 children wounded in the war. She, too, was a member of the shrapnel-lacerated people that Israeli Economics Minister Naftali Bennett accused of committing "self-genocide."

Most of the doctors I met in Al-Shifa were burned out from weeks of amputations and shrapnel extractions. A few even seemed to be on the brink of insanity. The director of the emergency room kept us seated in his office for a thirty-minute-long venting session. "We are human beings! Can't the world see that we're human?" he bellowed again and again as Ebaa rolled her eyes. She had grown frustrated with the Palestinians pleading for Western validation of their humanity, as if the value of their lives was not self-evident. On the hospital's second level, I encountered a mustachioed, middle-aged surgeon who demanded to know how much money Dan and I were making as journalists, accusing us of cashing in on Palestinian misery. A portly doctor chain-smoking on a couch nearby piped up to announce that he would not speak to another Western reporter, and that he would only speak Arabic to us. He repeated his declaration of refusal in near-perfect English.

We retreated to the courtyard in front of the hospital, where the medical intern Belal Dabour met us by a bombed-out ambulance and a row of refugees who had set up tents beside Al-Shifa. A few correspondents from Eastern European and Arab outlets milled around waiting for their broadcasts to begin. (American reporters were a scarce commodity at this point in the war.) Just before the ceasefire began, an Israeli drone had bombed Dabour's street, killing a ten-year-old boy. He apologized to me for his colleagues who had treated us with contempt but reminded me that they were coping with the effects of a war like they never experienced. Dabour expected that the trauma would catch up with him once the wartime adrenaline dissipated and life returned to whatever passed for normal in Gaza.

Suddenly, a row of cars barreled up to the hospital. In the first car, a man was hanging out the window waving a white shirt. In Gaza, this was the sign that vehicles were carrying dead and wounded civilians. As soon as they screeched into the parking lot, a woman sprinted from one of the vehicles with a limp infant in her arms towards the hospital's entrance. She dodged past a gurney carrying a man whose left leg had just been amputated and disappeared inside while the crowds milling around in the courtyard carried on as usual. It was just another afternoon at Al-Shifa.

A Funeral in Rafah

That night, after the forty-fifth day of war, Israel pounded Gaza with renewed ferocity. From my room, with the windows shut tight and the industrial fan cranked up to maximum speed, I could still hear the roar of F-16 jets as they coasted by, and could count the seconds before they struck their target—perhaps a rocket launching site or maybe some innocent family's home. I managed to drift off for a few hours before being ripped from my sleep by a series of explosions. It was 6 a.m. and the sun was beginning to rise over the Mediterranean.

I checked the Twitter timelines of local Gaza accounts for information on the bombings and found that most were reporting on a strike on a four-story home owned by Abu Hussein Kallab, a businessman in Rafah whose factory had been destroyed in a separate strike. Over a dozen bodies had been extracted from the rubble, including a little girl who had survived with a mouth full of concrete shards. The ferocity of the airstrike was on par with the attack aimed at Deif, a massive concentration of force on a single home that suggested top-level targets were inside.

By late morning, I learned that the dead bodies extracted from the rubble included three top Qassam Brigades commanders who had gathered inside the building to coordinate strategy. They were Raed al-Attar, the Qassam southern commander who oversaw operations in Rafah, his colleague, Mohammed Abu Shamaleh, and Mohammed Barhoum. Having led several operations in the field, including the tunnel ambush codenamed "Shattered Illusion" that brought the Israeli tank gunner Gilad Shalit into captivity, Abu Shamaleh was considered as a possible successor to Ahmad Jaabari when he was assassinated in 2012. Attar, for his part, was among Gaza's most revered figures for masterminding of the attack that captured Shalit. The deal for Shalit's release produced wild celebration across Palestine, but particularly in Gaza, as over a thousand prisoners were freed from Israeli jails and reunited with their families. Attar's hero status had been secured, as had his death sentence.

For his part, Barhoum was a veteran Qassam operative who helped coordinate the transfer of weapons through the tunnel network at Rafah. The three commanders played an arguably more important role than the partially crippled Deif in the day-to-day field operations of the Qassam Brigades. Indeed, Attar had overseen the operation to capture Lt. Hadar Goldin and was rumored to be one of the few people in Gaza who knew the whereabouts of Goldin's body.

With these assassinations, it seemed that the war would drag on endlessly. I was running low on cash and with the bombs falling again, my freedom of movement was severely compromised. That afternoon, I took a taxi to the Erez crossing and prepared to leave Gaza for a few days.

Inside the cavernous Israeli-run terminal, as I handed my passport to a young female COGAT administrator, she began pounding frantically on the bulletproof glass that separated us, ordering me to take shelter. A few seconds later, I heard something explode in the distance, likely a mortar round or rocket fired from Beit Hanoun. Watching well-protected Israeli soldiers panic was a surreal experience after witnessing the wholesale destruction they wreaked across Gaza.

In the parking lot outside Erez, an Israeli news crew from Channel 1 intercepted me and peppered me with questions about what I had seen inside Gaza. Did I see rockets fired from civilian areas? Was Hamas using human shields? What about the tunnels? Realizing this was more an interrogation session than an interview, I quickly found a taxi and headed straight to Ramallah.

That same afternoon in Rafah, 15,000 mourners marched through the streets of the war-torn southern city with the bodies of the three commanders wrapped in green Hamas burial shrouds. On sidewalks and in squares, men cried openly for the loss of those they saw as guardians of their city while colleagues of the three fallen commanders offered defiant tributes to them in a local mosque.

Attar and Abu Shamaleh had survived an assassination attempt in 2003 with the help of local farmers who hid them in an olive grove while Apache helicopters hunted them down. A year later, when Israeli special forces raided Abu Shamaleh's home, his neighbors helped him escape through the narrow lanes of central Rafah. This time, however, someone in the neighborhood had furnished the men's location to Israel's Shin Bet. Someone had been compromised by the intelligence services and induced into becoming a collaborator.

"My dad has spent his life fighting for the liberation of Palestine and today, my dad—they assassinated him," Abu Shamaleh's pre-teen daughter, Raba, told a local camera crew at her father's funeral. With tears streaming down her face, the distraught girl said, "It's all because of the collaborators and spies! And I tell my dad, God rest his soul, we'll go after them and we'll kill them."

The wartime anger directed at the occupier suddenly turned towards the traitors burrowing from within. The day after Abu Shamaleh, Attar, and Barhoum's assassination, a group of twenty-five accused collaborators that included two women was brought before a public crowd in al-Katiba Park in Gaza City. They appeared wearing masks, their identities concealed to guard their families from societal castigation. And then they were lined up against a wall and shot to death by members of the Qassam Brigades.

Photos of the execution were promptly disseminated to the media, presumably in hopes that the images would quell the anger overflowing across Gaza, and also as a warning to the collaborators who remained on the loose. Netanyahu's office seized on the execution scenes to portray Hamas as a gang of medieval fanatics no less barbaric than ISIS. By extension, he cast himself as the leader of the Westernized outpost on the front line against what he later described as "a world-wide network of militant Islamists" that "all share this fanatic ideology; they all have not only unbridled ambitions but also savage methods."

The image of spies dragged before firing squads is common throughout history, particularly among anti-colonial and revolutionary movements. But its appearance in Gaza exposed a depressing reality that was only discussed in whispers. Those who were executed had likely been among the most desperate of Gaza's dispossessed population. And before they became spies, they had been spied upon by the Israeli surveillance and cyberwarfare outfit known as Unit 8200.

An intelligence corps embedded within the Israeli military, Unit 8200 consists of several thousand of the army's most highly educated, technologically sophisticated soldiers. It is, in fact, the army's largest unit, comparable in its size and function to the US National Security Agency (NSA). Much of Unit 8200's work entails spying on everyone from Hezbollah and Hamas operatives to American citizens—the NSA handed over thousands of emails and phone communications to Unit 8200 of Arab and Palestinian-Americans, according to journalist James Bamford. In Gaza, Unit 8200 works with the Shin Bet to cultivate spies by compromising residents of the strip who might have fallen into difficult circumstances.

In a bracing September 12, 2014 joint letter declaring their refusal to serve any longer in the military, Unit 8200 veterans detailed how they preyed on innocent Palestinians, exploiting the weakest and blackmailing the most vulnerable. "If you're homosexual and know someone who knows a wanted person, Israel will make your life miserable," one of the Unit 8200 whistle-blowers explained to a reporter at the *Guardian*. "If you need emergency medical treatment in Israel, the West Bank or abroad—we searched for you. The state of Israel will allow you to die before we let you leave for treatment without giving information on your wanted cousin. If you interest Unit 8200 and don't have anything to do with any hostile activity, you're [still] an objective."

"All Palestinians are exposed to non-stop monitoring without any legal protection," the letter read. "Any Palestinian may be targeted and may suffer from sanctions such as the denial of permits, harassment, extortion, or even direct physical injury."

There was not a shred of sympathy to be found anywhere in Gaza for the poor souls who had fallen into circumstances that led them to collaborate. Though the Gaza-based Palestinian Center for Human Rights condemned the executions of the accused spies, a clear consensus in Gaza supported the death sentences. If I heard any dissenting opinions around Gaza, they were from those who believed the collaborators should not only have been executed, but brutalized as well.

Once again, Palestinians were pitted against one another through the machinations of their occupier. Palestinians killed Palestinians who had gotten Palestinians killed while Palestinian Authority President Mahmoud Abbas undercut the negotiating position of Hamas. Back in Tel Aviv, Netanyahu heaped praise on Shin Bet Chief Yoram Cohen for orchestrating the assassinations, while Amos Harel, military correspondent for the zealously anti-Netanyahu newspaper, *Haaretz*, proclaimed: "Assassinations of Hamas commanders could make Netanyahu the hero."

But Israel was hardly finished. As the war entered its denouement in the final week of August, the military readied a series of dramatic strikes aimed at the heart of Gaza City. The goal this time was to set the stage for the war's aftermath by provoking Gaza's middle class against Hamas.

CHAPTER 13

Bringing the Towers Down

Just after 7 p.m. on August 23, residents of the Zafer 4 and Zafer 1 towers in the central Gaza City neighborhood of Tel al-Hawa received a startling deluge of phone calls from strangers identifying themselves as members of the Israeli military. The ominous calls instructed the residents to immediately evacuate their apartments so the Israeli air force could bomb them without killing civilians. A drone was hovering overhead and F-16s could be heard roaring in the distance. The inhabitants of the two apartment buildings filled the streets carrying all the personal belongings they could quickly collect in the few minutes they had to escape.

As the evacuees assembled down the block, the drone launched a "knock-on-the-roof" rocket into a top floor of the building, sending sparks bursting into the night sky but doing little structural damage. Rockets like these contained light explosive payloads designed to frighten inhabitants out of their homes in advance of destructive missile strikes. Though their role in lowering the civilian death toll during the 51 Day War

Residents of Zafer 4 placed a sign on their ruined homes comparing Israel's attack on their building to Al Qaeda's attack on the World Trade Center. Photo by Dan Cohen.

was superficial at best, they helped Israel defend itself against growing charges that it was targeting civilians.

Fifteen minutes after the flurry of phone calls to residents of the towers, an F-16 swooped in to deliver the death blow to Zafer 4. With the first missile it fired, the Israeli jet left the high-rise wobbling like a punch-drunk boxer lurching for the ropes. With a second missile, it sent the monolith crashing to the ground, reducing twelve stories and the homes of scores of families to ash and ruin.

From the street, twenty-three-year-old Jehad Saftawi stared at the smoldering ruins of Zafer 4 and awaited the decimation of his home in Zafer 1. "Until now we are just watching and waiting for the Israeli warplane to target my building and my house," Saftawi said in a video diary he recorded on the scene. "I'm just waiting for the Israeli missiles to target my building and my house and to target my memories. I'm just watching and waiting."

A human rights researcher and videographer who did work for a New York City–based nonprofit, Saftawi had operated an online video livestream from his apartment balcony that recorded Israeli tank shells striking nearby buildings; he witnessed airstrikes on family homes in the distance and he saw the bright orange flash and billowing plumes of smoke rise in the air when Israeli jets bombed the administrative offices of Islamic University. The Israeli missiles would strike within meters of his apartment, destroying the tower across the street but leaving his building standing in the end.

As with Saftawi, the attack left the towers' residents alternating between confusion and despondency. They were the professional middle class of Gaza City, the doctors, engineers, journalists, and technocrats who had no affiliation with Hamas or Islamic Jihad. Though a Hamas-affiliated member of the Palestinian Legislative Council lived on the ground floor of Zafer 4, the building was honeycombed with Fatah supporters, including top-level security officials and a former advisor to Palestinian Authority President Mahmoud Abbas. Fatah is the Palestinian faction that controls the Palestinian Authority, the US-backed entity that Israeli intelligence and cabinet-level officials hoped to reinstall as the governors of Gaza. So why was Israel targeting its Gazan power base?

Despite having overseen the assassinations of three top-level Al-Qassam Brigades Commanders three days before, Netanyahu's popularity remained dangerously low by this point in the war, with only 38 percent of Jewish Israelis expressing approval of his performance. Rocket and mortar barrages continued to batter southern Israeli communities, demonstrating the Israeli military's failure to undercut Al-Qassam's deterrent capacity. On August 22, the day before the military targeted Zafer 4, a mortar round fired from Gaza killed Daniel Tragerman, a four-year-old resident of Nahal Oz. The outpouring of grief for the first child casualty of the war that Jewish Israeli society could identify brought renewed political pressure on Netanyahu. He needed to strike hard and soon, as the negotiators in Cairo seemed to be nearing a deal.

With the military's target bank virtually exhausted, Netanyahu and his kitchen cabinet of security advisors and military chieftains had resolved to extend the war into the sector of Gazan society that had the least involvement in the conflict. "Nothing is immune, even if a fourteen-story building has terrorist activity, the building will be damaged and will collapse," an Israeli military official declared on August 23. That day, in addition to destroying Zafer 4, Israel brought down the Rafah commercial center, obliterating all four floors of a downtown shopping mall that was home to forty-seven shops.

As night fell, Israeli intelligence services hacked into the signal of the Hamas-run Al-Aqsa TV to deliver an ominous threat. White Arabic script appeared against a black and yellow Star of David, the logo of the Israeli military. The lengthy message concluded:

"For your own safety, prevent the terrorist groups from using your facilities for their purposes and move away immediately from the places where the terror groups are active. People of Gaza—the war is not over yet. You are warned."

Earlier on August 23, the leader of the Hamas delegation to Cairo, Mousa Abu Marzouk, had suggested that the war had become a stalemate and hinted that Hamas was prepared to accept a truce. A few days later, on August 25, Islamic Jihad officials in Cairo told reporters that they were ready to sign a ceasefire agreement. But even with the war's end on the immediate horizon, the Israeli air force bombed the passenger terminal at the Rafah crossing—the only way out of Gaza for most of its residents. Then it homed in on another of Gaza's landmark towers.

In the early hours of the morning that same day, an Israeli drone hovered over the Italian Compound in Gaza City's Rimal neighborhood while residents came pouring out of the sixteen-story apartment tower following a flurry of ominous phone calls from the Israeli military. Built by an Italian company, the tall green and white tower was a local landmark, housing more than fifty families who formed the spine of Gaza's educated middle class. At the tower's base was a block-long row of cafes and restaurants.

As the Italian Tower residents watched from the street in their nightclothes, F-16s swooped in for the pre-dawn attack, blasting the walls of the tower with a series of missile strikes. The jets failed to bring the well-constructed tower to the ground, leaving it as a ravaged pillar chewed to its core by shrapnel and high explosives, a monument to the final stage of malevolence.

Days later, after I re-entered Gaza, Dan Cohen and I met Hatem Yahya Al Barawi in an empty lot in front of the Italian Compound. Barawi was a thirty-eight-year-old lawyer who had fled his neighborhood in the eastern Gaza City neighborhood of Al-Tufah after Israeli shelling destroyed most of the buildings on his block. He and his family had taken up residence in the Italian Compound less than a week before it was struck by the F-16s. "This is not a rocket factory and it is not a weapons storage building," Barawi protested. "The people here are civilians. They are doctors, teachers, businessmen—they're the best of society. So why else destroy this tower but for the savagery and barbarism of the Israelis that target everything on this land: humans, stones and plants? Why else but to plant terror and fear and kick people out of their land?"

Israeli violence had become such a consistent feature of Gazan life that few of Barawi's neighbors were terribly shocked by the destruction of their homes. "We actually got used to all the explosions," he reflected. "Everyone was prepared for their ceilings to collapse on them so they sat in their apartments and played with their kids and did what they normally do. We prepared while watching TV or doing mundane things just to move from this world into the next."

Silencing the Media

Three hours after decimating the homes of seventy families in the Italian Compound and blasting cafes and commercial shops at the building's base to ruin, the Israeli air force moved on to another civilian target in the area. It was Al-Basha Tower, Gaza City's oldest and most notable high-rise complex and the home to dozens of media organizations. Basha Tower was the base of operations for virtually any working journalist living in the strip. International correspondents also made use of the building; when Bloomberg sent foreign staff to Gaza, they worked from the Basha Tower office of Saud Abu Ramadan, a fifty-year-old reporter who regularly published with the American news organization.

In the early hours of the morning of August 26, the doorman at Basha Tower received a phone call from the Israeli military informing him that the building was about to be destroyed.

When the doorman demanded proof he wasn't being pranked, the caller addressed him by name. Five minutes later, a drone fired a warning rocket into the side of the building, provoking media staff to rush out through the front door and into the street with any equipment they could carry. Families who had taken shelter in the building after losing their homes in Shujaiya and Beit Hanoun were about to become homeless all over again. As evacuees filled the streets, they rushed into adjacent apartment blocs to warn residents that the thirteen-story monolith was about to fall, and that it might destroy their homes as well. Just moments before, the journalists had been covering Israel's attacks on towers. Now they became the story.

At 4:30 a.m., Israeli F-16s launched a fusillade of precision guided missiles into Basha Tower, sending it crashing into the ground. "That pilot was a fucking engineer!" a local driver who witnessed the attack marveled to me. "Man, he carved that building up like a cake." Mohamed Omer, the Gaza-based journalist who had closely documented the past two wars, reported that the Israeli military had used 5,000-pound GBU bunker buster missiles in its attempt to kill Mohammed Deif. The swift and comprehensive destruction of tall and well-constructed towers in central Gaza City raised questions about whether GBUs designed to penetrate thick layers of reinforced concrete had been used again, against civilian targets.

In fact, in 2012, the US Department of Defense had authorized a $647 million ordinance shipment to Israel that provided its air force with 1725 BLU-109 and 3450 GBU-39 bunker buster bombs. The shipment of munitions was designed to replenish the supply that Israel had exhausted during the November 2012 military operation that left more than a hundred civilians dead in Gaza. Before a US sale of GBU missiles to Israel in November 2009, diplomats from both countries privately concluded that "the transfer should be handled quietly to avoid any allegations that the USG [government] is helping Israel prepare for a strike against Iran," according to a cable later published by WikiLeaks. As one civilian high-rise after another came crashing down in Gaza, however, it appeared that Israel had found uses for the weapons against targets much softer than underground nuclear facilities.

Outside the rubble of Basha Tower, next to a tent that functioned as his makeshift office, I met Basel Qananeh, a youthful news anchor for a local radio station called *Voice of the People*. Qananeh was among those who went from reporting on the attacks to fleeing from them. It was not until hours after the bombing, when he saw the smoldering ruins of Basha Tower, that he was able to recognize the gravity of the assault. "I turned on the TV and saw the tower where I worked for eight years, that we don't just see as a media institution—it's part of our souls—completely destroyed!" Qananeh recalled.

Qananeh viewed the destruction of Basha Tower as an attack on Gaza's entire journalist community. "They target journalists and civilians to silence the media outlets that hurt the occupier in front of world opinion," he told me. "For us in the media, this isn't the first time and it won't be the last time that the enemy targets journalists or journalism headquarters. The occupation does not distinguish between a civilian, a journalist, and a child. They just target Palestinians in a barbaric manner. This is not going to affect us. We will continue to cover all of the crimes of the occupation. As journalists, we have to be the messengers and deliver the news."

Aside from Netanyahu's demagogic references to "terror towers" in a meeting with the regional council heads from the south, the Israeli government offered little justification for bringing the residential apartment blocks and commercial centers down. A report published on the attacks in December 2014 by Amnesty International concluded that Israel was guilty of "deliberate destruction and targeting of civilian buildings and property on a large scale, carried out without military necessity."

Basha Tower's destruction was the final indignity for a Gazan media that lost sixteen members during the war, including several who literally died on camera. Curiously, the attacks on journalists and their offices generated little outrage in the West, even when those journalists worked for major Western media outlets. Israel's bombing of the office owned by the independently contracted stringer for Bloomberg News, Saud Abu Ramadan, was not mentioned in Bloomberg's coverage of the war. When Israel attacked the Mushtaha building, another office complex in central Gaza City that housed the offices of major foreign news agencies like Andalou and Xinhua, local photojournalist Wissam Nassar told Dan Cohen that the bombings destroyed his car. Nassar's photography regularly appeared in the *New York Times* during the war, however, the attack that ruined his vehicle and destroyed a building filled with media offices was absent from the paper's coverage.

Signing Off

During the 2012 military escalation in Gaza, then-Egyptian President Mohammed Morsi mediated negotiations that compelled Israel to halt its assassinations of Palestinian leadership, helping to bring the fighting to an end before it spiraled out of control. But with Egypt now under the control of Abdel Fattah Al-Sisi's military junta, the Israeli military had been granted virtually unlimited space to act. It was not until the morning of August 26 that Israel agreed in Cairo to halt its policy of assassinating the leadership of political and military factions in Gaza. That same day, Palestinian negotiators signed an agreement to bring the 51 Day War to its conclusion. The truce would begin on August 26 at 7 p.m.

The truce as it was detailed by negotiators on all sides appeared to contain few concrete provisions for improvements to the conditions of life in Gaza. Negotiations on major demands like the rebuilding of Gaza's airport and the construction of a seaport were left for a later date, leaving many Palestinians to wonder if Hamas had agreed to the hollow peace that Egypt, the Palestinian Authority and the US had demanded it accept at the beginning of the war.

Among the only concessions to Gaza's civilian population was an expansion of the fishing zone from three miles to six miles from Gaza's shore. How the new terms would be enforced if Israel's navy decided to abrogate them as it had consistently done in the past was left unexplained. The deal also contained vague language about increasing traffic through the perpetually sealed Rafah Crossing, but there was little indication that the ferociously anti-Hamas Egyptian regime would honor such concessions. From Jerusalem, Netanyahu boasted to a wary public that Hamas had "agreed to the same Egyptian ceasefire proposal that we were ready to accept directly at the outset [of the war] without time constraints and without any of the conditions that they set. They got to this point the hard way. They kept testing us and every time we struck them but the last time, given this accumulation of blows, they were persuaded."

As the truce deadline approached the fighting intensified. On the afternoon of August 26, while Israel struck mostly civilian targets in Gaza, Al-Qassam Brigades fighters launched more mortar attacks on the mostly empty Israeli communities on Gaza's periphery where Israel's military remained massed. Unlike rockets, the mortar rounds were impervious to Israel's Iron Dome system, and rarely triggered warning sirens. Two Israeli civilians were killed and five wounded by a mortar attack on one of the southern kibbutzim, compounding the anger of the southern Israeli community council heads who had spent the day raging at Netanyahu for signing what they called a "surrender to terrorism."

In the minutes leading up to the 7 p.m. ceasefire, Gazans poured from their homes and filled the streets of cities across the battered strip, if not to commemorate a decisive military victory, then to celebrate their survival of 51 days of violence that left no one unscathed.

CHAPTER 14

Defiance in the Rubble

On August 26, the night the ceasefire took effect, the streets of Gaza City filled with tens of thousands of people. Exhausted by 51 days of war, they were ready to return to life under conditions they hoped would be at least marginally better than before. But they also seemed to have accepted that life in Gaza would never be the same again.

The boisterous procession through Gaza City was not a victory parade in any traditional sense; it was a display of popular defiance, an opportunity for common Palestinians to exhibit their solidarity with Gaza's fighters and their determination to resist at any cost. Among the crowds, a stout middle-aged woman summoned my colleague Dan Cohen to the van where she sat surrounded with children waving the green Hamas banners. "I'll die and I'll give [up] all my sons if that's what we have to do to liberate Palestine," she declared vehemently. Clutching an expressionless little boy by his shoulders, she exclaimed, "This is my youngest son and I'm prepared to give him up, too, if that's what it takes!"

Beside a Palestinian flag, the names of the past three military conflicts; beside Israel's flag, graffiti reads, "You have been defeated."

Throughout Palestine, victory was understood not necessarily as a decisive military triumph, but as a forceful demonstration of qualities like *sumud* (steadfastness), *fidaa* (sacrifice/redemption), and *ebaa* (stubbornness in the face of power) during a prolonged trial. This attitude has, of course, been a feature of anti-colonial struggles throughout history, from Vietnam to Algeria to South Africa, but it was especially pronounced in Gaza, where 1.8 million ghettoized refugees were taking heavy losses against a nuclearized army equipped and financed by the superpowers of the West. I witnessed the clearest distillation of this defiance in Beit Hanoun, the decimated northern border city. There, during the mid-August ceasefire, I met a family gathered above the ruins of their home, a four-story structure that had been transformed into a massive crater by a direct hit from an Israeli fragmentation bomb. On a flat slab of concrete that sat above the gargantuan sinkhole, graffiti read "3 to 0," portraying the Palestinian armed factions as the victors of the last three military conflicts in Gaza.

The celebratory gunfire that punctuated Gaza's victory processions—and which caused dozens of injuries and even a few deaths—was an important component of the exhibition of defiance. Among Israel's key demands at the start of the war had been the full demilitarization of Gaza, with Interior Minister Yuval Steinitz predicting that "Gaza will be exactly like Ramallah." By displaying their automatic rifles and letting rounds off into the sky, the young men of Gaza distinguished themselves from their counterparts in the West Bank who had been disarmed and were now policed by the security forces of Palestinian Authority President Mahmoud Abbas that coordinated directly with the Israeli army. A group of young male revelers reinforced the point, chanting, "Abbas is a traitor!" as they cheered a Qassam fighter passing by atop a pickup truck bed.

Besides Al-Qassam, the Al-Quds Brigades of Islamic Jihad planned a victory parade of its own the following day. The local wing of the Al-Aqsa Martyrs Brigade of Fatah, the group that controlled the West Bank, also participated in the fighting alongside the Popular Resistance Committees, a faction founded by ex-Fatah fighters who had refused to demilitarize as their comrades in the West Bank had done. The Popular Front for the Liberation of Palestine (PFLP), a traditionally left-wing party that had faded into the margins as Hamas and Fatah competed for control of the Palestinian polity, saw a resurgence during the 51 Day War as its Abu Ali Mustafa Brigade complemented operations by the better equipped armed factions. The battlefield had provided the various parties with a momentary relief from the painful rifts that had plagued the Palestinian national movement over the years. With Hamas's political leadership emerging from bunkers and returning from Cairo, however, politics quickly returned to the fore.

Mahmoud al-Zahar was among the first to address the crowds in Gaza City. A sixty-nine-year-old surgeon with a salt-and-pepper beard and shock of gray hair combed across his scalp, Zahar was one of Hamas's most veteran leaders and the key link to the movement's military wing. Having spent the war underground, he returned to a home that had been reduced to rubble for the second time since the Second Intifada. Before the celebrating crowds, Zahar set out to assuage doubts about the deal Hamas had just signed. "We will build a seaport and an airport. We don't need anyone's approval for that," Zahar pledged, sending gales of cheering through the crowd. He even vowed that the Al-Qassam Brigades would "attack the ports of anyone who attacks ours."

But there was little indication Israel would stand aside and allow Gaza to restore its bombed-out airport in Rafah or build a seaport. And it was unclear how a lightly armed guerrilla force like Al-Qassam could deter attacks on either construction operation from a blue water navy and one of the world's most advanced air forces.

On August 27, following the popular celebrations the night before, a crowd of more than ten thousand filled the vast concrete lot in front of Gaza City's parliamentary building for Hamas's official victory celebration. It was a festive scene, with food vendors clustered around the lot to serve up grilled meats and juice to the families who descended on the celebration with green Hamas banners in hand. Some parents had dressed their children in military garb, with custom-made camouflage outfits and plastic toy guns. A young government official caught me photographing a father adjusting the mock uniform of his son, who looked to be about five years old. "I'm against this," he whispered to me, side-eyeing the battle-dressed kids.

The event's highlight was the appearance of Ismail Haniyeh, the former Prime Minister of the Palestinian Authority who voluntarily resigned from his position when Hamas agreed to

A Qassam fighter at the official Hamas victory celebration on August 27 in Gaza City. Photo by Dan Cohen.

the unity government with Fatah. One of Hamas's more pragmatic and politically ambitious figures, Haniyeh had spent the war in a bunker, evacuating his home before the Israeli air force obliterated it with a missile strike. His reemergence before the massive crowd was a carefully staged event designed to wed the most visible local leader of Hamas with the universally revered fighters of the Qassam Brigades. As soon as Haniyeh appeared at the podium, a long procession of masked fighters proceeded through the crowd, ascending dual staircases beside the dais and assembling along the walls that rose above Haniyeh's audience. The fighters were joined by exuberant girls in plain clothes and little boys in mock uniforms, including one clutching a model of a M-75 rocket.

The optics deflected attention from the political consequences of the deal the Palestinian delegation had just signed in Cairo. In fact, Haniyeh did not mention the deal at all in his thirty-minute address to the crowd. Instead, he focused on the role Hamas played in shoring up the capacity of Gaza's armed factions. "We are proud to have embraced the resistance and even after years of being in power, we did not shy away from helping it. Even after years of governing we did not shy away from embracing the resistance forces," he declared.

Gasping between sentences in the sweltering afternoon heat, Haniyeh went on to thank the residents of border areas like Beit Hanoun and Shujaiya who had lost their homes and were still living in shelters. "The bravery of Shujaiya and Beit Hanoun and the other border towns allowed us to defeat the army of the Zionist enemy. And it was on the borders of Gaza that we crushed the myth of the invincible army," he announced, prompting the war's popular battle anthem, "Here We Prepare," to pump through the PA system.

"The *sumud* of Gaza will be rewarded with victory!" Haniyeh promised. But how? How would the military achievements of Gaza's armed factions and the titanic sacrifices of its civilian residents be converted into concrete gains, especially when a global juggernaut pressed against the gates of Gaza with all of its weight? Hamas had fewer allies in the region than ever and powerful antagonists among the Saudis, the United Arab Emirates, and the Egyptian regime, not to mention the EU and the US. So far, the answer was elusive.

"Talk is vain and victory cannot be captured in words," Haniyeh concluded.

No Longer Orphans

Hours after the official Hamas victory parade on August 27, the Al-Qassam Brigades gathered in the ruins of Shujaiya for a dramatically staged press conference. The setting was chosen for its

Qassam fighters hand rifles to two female supporters seeking a victory selfie. Photo by Dan Cohen.

symbolic value; it was here that Qassam and an array of armed factions from across Gaza's political spectrum dealt the Israeli army a bloody nose in one of the war's most intense battles. And it was from Shujaiya that a group of Qassam fighters staged its stunning raid of the Israeli military base at Nahal Oz. From this decimated city, Abu Obeida was expected to use his first post-war appearance to consolidate the legend of Gaza's resistance.

As darkness descended, I followed a long procession of families and young men past the seemingly endless skeletons of bombed-out four-story homes towards Al-Qassam's press conference. The hundreds of onlookers gathered before a dirt mound at the eastern edge of Shujaiya that had been transformed into a stage for the press conference. Generator-powered spotlights illuminated the stage while the rest of the neighborhood fell into complete darkness. In the distance, further to the east, just beyond the concrete walls that encircled Gaza, the lights of Nahal Oz glittered. The hum of the ever-present drone could be heard overhead. As the media assembled its cameras before the stage, fifty or so masked fighters attempted to clamber up the dirt mount and gather around the makeshift podium. They wound up tripping over one another and nearly caused an embarrassing pileup. "Two fighters from each faction!" a man barked through a megaphone, attempting to coax a few fighters down from the mound as a stray gunshot sounded nearby.

At the base of the makeshift stage, Al Qassam had laid out its panoply of weapons. A masked fighter in black battle dress uniform balanced a Yasin rocket launcher on his shoulder, displaying the homemade RPG honed by the assassinated weaponsmith Adnan Al-Ghoul. Another fighter clad in a ghillie suit—an outfit layered with camouflaged strips that resembled a Swamp Thing costume—posed with the long-barreled, homemade Al-Ghoul sniper rifle that was responsible for several long-distance kills during the battle of Shujaiya. Next to me, a fighter palmed a high explosive mortar round identified with English markings.

Though Al-Qassam fighters assumed a prominent position on stage, the scene was carefully choreographed to present an image of factional unity. Thus the red flags of the leftist PFLP fluttered beside the green banners of Hamas. Next to them were the white-and-yellow flags of the Fatah-affiliated Al-Aqsa Martyrs Bridgade and the black banners of Islamic Jihad's Al-Quds Brigades.

In his characteristic red keffiyeh mask, Abu Obeida emerged in the center of the fighters with a wireless microphone in one hand and a handwritten statement in the other. He spoke eloquently in ornate Arabic. "Our people have lived what it means to be orphans," Obeida proclaimed. "They've been oppressed and defeated. And today, from Gaza, the symbol of perseverance and victory, it has become clear to the whole world that we are no longer orphans. The orphans have grown up. The resistance has become strong. And they will not allow anyone, whoever they are, to oppress them or to behave towards them like tyrants."

Obeida's speech highlighted the psychological importance of the armed struggle. For those who had suffered at the hands of the Israeli military with the deaths of multiple family members, the destruction of their homes and the loss of their livelihoods, Al-Qassam's headlong battles with Israeli soldiers and persistent rocket salvos provided a sense that their sacrifices had not been in vain. Next to Obeida stood a stocky fighter brandishing the Tavor rifle that had been captured from an Israeli soldier in the now famous Nahal Oz raid.

While Abu Obeida hyped wartime achievements, he slipped in a pointed message to the Palestinian political leadership that had kept a safe distance from the battlefield. Crafted with apparent input from figures outside of Qassam's ranks, and delivered in the name of the united armed factions of Gaza, the Qassam spokesman struck a populist tone.

"The resistance unifies us and brings us together and ends our differences," he bellowed before the crowd of mostly young men packed around the dirt mound where he stood. "This is our greatest achievement through this great battle. It marks a red line that our people will never allow anyone to cross ever again. And we will look with suspicion at anyone who steps over it. We will not return to divisions and differences, exchange accusations or abdicate responsibilities. From now on, no one is allowed to return to the painful past."

His message could have been aimed at Mahmoud Abbas, whose Palestinian Authority had avoided paying Hamas government employees after it entered the unity government in June. Or it could have been applied to the political leadership of Hamas that had summarily stripped Fatah employees of their positions once it consolidated power in Gaza in 2006. Abu Obeida criticized those who continued to "exclude sections, factions and resistance groups of our people. We need an immediate and serious effort to restructure our national institutions so that they are more inclusive and can represent our legendary people in the best way," he declared.

A spontaneous chant rose from the crowd, "Unity! National, national unity! Our identity is Palestinian! Our resistance is Islamic!"

As soon as the press conference dispersed, young men rushed forward for selfies with the masked fighters like sports fans asking their favorite athletes for autographs. The fighters eagerly obliged, posing with ramrod straight torsos and Kalashnikovs across their chests. Near the stage, a group of young men grabbed Al Jazeera Arabic's star correspondent Tamer al-Meshal and hoisted him up to the sky with celebratory cheers. Meshal's coverage of the massacres in Khuza'a and Shujaiya and his special report on the Al-Qassam Brigades were some of the most widely viewed pieces of broadcast journalism any Arabic-language reporter produced during the war. Though he is virtually unknown in the West, the young correspondent had become a local hero who told Gaza's story from a literally underground-level perspective.

I wandered away from the festivities and back into the blacked-out streets of Shujaiya, which were lit only by the light of cellphones and piles of broken furniture set aflame. The footsteps of Qassam fighters as they sprinted towards waiting pickup trucks resounded in the night. I turned a corner and found a burning couch at the entrance to the rubble-strewn street where Salem Shamaly was cut down as he searched for his missing family. A dozen young men stood around in silence, staring at the bonfire and the shadows that danced against the pockmarked walls of the homes they used to live in.

CHAPTER FIFTEEN

Dodging Death

Children play in Gaza City's port the day after the victory parades.

On August 28, the day after the victory parades, the gunfire in the sky, the stentorian speeches, the ululations and the celebrations, uniformed policemen were back in the busy streets of central Gaza directing traffic. The seaport was full of families again, with children frolicking in the shallow shores off the rock outcroppings that encircled the inlet. Further south, where the flow of raw sewage from Gaza's shattered sanitation system was less extreme, the beaches were full. I spent an afternoon wandering around the Gaza City port and making small talk with some of the locals enjoying the sultry day.

As I watched a fishing crew load nets for the evening's catch, I fell into conversation with a twenty-year-old man from Shujaiya whose right arm was in a cast. Broad shouldered and with an athletic bearing, he told me he had lost a contract to play professional soccer in Jordan when Israeli shrapnel shattered his arm. His home was destroyed along with his entire neighborhood. He was among the untold number of athletes in Gaza who lost their careers and even their lives, like Ahed Zaqout, killed in his sleep by an Israeli attack on his apartment. Zaqout was among two active coaches killed during the onslaught of as many as twenty athletes.

"We are already dead," the young footballer said, staring off at the bustling port.

Later that day, Dan Cohen and I were joined at our apartment on the port by Jesse Rosenfeld, a journalist from Toronto and longtime friend who had covered the most gruesome stage of the war, during the ground invasion, when scorched bodies were literally piling up in the streets. Jesse was one of the first Western journalists to report on the summary executions that took place in Khuza'a in the home of Hani al-Najjar. Now he was back to investigate the circumstances of the killings and search for the identities of the victims. He brought with him the borrowed laptop he relied on throughout the war after his computer broke: an old MacBook with a shattered screen that could only display documents in the bottom left corner.

A few days later, on August 30, Jesse, Dan and I were among the only international journalists in attendance at a ceremony in central Gaza that honored the sixteen local reporters killed by the Israeli military during the war. By the time we learned about the ceremony and arrived at the downtown office lot where the modest event took place, we found the journalists' family members filtering out with small bouquets of flowers in hand while a group of local correspondents assembled in a triumphant pose. These reporters had been closer to the fire than most outsiders—many were targeted in their homes and offices—and produced some of the most bracing coverage of the war as a result. Unlike those of us who came from abroad, the Israeli military did not seem to view local correspondents as journalists deserving of any special protection. They were simply Palestinians who could be eliminated like anyone else, and whose deaths did little to generate international outcry or profuse exhibitions of solidarity. During the military escalation in Gaza in November 2012, when Israel targeted reporters working for the Hamas-run Al-Aqsa TV for assassination, the Israeli army spokesperson's unit declared that any reporter in the vicinity of Hamas "positions" was a potential target. During the 51 Day War of 2014, Israeli forces targeted and destroyed Al Aqsa TV's offices in Gaza City.

On most nights in the week after the war, we found ourselves unwinding at an apartment on a top floor of the Zafer 1 residential tower that belonged to Jehad Saftawi. A wiry twenty-four-year-old writer and researcher with deep-set eyes and a confidence that belied his age, Jehad had committed himself to bringing the war to an international audience from a ground-level, real-time view through the online livestream he operated. Saftawi's father, a former Islamic Jihad leader who ultimately quit the group, was still in jail after his imprisonment

Jehad Saftawi and Aburamadan on their balcony in Zafer 1. Photo by Dan Cohen.

fourteen years ago by the Israeli government in violation of the Oslo Accords, which were supposed to have provided him with amnesty from prosecution. Jehad's wife, Lara Aburamadan, was an artist who hoped to dedicate herself to painting and jewelry-making. Unable to find an adequate supply of beads and art materials to pursue her craft under the Israeli-Egyptian siege, she scraped by as a journalist and translator. Every month, Aburamadan hosted a party for her girlfriends, who showed up in stylish, tight-fitting dresses and danced in the salon while Saftawi and his friends hung out in the kitchen. It was the closest thing to a night of clubbing that the Gaza Strip had to offer.

During the last days of the war, Dan and I had subsisted on falafel, the occasional kebab sandwich and the corn flakes we bought at our local corner store. But now that Gaza's fleet of rickety fishing boats were back in the water after 51 days of inactivity, we found ourselves seated around Saftawi's kitchen table before an Alexandrian-style fish meal. We were joined at the table by Jehad's older brother, Hamza, and Mohammed Suliman, a researcher for the Al Mezan Center for Human Rights who at age twenty-four held a master's degree in Human Rights from the London School of Economics. Unlike the rest of us who showed up in shorts or dusty jeans and sat around shirtless in the sweltering heat, the bespectacled Mohammed always appeared in business attire, with a striped shirt tucked into neatly pressed khaki pants. Having spent the last two months producing daily reports for Al Mezan on the casualties across Gaza, and literally dodging airstrikes on his way to work, I assumed Mohammed would want to discuss something other than death and destruction. But the war seemed to be the only topic on his mind. As he polished off the last piece of fish, he reflected on the killing of a co-worker.

"Anwar Zaaneen, he made the coffee at Al Mezan and in the end, when he lost his confidence, he lost his life," Mohammed recalled. "When the war started [Zaaneen] left his home in Beit Hanoun and stayed at our offices at Al Mezan. It was a supposedly safe place where he could stay with his family from day one of the war to the end, because of how fearful he was. After the first three-day truce, he decided to go back to Beit Hanoun just to get his motorcycle cause he wanted to move it. He didn't drive it because it was dangerous, he just walked it carefully through the streets. And then, he saw a group of municipality workers and he was going there to talk to them about an issue about his house, when a bomb just directly hit him."

"It was another day at Mezan working on our press release and all of the sudden then the news comes: 'Anwar Zaaneen was just targeted in Beit Hanoun.' *Anwar Zaaneen?* I couldn't believe it!" Mohammed said. As shocked as he was by his co-worker's killing, it was the normalization of death that disturbed him the most: "Everyone was just carrying on with their work as if there's no news. I was the only one. Everyone was just working and carrying on! Afterwards I realized they just were so unprepared to receive this news that they just ignored it."

Jehad experienced a similarly unsettling feeling when he received a call from the Israeli military ordering him and his neighbors to evacuate their homes in Zafer 1. "I grabbed all the most important documents and all the new clothes in my apartment," he recalled. "I went out to go to my family's house, but ten minutes later they completely destroyed a tower next to ours that was twelve floors high. And this didn't even shock me because I was waiting for them to hit my building. I was too busy thinking of getting the important papers out and the passports."

Outside Jehad's window lay the ruins of Zafer 4 and beside it, a row of tents erected by its former residents.

"We were living in a maze of death," said Mohammed. "You just needed to walk carefully for fifty-one days. It was raining death in Gaza. Like, huge bombs, man! It's raining bombs and you're just dodging death. This is how we survived."

"It's about confidence," Jehad emphasized. "The people who lost their confidence, they just got killed."

Leaning against the counter and gnawing on a piece of leftover fish, Jehad's older brother, Hamza, wondered how the trauma of war would affect him. "You feel in the war like you're all alone on Earth," he said. "No one cares what happened to you. You have to just take care of yourself and hope you make it through the day. You become afraid to face the day; you become afraid to find out one of your friends is dead. And that's what will make you go completely psycho!"

"In the first two wars, they didn't hit us here, right in the center of the city," Hamza continued, with wide eyes and a look of astonishment across his face. "Every time, death gets closer and closer. We need to enjoy ourselves, to be happy, to just go on, because in the next war, they could kill us all."

After a long minute of silence, Mohammed piped up: "In three months' time, no one will be talking about what happened in Gaza. So we'll move on. We'll move on; we don't care about death. We know death!"

CHAPTER 16

The Deadliest Catch

Among the only conditions the ceasefire agreement spelled out in concrete terms was an extension of Gaza's fishing limit from three to six miles. In fact, this condition was outlined in the treaty that brought the November 2012 military escalation to an end, but it was never honored by Israel. For the fishing captains who remembered when it was possible to fish as far as twenty miles off the coast in the years before the 1993 Oslo Accords set into motion a gradually tightening regime of separation, another promised extension of the limit meant little. The best catches lay in the blue depths of the Mediterranean, but the Israeli naval cordon consistently sent Gaza fishing crews back to port with miserable hauls before they even reached six miles at sea. Having been transformed by the siege into a literally captive market, Gazans are often forced to buy fish imported from Israel at inflated prices, even if it was caught just a few miles from their coastlines. Meanwhile, the 40,000 or so Gazans who depend directly on the fishing industry continue to sink into spiraling depths of poverty and despair.

Less than a week after the ceasefire took effect, I arranged to join a local crew for one of the first overnight fishing voyages since the ceasefire. The trip would test the new limits and foreshadow the humanitarian landscape of the post-war era. If the status quo remained entrenched, it would not be difficult to predict another round of "mowing the lawn" at some point in the next two years, or that the next operation would strike even deeper at the roots of Gaza's civilian population.

When I arrived at the port with Dan Cohen in the late afternoon of September 1, we passed the storehouses the fishing crews had used to hold their spare parts and the nets they would cast in the winter season when different breeds of fish entered the sea. The single-story units had been reduced to rubble by Israeli missiles, their contents comprehensively torched. On a busy dock, as crews loaded their nets for the night's journey, a veteran member of the Gaza fisherman's union named Zacharias Bakr told us that he and other boat owners had been worried Israeli naval cruisers and F-16s would bombard their boats, so they took a gamble and tucked everything away in the storage units. Now it was all gone; Zacharias estimated losses at $1 million in destroyed equipment and $5 million in lost work for the entire port. He was a member of the famed Bakr clan that dominated the local fishing industry, and which lost four of its young sons in one of the most widely publicized massacres of the war. After seven years of siege and three devastating military assaults, this once prosperous family had been driven to the brink of ruin.

We boarded a rickety diesel boat at sunset with Zacharias and rumbled out into the Mediterranean. At the middle of the boat was his cousin, Raed Bakr, who would be the captain for the night. Raed manned the wheel while a shipmate with one

Heading out to sea from Gaza City's port. Photo by Dan Cohen.

hand—the other looked like it had been burned off—repaired wires in the navigation system with electrical tape and scissors. Other members of the crew sat cross-legged on the deck sewing broken line.

Even as I struggled with the onset of seasickness as we bobbed in the sea like a cork, the experience of watching the concrete bloc buildings and traffic-choked streets of Gaza City fade into the distance was exhilarating. I watched the sun sink below the horizon, sending a fiery orange hue shimmering across the waves, and imagined sailing to a foreign port, perhaps to one of the Greek isles or maybe north to Beirut, and feasting on the fish that we hauled in along the way. I had to remind myself what Zacharias told me when we were chatting on the dock: He had not been permitted to leave the Gaza Strip for a single day since he was arrested and locked in an Israeli jail forty-one years ago.

As the night set in and the tiny lights of Gaza City dissolved to black, the first stage of the fishing operation began. Like every other boat that embarked from Gaza's port, this one was affixed with flood lamps that illuminated the sea around the boat, attracting schools of sardines to its immediate perimeter. Once we were two or three miles at sea, the ship came to a halt and the lights flashed on, turning the sea aqua blue. For almost an hour, we bobbed in the gentle sea while the crew patiently waited for the fish to gather. Some among the crew used the downtime to snare fish with single lines strung to plastic water bottles, while others smoked and hung out. At various intervals throughout the night, there were prayers at the bow and meals at the stern.

Dan and I joined a few crew members around a rug for a modest mezze dinner with Raed Bakr. Seated in a plastic chair, the captain proceeded to outline the perils of fishing under siege. "We are facing enormous problems," he explained. "We get kidnapped by the Israelis all the time." He pointed at a lanky member of his crew perched on the stern with an impassive gaze. "He was kidnapped," Raed said. "I was kidnapped. Many of these guys have been put in jail. When we got locked up, I got one year and he got six years," he added, motioning back to the crew member on the stern, silent and expressionless.

Israeli naval patrol ships routinely circled his boat at eighty kilometers an hour, Raed said, threatening to capsize it in the terrifying wake they created. On other occasions, the ships cut his nets and blew out his flood lamps with machine gun fire. The Israelis patrolled Gaza's coastline in Shaldag class fast patrol boats and corvette class cruisers provided to the military at a deeply discounted price by the German government. The boats had been used to shell civilian homes throughout the 51

Day War, but now they had returned to the mundane duty of harassing Gaza's fishing crews.

"Sometimes when they arrest me," Raed said, "they call me through the megaphone and give me orders. If you don't follow them they can shoot at the boat. If they want to arrest someone on the boat, they make him strip naked, and whether or not the sea is quiet or stormy—they don't care—they make him jump in the water. He then has to swim eight hundred meters to the Israeli boat."

Would the presence of international reporters and activists on the boat shield him from Israeli violence? I asked Raed.

If we encountered the Israeli navy tonight, he explained, they were less likely to attack the boat. However, if he tested the fishing limit with internationals on board, he could expect harsh repercussions the next day. According to Raed, each time he attempted to fish beyond the limit with internationals aboard, the Israeli navy would seek his boat out the following night and exact revenge with gunfire or by kidnapping members of his crew. To head off any future retribution by the Israelis, he planned to approach the naval cordon with extreme caution tonight.

After an hour spent waiting for the catch to gather around the boat, it was time to run the nets. A crew member set out in a small motorboat, circling the boat and expanding the net into a basket that scooped up the sardines. Zacharias paddled behind him in a skiff, coordinating between the main fishing boat and the motorboat by shouting commands. Once the nets were out, the crew gathered at starboard and began hauling them in by hand. Practiced during the pre-occupation days, when Gaza's fishermen navigated the sea in wooden sailboats, free from the fear of Israeli harassment, this simple method had been passed down through the generations.

As the crew hauled the nets back onto the ship, a flurry of little fish shot out onto the deck; some hit me square in the face as I took video of the operation on my iPhone. It seemed to me that Raed and his crew had hauled in a sizable catch, but when the fish and assorted sea creatures were finally packed away in plastic crates, the depressing reality sank in.

"This catch should be triple what it is," Raed grumbled as he flicked a cigarette butt into the murky sea. "We lost so much money during the war when they bombed our storage spaces. I was sitting home for fifty days praying to God for the chance to fish. I spent fifty days not working, plus the stress of being under the bombs the whole time. We fishermen, we live day by day. If we work today and get fish, I'll be able to live. I can go to the market and get vegetables for my family. If I don't get fish, I can't do anything. And if I can't get past four miles at sea tonight, I won't get anything."

The routine continued through the night: Flood lamps lit up the sea, the crew passed the time with cigarettes and small talk while the sardines gathered, the skiffs ran the nets, the crew yanked in the lines, the fish flopped across the deck, and at the end of it all, Raed was left grimacing about another miserable haul. At around 2 a.m., about half the crew had dozed off on mats and rugs laid out around the bow of the boat. Others sat along the boats edges, sipping on coffee and heavily sugared tea. In spite of the imminent financial loss their trip would incur, the crew was unfailingly good natured, treating their guests to coffee and sweets throughout the early hours of the morning.

With the night nearly at its end, Zacharias was back in the skiff guiding the net around the boat while the crew gathered at starboard to haul the lines back in for a final time. Instead of pushing the boat closer to the six-mile limit, Raed seemed to be playing it safe. But even at just over four miles at sea, he had run up against Israel's iron wall. An Israeli patrol boat darted in from the distance, parked a few hundred meters west of our boat, and flashed a blinding spotlight on us. It was clear the crew was accustomed to these unpleasant encounters with the navy, as they continued their work undisturbed, muscling the nets in and packing the sardines with efficiency. Within fifteen minutes, Raed had the boat chugging back to port.

"We're all in a prison here," Zacharias Bakr grumbled to me. "Even when we're at sea."

Back at the port, as his crew loaded the plastic crates of sardines and prawns into the back of rickshaws on their way to the nearby fish market, Raed assessed the damage. The journey had cost him about 2,500 shekels (just over $600) but the haul would only garner 500 shekels ($125) at the market.

"I was out there for fourteen hours, leaving my family behind while they pray that I can bring some kind of livelihood to them," Raed lamented. "And now I have nothing. In fact, I have a huge loss. And I'm not alone. I have more than a hundred people who depend on this boat—entire families depend on this boat to bring them the basics for life."

I asked Raed if the international community could do anything to help him. "Our message is simple," he responded. "We don't need any aid or anything. Just put pressure on the Israelis so they get out of the sea and let us fish and bring a livelihood to our families again."

By October 2014, attacks on Gazan fishermen within the six-mile fishing limit had become routine. The Palestinian Center for Human Rights documented eighteen shooting incidents in the two months after the ceasefire and at least four instances in which fishermen were arrested while working inside the six-mile line. On October 22, the Israeli navy chased two boats fishing off the coast in northern Gaza, peppering the crews with rubber-coated steel bullets and arresting seven of them. Not a single rocket was fired into Israel from Gaza in these two months. Amidst the one-way ceasefire, the *New York Times* described the atmosphere as "a fragile calm."

As the suffocating monotony of siege returned to Gaza, diplomats gathered again in Cairo on October 12, this time to consider raising the funds necessary to rebuild the Strip's shattered infrastructure, and to mull the possibility of replacing its pulverized factories with sweatshops.

CHAPTER 17

Singapore or Darfur

A 2013 United Nations Relief and Works Agency report found that the Gaza Strip would be uninhabitable by 2020. Thanks to the 51 Day War, however, this terrifying forecast may have been realized prematurely.

The Israeli military had not only torn through the civilian population of Gaza like a buzz saw during the 51 Day War, killing some 2,200 people—more than 70 percent were confirmed as civilians—and wounding well over 10,000; it had pulverized Gaza's infrastructure. Over 400 businesses and shops had been damaged in targeted Israeli strikes, and at least 120 were completely obliterated; 24 medical facilities were damaged, including the Wafa Hospital in Shujaiya, Gaza's only geriatric rehabilitation facility, whose top three floors were razed by tank shelling. A full one third of Gaza's mosques were bombed, from the Al-Amin Muhammad Mosque, a stately structure built in the center of Gaza City with donations from a Malaysian Muslim charity, to the Al-Omari Mosque, a historical treasure that had stood in the same spot in Jabalia since

In central Gaza City, one of the more than 160 mosques bombed by Israel during the 51 Day War.

647 AD until it was brought to the ground by Israeli missiles on August 2. Gaza's lone power station was decimated by Israeli airstrikes on July 29, leaving most of Gaza without electricity for over 18 hours a day, and sometimes longer. Perhaps the most disturbing figure was the more than 18,000 civilian homes the Israeli military leveled during its assault on Gaza, leaving at least 100,000 homeless or forced to cram into the already overcrowded homes of relatives.

The violence was not limited to human life. When I visited the Bisan Zoo in Beit Hanoun after the war, I found battered cages full of exotic animals shredded by Israeli shrapnel and decomposed monkey carcasses splayed out on a toe path—the small chimpanzees had apparently been blown out of their cages. The rest of the animals seemed to have been driven crazy by weeks of bombings. In a small cage at the rear of the zoo, I discovered a group of dust-ridden foxes running in a seemingly endless circle. It was almost as hypnotic to watch them as it was depressing. In October, the surviving animals were shipped to Jordan, bringing Gaza's only zoo to an end.

In the wake of all this destruction, the representatives of the international community returned to Cairo on October 12. It was expected that they would pledge the necessary funds to repair the more than $7 billion in damage that Israel had exacted on the Gaza Strip through its Operation Protective Edge, just as they had done after Operation Cast Lead in 2009 and Operation Pillar of Defense in 2012.

Yet as soon as they arrived, the diplomats were assured from Jerusalem by Israeli Minister of Transportation Yisrael Katz that their efforts at planning reconstruction were utterly futile. "The Gazans must decide what they want to be: Singapore or Darfur," Katz remarked, inadvertently comparing the Israeli army to the Sudanese Janjaweed accused by the US Department of State of committing genocide in Darfur. He continued: "They can pick between economic recovery and war and destruction. If they choose terror, the world should not waste its money. If one missile will be fired, everything will go down the drain."

The message was not lost on the diplomats. As one Western diplomat told Agence France-Presse on condition of anonymity, "We have seen infrastructure projects that we have contributed to which have been destroyed." The diplomat complained that the sustained Israeli assaults on Gaza's infrastructure had prompted "considerable donor fatigue."

Johan Schaar, the head of Development Cooperation for the Swedish Consulate in occupied Palestine, conceded during the conference that the inevitability of another Israeli assault on

Gaza had rendered the whole rebuilding exercise futile. "No one can expect us to go back to our taxpayers for a third time to ask for contributions to reconstruction and then we simply go back to where we were before all this began," he complained. "That is out of the question."

Only about half of the $5 billion pledged at Cairo would actually be budgeted towards Gaza reconstruction. The rest, according to Palestinian Authority Prime Minister Rami Hamdallah, would help keep his unelected government afloat in the West Bank, where 30 percent of the government's budget is spent on the security forces that are paid to police fellow Palestinians on behalf of Israel's occupation. Under the guise of restoring the basic functions of Gaza, the diplomats in Cairo found a backdoor channel to sustain the police state that rules the West Bank's ever-shrinking cantons.

"Without a [political breakthrough] I think we'll probably end up giving but it will be repackaging the assistance that we already give," a European diplomat told the news service, IRIN. "In reality none of it will be new money. There isn't a terrible amount of political commitment or hope."

Throughout the conference in Cairo, the diplomats discussed the destruction of Gaza as though it was the result of a natural disaster—as though the missiles that reduced the strip's border areas to rubble were meteors that descended from outer space. Indeed, Israeli violence against Gaza's civilian population was scarcely mentioned at all, nor were any diplomatic measures against it proposed. And with Hamas barred from participation in the conference by Egypt and the US, which refused to negotiate directly with the group, the elected government of Gaza was unable to raise the issue.

When Kerry appeared at the lectern, he pledged a piddling $212 million to Gaza, nearly $700 million less than the US gave after the 2008–09 Israeli assault known as Operation Cast Lead. He then proceeded to effusively compliment Sisi's "efforts."

"But President Sisi's efforts, I think it's fair to say, have really helped to reaffirm the pivotal role that Egypt has played in this region for so long," said Kerry, lending the despot the legitimacy he was desperately seeking. The military coup and subsequent massacres of peaceful protesters that Sisi oversaw were now forgotten, as were the 40,000 political prisoners languishing in Egyptian jails. Hours after the event, Kerry met privately with Sisi to promise a shipment of ten Apache attack helicopters that would later be used to reinforce the Egyptian army's onslaught against the city of Rafah. There, Sisi planned to order the demolition of 1200 civilian homes and the forced relocation of their inhabitants in order to tighten the siege of Gaza.

Having already praised the Egyptian military junta for "restoring democracy," Kerry praised Israel as a generous nation taking "positive steps" to help sustain Gaza's economy and get the beleaguered territory back on its feet. He trumpeted "new measures that should allow increased trade in agricultural goods between Gaza and the West Bank, and more permits for Palestinian business leaders to enter Israel," omitting the fact that Israel had banned rebuilding materials to Gaza, indefinitely delaying sixty truckloads from entering in October. "We hope to see many more positive steps announced and implemented in the coming weeks and months," Kerry declared.

Finally, Kerry dusted off an obscure and little-understood economic plan called the Initiative for the Palestinian Economy, claiming it was a recipe for reducing Palestinian unemployment to 8 percent—the same rate as in the US. (Unemployment in Gaza after the war had topped 50 percent.) He credited McKinsey & Company, the US-based corporate management consulting firm that helped Enron exploit California's energy crisis, with producing the initiative's analysis of the Palestinian economy.

"We're talking about real investment that produces real jobs and opportunities for thousands of Palestinians," proclaimed Kerry, "and that is what is going to make the difference over the long term."

The Sweatshop Initiative

When he rolled out the Initiative for the Palestinian Economy at the 2013 World Economic Forum in Jordan, Kerry hailed it as "a new model of development . . . that is bigger and bolder than anything proposed since the Oslo Accord," promising a $4 billion injection of investments into the Palestinian economy.

Implementation of the plan was placed into the hands of Tony Blair, the former British Prime Minister and business-inclined Quartet Representative whose corporate network had raked in close to $100 million advising a vast web of corporations, banks, and dictators from Kazakhstan's Nursultan Nazarbayev to Egypt's Sisi. While tendering a $2 million paycheck to consult for JP Morgan, Blair took credit for persuading Israeli administrators to open up radio frequencies to allow the Palestinian telecom company, Wataniya, to provide service in the West Bank. The deal reaped a major windfall profit for Blair's employer, JP Morgan, which happened to have provided the $2 billion loan that brought Wataniya into existence through the Qatari telecom giant QTEL—one of JP Morgan's top clients. Through his role as one of the world's top peace processors, Blair expanded the crony capitalist network that had earned his network of businesses over $90 million since leaving office.

To lend the economic initiative a prominent Palestinian promoter, Kerry recruited Munib al-Masri, the Palestinian tycoon who lived high above the poverty stricken Balata Refugee Camp in an Italian revival-style mansion. He had also enlisted the financial know-how of Tim Collins, a major Democratic Party donor and venture capitalist whose Ripplewood Holdings leveraged buyout firm had liquidated food company Hostess, sending 18,500 unionized workers into the ranks of the unemployed. Earlier in 2014, Collins had purchased a $30 million stake in one of Egypt's top property developers. "We are very interested in being a part of the recovery of the Egyptian economy," Collins said at the time.

Little was known about the plan at the time Kerry unveiled it at the World Economic Forum. My email and telephone queries to Ruti Winterstein, Blair's Political and Policy Advisor at the Quartet offices in Jerusalem, went unanswered. Despite his optimism, Kerry stonewalled reporters seeking details about the initiative. Nevertheless, I managed to secure some details of the Initiative for the Palestinian Economy through a Palestinian businessman who furnished me with a fourteen-page paper that he said was produced on behalf of the Quartet by McKinsey & Company. The paper was a classic document of neoliberal thinking that analyzed the occupied Palestinian territories as though it was a normal developing nation whose economic performance could be optimized with just a little technical know-how, some innovative marketing strategies, and a whole lot of international corporate involvement. Israel had provided the shock, and McKinsey arrived with the doctrine.

The consultants concluded in the paper that the walled-in Gaza ghetto "underperforms on key tourism metrics," but the analysts couldn't seem to explain the reason, alluding only to "regional instability" and "low awareness of existing tourism destination sites." Ignoring the Israeli siege, the factor that made literally everything they proposed a total fantasy, the firm suggested "a range of new hotel offerings...underpinned by aggressive marketing." If only Gaza could find a winning brand, according to McKinsey, boutique spas would suddenly blossom along its coastline, providing stunning vistas of Israel's naval blockade.

To bring Gaza's beleaguered economy back to life, the consultants called for the proliferation of what were effectively sweatshops that would churn out zippers and buttons for "high-end designers in Israeli clothing markets requiring relatively small, customized orders not handled well by bulk-order manufacturers." So much for Singapore on the Mediterranean. Under international guidance, Gaza would become an occupied Bangladesh, producing accoutrements for trendy Tel Aviv fashionistas.

Nearly every construction and agricultural project envisioned in this summary analysis had been rendered impossible by Israel's siege and its accompanying military assaults. Not a single dollar has been pledged to the Northern Gaza Emergency Sewage Treatment Project, which was highlighted in the document as one of the Quartet's major achievements. And with tens of thousands of homeless crammed into UN schools, the affordable housing units described as "an aspiration" were just that.

At no point in the Quartet's paper on the Initiative for the Palestinian Economy was the Israeli occupation or siege of Gaza mentioned.

Even as he conceded at the Cairo donor conference that aid to Gaza was a "band-aid fix," Kerry offered no political remedies beyond the framework plan for two states that the Israeli government had resoundingly rejected earlier in 2014.

As the diplomats in Cairo left Egypt wringing their hands, Israeli officials issued further threats. "If one Protective Edge was not enough, you will get two and three until Hamas terror ends," Transportation Minister Katz warned. "I prefer one thousand Palestinian mothers crying than letting one Jewish mother cry."

The Conflict Management Approach

By the time the punishing winter storms were lashing Gaza in early 2015, the charade in Cairo was all but forgotten. And nothing had changed on the ground. This was no thanks to the United Nations, whose blueprint for reconstruction was described by a disillusioned UN official as "the next stage of Israel's blockade of Gaza." The official concluded: "It started with a very crude blanket blockade, where pencils and coriander were not allowed in, but now it is becoming much more sophisticated, like the occupation of the West Bank. And now, the international actors are being embedded and made complicit in the siege."

The official revealed that the UN plan would mandate that all materials entering Gaza be vetted by the Israeli military authorities that administered the siege of Gaza. Any family who wished to have their home rebuilt would have to submit their private information to the Palestinian Authority, which would then supply it to the Israeli military for approval. Every piece of material down to bags of cement would be carefully tracked by the UN, and by extension, the Israeli military it was coordinating with. And each family that received rebuilding material would be subjected to careful monitoring.

"The tight, almost dystopian new controls envisioned in the [UN plan for Gaza reconstruction] underline Israel's approach to the Strip as being first and foremost a gigantic prison—only it is being upgraded from a third-world prison camp to an American cutting-edge SuperMax facility," the Israeli analyst Dimi Reider concluded in *Middle East Eye*.

Ron Ben-Yishai, a military correspondent for the Israeli daily *Yedioth Ahronoth* who was privy to details of the UN plan, named its authors as the UN Special Coordinator for the Middle East Peace Process Robert Serry, Egyptian intelligence chief Mohammed Farid el-Tohamy, Palestinian Authority Prime Minister Rami Hamdallah, and Yoav Mordechai, the Israeli major general in charge of coordinating the occupation of Palestinian territory. Yishai described the plan as a blueprint of "the conflict management approach."

By January 2015, little of the $5 billion pledged by international donors in Cairo had reached Gaza and almost nothing had been rebuilt. The UN plan was a nonstarter, rejected by Hamas and Gaza's private sector as a retrenchment of the siege. While Chris Gunness, the spokesperson for UNRWA (the agency in charge of caring for Gaza's refugee population) warned that Gaza was "submerged in despair," Serry, the UN Special Coordinator, blamed Palestinians for refusing to accede to the rebuilding plan he helped create for them. "We need a government... that is able to take responsibility," he complained.

In February, UNRWA funds for Gaza reconstruction had dried up altogether, forcing the agency to suspend its cash assistance program for those who had lost their homes to Israeli strikes during the war. Rebuilding was frozen even before it began in earnest, and there was no sign that it would ever begin. Forty-two thousand government employees in Gaza had gone six months without receiving their salary. As Israel re-

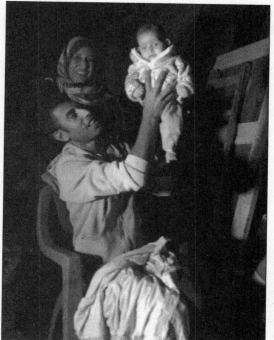

Wadie Abu Khesi at 3 months old. He froze to death three months later. Photo by Dan Cohen.

fused a Turkish offer to provide an offshore electricity station for Gaza, the Strip remained without electricity for eighteen hours a day. The Rafah border crossing was kept shuttered by the Egyptian regime, prompting a crowd of thousands to rush its gates when it finally opened for three days.

In December, Dan Cohen met the Abu Khesi family in the rubble of their home in Shujaiya. They had been left homeless by the war and were left to shelter themselves against one of the harshest winters in Gaza's history with little more than nylon sheets, scrap metal and blankets. Dan found the family's youngest child, Wadie, captivated by the bright light he had affixed to his camera. Born during the war, Wadie had never seen light produced by electricity—he had only known the illumination produced by the nightly fires the family lit to keep warm.

On January 15, about a month after Cohen's visit, five-month-old Wadie froze to death, making him the fifth child to die of exposure in the punishing winter.

A sense of abandonment and despair had consumed Gaza, igniting the flames of rage and spreading radicalization like wildfire. Almost as soon as the curtains closed on the 51 Day War, the stage for the next war was set.

CHAPTER 18

The Teacher

Just a few months before I traveled to Gaza to cover the 51 Day War, I was dining at an upscale Italian restaurant in Berkeley, California with the literature professor Refaat Alareer, who usually lives in Gaza City. We had been invited there by the Lannan Foundation, a Santa Fe, New Mexico–based foundation that supports a mix of artistic endeavors and progressive political causes. I had just delivered a talk on my book, *Goliath: Life and Loathing in Greater Israel*, in San Francisco, beside the Palestinian-American author and activist Ali Abunimah. For his part, Refaat had been touring the US with a group of Palestinian authors from Gaza to promote the compilation of essays he had edited, *Gaza Writes Back*.

We had followed closely on each other's heels throughout our book tours that spring. When I spoke at Western Washington University, a picturesque campus on the US border with Canada, I was peppered with questions by a Jewish-American undergrad who seemed to have never encountered a critical analysis of Israel or Zionism and was clearly anguished by my presentation. A week later, I learned from Refaat that the same student had cried openly as he and two other young writers from Gaza, Yousef Aljamal and Rawan Yaghi, described growing up under siege to the campus audience.

By the time we gathered at the long dining table in downtown Berkeley, everyone seemed to be struggling with varying levels of exhaustion and bewilderment from our long cross-country tours. I felt slightly uncomfortable seated beside three young people on a brief furlough from the Gaza ghetto before crystal goblets of Merlot and smooth wooden boards of artisanal cheeses spread out on white tablecloths. But I quickly forgot my unease as I fell into conversation with Refaat.

We spent the next hour chatting about his impressions of the vast and blindingly colorful country he had just barnstormed across. The American landscape had offered Refaat the chance to meet Jews who did not greet him from behind the barrel of an M-16, from inside the cockpit of an F-16, from the turret of a Merkava tank, or behind an occupation administrator's desk. Refaat described how life under occupation in Gaza had produced his "Malcolm X moment," and how his visit to the US helped him emerge from it, just as Malcolm X began questioning his prejudices after experiencing fraternity with the whites he met on his pilgrimage to Mecca.

"When Malcolm X was in prison, his sister told him, 'Elijah Muhammad said Islam is the true religion of black people and the white man is the Devil.' He thought of every white person he had ever met in his life and realized that he had been harmed in one way or another by every one of them," Refaat explained. "This is what's happening to us in Palestine, because you never come face-to-face with a Jewish person who's not armed to the teeth trying to kill you. And that makes it very hard to break with your prejudice."

When Refaat traveled across the United States, he met for the first time with Jews who treated him with empathy. "When you talk to Jewish people about their lives, they host you in their homes, you spend time with their families, they can educate you in ways beyond imagination because they know about Israel, about Jewish life, about Zionism," he marveled. "You learn so much because they are insiders. It was the tour to America that changed me in so many ways."

Even as it stimulated his imagination and broadened his perspective, Refaat's trip to the US summoned pangs of regret. Like any other Palestinian academic, the occupation had cost him countless opportunities to study abroad and form relationships with his intellectual counterparts. In 2005, Israeli authorities refused to allow him to complete his master's degree in the UK. He lost an entire year of his studies along with his scholarship. Over the following two years, the Israelis refused to allow him to leave Gaza on ten separate occasions. He remembered telling them, "If you have something against me, just put me in prison!"

When Refaat finally managed to secure permission to travel to the US in 2014, Sarah Ali, a twenty-two-year-old English literature student and teaching assistant at Islamic University who had contributed to *Gaza Writes Back*, was refused a permit to join him on the book tour. Thus, at events around the country, Refaat and his fellow Gaza writers, Yousef and Rawan, delivered lectures next to a chair with a cardboard cutout that read: "Sarah Ali Should Be Here."

"Israel wants us to be closed, isolated—to push us to the extreme," Refaat reflected. "It doesn't want us to be educated. It doesn't want us to see ourselves as part of a universal struggle against oppression. They don't want us to be educated or to be educators."

When Refaat returned to Gaza from the US, he redoubled his efforts to educate Gaza youth out of the narrow prejudices spawned in the seedbed of siege and occupation. At Islamic University, the conservative higher education institution co-founded by the assassinated Hamas leader Sheikh Ahmed Yassin in 1978, Refaat introduced his students to Hebrew literature. Among the Jewish Israeli writers he assigned them was Yehuda Amichai, the legendary poet whose famed work, "God Has Pity on Kindergarten Children," tells of short lives consumed in war and punctuated by intimate encounters with violence. The poem's opening stanzas resonated easily with Refaat's students:

God has pity on kindergarten children,
He pities school children — less.
But adults he pities not at all.

He abandons them,
And sometimes they have to crawl on all fours
In the scorching sand
To reach the dressing station,
Streaming with blood.

Refaat also assigned his students *The Merchant of Venice*. He encouraged the class to view Shylock, Shakespeare's Orientalized, avaricious Jewish character, as a sympathetic figure who had struggled to retain a modicum of dignity under an apartheid-like regime.

When his students finished reading the play, Refaat asked them which Shakespearean character they sympathized with more: Othello, the Venetian general of Arab origin, or Shylock, the Jew. He described their response as the most emotional moment of his six-year teaching career: One by one, his students declared an almost visceral identification with Shylock.

In her final paper, one of the Refaat's students reworked Shylock's famous *cri de coeur* into an appeal to the conscience of her own oppressors:

> *Hath not a Palestinian eyes? Hath not a Palestinian hands,*
>   *organs,*
> *dimensions, senses, affections, passions; fed with*
> *the same food, hurt with the same weapons, subject*
> *to the same diseases, heal'd by the same means,*
> *warm'd and cool'd by the same winter and summer*
> *as a Christian or a Jew is? If you prick us, do we not bleed?*
> *If you tickle us, do we not laugh? If you poison us,*
> *do we not die? And if you wrong us, shall we not revenge?*

Refaat stored his students' papers in his desk at Islamic University's English Department like small treasures. On August 2, the Israeli military bombed his department along with the university's administrative offices, sending those papers up in flames. The office where students met him during office hours was pulverized and the student library next door was decimated. When Israeli army spokesman Peter Lerner claimed that the air force had targeted a "weapons development center" in the school, Refaat's students responded with sardonic humor, joking about the PMDs, or Poems of Mass Destruction, they had been storing on campus.

"Open minded Palestinians are more dangerous," Refaat said. "That's why [Israel] attacks the Islamic University. That's why it attacks other colleges. Of course, they lied when they attacked it."

Refaat had seen his school attacked by Israeli forces before, he watched it be rebuilt, and he assumed it would be repaired again.

But there was little that could console him over the violence that had sheared branch after branch from his family tree. During the war, he lost his brother-in-law, who also happened to be his best friend. He also learned that his cousins had been massacred in Shujaiya — Fathi al-Areer was among the survivors of Refaat's extended family whom I interviewed in the rubble on August 14. Next, he received news that his brother was killed.

In the months after the war, his brother's young son, Ranim, slipped into a state of desolation. "I hate Dad," Ranim would mutter on a routine basis. "He won't come back."

Holy Work

In early 2015, as electricity shortages plagued Gaza, I struggled to stay in touch with Refaat. His electricity came on for less than six hours at varying times depending on which day it was, leaving us with only a brief window of time to connect on Skype. When I finally reached him in late January, I found him coping with the malaise spreading all across Gaza after the war. His house and his neighbor's house had been bombed, forcing him to spend days at UNRWA offices attempting to negotiate the reconstruction process. It had taken three months to demolish a section of his family's home that threatened to collapse atop passersby. "If it took that long, imagine how long the bureaucracy of getting it built again will take," Reefat sighed.

One of Refaat's brothers lost his job when the ice cream factory he worked in was bombed by Israel. He was left to scramble to collect enough money just to pay his monthly rent. His father, who had not been able to find work in twenty years, depended on help from his unmarried sons. As dire as their situation had become, Refaat's family members considered themselves lucky compared to the thousands of government employees who had not worked in months and had no family assistance. "We always ask ourselves how they survive," Refaat said of the unpaid workers. "You get to the point that you will do anything for a buck. It's no surprise that crime is up, that domestic violence is up, that divorce is skyrocketing. Does the PA or Israel understand that sooner or later this will lead to an explosion?"

With the Rafah border crossing almost hermetically sealed by the Egyptian junta, Refaat had little chance of escaping Gaza to complete his PhD. His only release from frustration was in the classroom. As the siege tightened in the immediate aftermath of the war, he returned to Islamic University and redoubled his efforts to expand his students' intellectual horizons. "I find myself releasing most of my anger at the situation by teaching young people about the struggle and about being creative in the way we fight for our rights and freedom," Reefat said. "It's very rewarding."

In December 2014, Refaat's class played host to my colleague Dan Cohen. Dan observed as Refaat presented his class with a story by one of his students, Noor Elborno, written from the perspective of an Israeli veteran of an assault on the Gaza Strip. The soldier character had returned to his family in Israel plagued with post-traumatic stress disorder and consumed with nightmares about the children he had killed back in Gaza. As the Palestinian children in his nightmares morphed into his own children, the soldier descended into madness. Had the story been written by an Israeli, it would have fit neatly into the country's hackneyed shooting-and-crying literary sub-genre, the most notable example being *Waltz With Bashir*, in which soldiers sought personal absolution through anguished confessions of crimes they committed against Palestinians and Lebanese civilians. Authored by a young Palestinian in Gaza taking on the perspective of an Israeli directly engaged in violence against her society, however, the narrative reflected an unusual yearning to understand the psyche of the occupier.

Refaat turned to his class and asked them if they could sympathize with the soldier in the story. A few students said they might be able to, but only on the condition that they were first released from the bonds of occupation. Others protested that the soldier was complicit in their oppression, that he was a baby killer who deserved to suffer for his crimes. The angry voice of a young woman suddenly rose above those of her classmates. "I hate them all!" she exclaimed. She emphasized that she was referring to all Jews.

Refaat took the opportunity to explain to the class that not all Jews were Zionists, and not all Zionists were Jews. He challenged them not to implicate an entire group for the cruelty of a state that claimed to be acting in the name of world Jewry. "I told my students about my time in the US staying with Jewish friends, being with their families, about seeing them defend Palestinians," he recalled to me. "It's abstract to them because Israel won't even let my students travel to meet other people. Actually, three of my students have been prevented from leaving recently. But if these kinds of discussions help ten percent that's wonderful, because later on, when they get to break the walls of isolation that the occupation and Egypt are creating, when they meet Jewish people who are working for our cause, it's going to make all the difference."

Towards the end of the class, Refaat asked his students to raise their hands if they had lost their home or friends and family during the war. Most in the room threw a hand in the air. The young woman who declared her hatred for Jews had, in fact, lost her home in Shujaiya and witnessed the deaths of family members and neighbors. "It clearly showed how Israeli violence is pushing everyone to the extreme," Refaat said. "This war was so horrible, it really touched everyone."

When class was over, fifteen young women in colorful head-scarves and long dresses immediately surrounded Dan and began peppering him with questions. "The class had apparently known that I was a Jew," Dan told me, "and they wanted to know what I thought about them, about Gaza, about my life in the US. They had never met a Jew before and they really showed me a lot of respect."

The following day, the young woman who declared her hatred for Jews approached Refaat to express her regret. Hearing herself verbalize her resentment left her feeling ashamed and the meeting with Dan after class had provoked her to consider redirecting the anger that had gripped her after the war.

"Gaza is the most maligned place in the world, and if we were to believe what we're told by established Jewish groups in the US and mainstream media, we would think that a Jew in Gaza would be ripped apart, that Gazans are running around looking for a Jew to kill," Dan reflected. "In this supposed hotbed of anti-Semitism, everything was completely the opposite of the way I was told it was going to be. What I found were people like Refaat fighting to keep the violence that had consumed the physical lives of his students from consuming them internally. What he's doing is holy work."

While some youth discovered outlets in intellectual life and online with social media, no one, no matter how educated or worldly, could escape the cloud of despair that settled over Gaza after the war.

Leaving Gaza

In the months after the 51 Day War, thousands of Palestinians driven into ruin by the onslaught attempted to escape Gaza through tunnels into Egypt, where they paid exorbitant fees to smuggling gangs for a place on a rickety boat to Europe. In September 2014, near the island of Malta, a rival smuggler rammed a boat filled with Palestinians fleeing Gaza and capsized it. Five hundred passengers perished in the disaster. "This has never happened before," said Sara Roy, a senior research scholar at the Harvard University Center for Middle Eastern Studies and a leading expert on Gaza's humanitarian situation. "Even in the worst of times, people never considered abandoning the Gaza Strip."

As one of the harshest winters in recorded history descended on Gaza, electricity was reduced from eight hours a day to around four. Cooking gas was widely unavailable, even in central Gaza City, prompting some to consider lighting campfires in their freezing apartments. When he returned in January 2015 to the bloodlands of Khuza'a, Dan Cohen found homeless families huddled in freezing shipping containers in the shadow of an Israeli sniper tower two hundred meters away. Despite their desperate straits, one family boasted to Dan that the next time he visited them, their home would be rebuilt and grander than ever.

"All I could say was, '*insha'Allah*,'" Dan recalled. "Because the reality is they are sentenced to life in those shipping containers.

"Being back with the rubble people reminded me of watching ants after some toddler kicked their anthill and they're trying to put it back together," he continued. "And then the toddler comes and kicks it again. People are trying to put their anthill back together. And waiting for the next round that's going to completely destroy it."

Our colleagues, journalists Jehad Saftawi and Lara Aburamadan, were among those seeking a way out of Gaza. The couple was preparing for a trip to the US, where they hoped to have a child whose American citizenship might afford it the freedom of movement and rights they had been denied. Mohammed Suliman, the young human rights researcher who spent nights hanging out with us in Jehad's apartment, was planning to pursue his PhD in Australia. One by one, the best and brightest of Gaza were planning their escape. But so far, neither Jehad and Lara nor Mohamed had reached the end of the bureaucratic maze they needed to navigate to secure exit visas.

As I write this, I have discovered that another Gazan friend, the journalist Mohamed Omer, was kidnapped outside his Gaza City home by thugs identifying themselves as affiliates of the Islamic State (IS). Omer said he was interrogated and tortured for several hours before being released at Al-Shifa Hospital. Amid a wave of mysterious bombings, the presence of IS-like elements in the tightly controlled enclave had spawned an array of theories about foreign meddling and intrigue aimed at destabilizing Hamas. More crucially, it has highlighted the intensification of the political radicalization borne from rising desperation.

As Israel headed for national elections in March 2015, Tzipi Livni, a leader of the supposedly left-of-center Zionist Camp, suggested that war with Gaza was Israel's only option: "Hamas is a terrorist organization and there is no hope for peace with it... The only way to act against it is with force." She was echoed by her right-wing rival, Foreign Minister and Yisrael Beiteinu Party leader Avigdor Lieberman. "A fourth operation in Gaza is inevitable," he declared, "just as a third Lebanon war is inevitable."

Who will live when the next war comes down on Gaza, and who will die?

In the time of the siege, Israel will decide.

NOTES

Notes to the Introduction

2 *A majority are,* Gaza Strip Demographics Profile 2014, Index Mundi, http://www.indexmundi.com/gaza_strip/demographics_profile.html.

3 *Gaza's refugee population,* United Nations Relief and Works Agency, Where We Work—Gaza Strip, http://www.unrwa.org/where-we-work/gaza-strip.

3 *"Superfluous young men,"* "Harvard Fellow calls for genocidal measures to curb Palestinian births," *Electronic Intifada,* February 22, 2010, http://electronic intifada.net/content/harvard-fellow-calls-genocidal-measure-curb-palestinian -births/8692.

3 *Dayan's eulogy,* Benny Morris, *Israel's Border Wars: 1949–1956,* Oxford University Press, 1997, p. 396.

4 *Grossman on Sharon,* David Grossman, "How Sharon won Israel's trust," *LA Times,* January 6, 2006, http://articles.latimes.com/2006/jan/06/opinion /oe-grossman6/2.

4 *Weisglass on disengagement,* Ari Shavit, "Top PM aide: Gaza plan aims to freeze the peace process," *Haaretz,* October 6, 2004, http://www.haaretz .com/print-edition/news/top-pm-aide-gaza-plan-aims-to-freeze-the-peace -process-1.136686.

5 *"Kill and kill and kill,"* Max Blumenthal, *Goliath: Life and Loathing in Greater Israel,* Nation Books, 2013, p. 92.

5 *"Free and fair" election,* Aaron Pina, CRS Report for Congress, Palestinian Elections, February 9, 2006, http://fas.org/sgp/crs/mideast/RL33269.pdf.

6 *US shipment of arms to Fatah security,* David Rose, "The Gaza Bombshell," *Vanity Fair,* April 2008, http://www.vanityfair.com/news/2008/04/gaza 200804.

6 *Daily calorie intake,* "Israel calculated Palestinian calories for Gaza blockade."Ma'an News Agency, October 17, 2012, http://www.maannews.com /eng/ViewDetails.aspx?id=529743

6 *Fatalities in 2008–09 assault,* Fatalities in Operation Cast Lead, B'tselem, http://www.btselem.org/statistics/fatalities/after-cast-lead/by-date-of-event.

6 *Fatalities in 2012 escalation,* Fatalities in Operation Pillar of Defense, B'tselem, May 9, 2013, http://www.btselem.org/press_releases/20130509 _pillar_of_defense_report.

Notes to Chapter 1

7 *Hermes 450 drones,* Yaakov Katz, "Israel believed to be using armed UAVs," *Jerusalem Post,* August 8, 2012, http://www.jpost.com/Defense/IDF -believed-to-be-using-armed-UAVs.

7 *Further than three miles,* http://gisha.org/updates/1899.

7 *Buffer zone,* Fares Akram and Jodi Rudoren, "Gaza Farmers Near Fence With Israel Remain Wary," *New York Times,* June 7, 2013, http://www .nytimes.com/2013/06/08/world/middleeast/palestinian-farmers-in-gaza -buffer-zone-remain-wary.html?_r=0.

7 *Permits to enter,* Movement of People Via Rafah Crossing, http://gisha.org /graph/2399.

7 *Storm the Rafah crossing,* Chat2Gaza, Hundreds of Palestinians storm the Rafah crossing: A personal account from *Gaza Today,* September 29, 2013, http://chat2gaza.com/2013/09/29/hundreds-of-palestinians-storm-the-rafah -crossing-a-personal-account-from-gaza-today/.

7 *Unemployment rates,* Unemployment in Gaza: highest since 2009, Gisha, May 25, 2014, http://gisha.org/updates/2901.

7 *Child malnutrition rates,* World Health Organization, Health conditions in the occupied Palestinian territory, including east Jerusalem, and in the occupied Syrian Golan, Report by the Secretariat, May 11, 2012, http://reliefweb .int/sites/reliefweb.int/files/resources/Full_Report_3973.pdf.

7 *Israeli assaults on Gaza,* http://www.ibtimes.co.uk/israels-operation-protective -edge-body-count-multiple-gaza-attacks-1456029.

8 *Bennett threatens to bolt,* Gil Hoffman, "Bennett Privately Threatened PM to Quit Coalition," *Jerusalem Post,* 4 April 2014, http://www.jpost.com /Diplomacy-and-Politics/Bennett-privately-threatened.

8 *Palestinian prisoner release,* Michael Wilner, Herb Keinon "US: No Palestinian prisoner release is violation of terms of talks," *Jerusalem Post,* March 19, 2013, http://www.jpost.com/Diplomacy-and-Politics/US-to-Israel-No -Palestinian-prisoner-release-is-violation-of-terms-of-talks-346878.

8 *Netanyahu refuses to release prisoners,* Herb Keinon, "Israel Cancels Fourth Prisoner Release," *Jerusalem Post,* 4 April 2014, http://www.jpost.com /Diplomacy-and-Politics/Israel-cancels-fourth-prison.

8 *Indyk blames Netanyahu* Nahum Barnea, "Inside the Talks' Failure: US Officials Open Up," Ynet, 2 May 2014, http://www.ynetnews.com/articles /0,7340,L-4515821,00.html. Also see: "How Martin Indyk went from AIPAC man to blaming Israel," *The Jewish Daily Forward,* May 15, 2014, http://www.haaretz.com/jewish-world/jewish-world-features/1.590813.

8 *Netanyahu and his inner circle outraged,* Attila Somfalvi, "Israel Caught off Guard by US Support of Palestinian Unity," Ynet, 3 June 2014, http://www .ynetnews.com/articles/0,7340,L-4526668,00.html..

8 *Rogue Hamas cell,* "Mashaal admits Hamas members kidnapped and murdered Naftali, Gilad and Eyal," *Jerusalem Post,* August 23, 2014, http://

www.jpost.com/Arab-Israeli-Conflict/Mashaal-admits-Hamas-members
-kidnapped-and-murdered-Naftali-Gilad-and-Eyal-371997.

8 *Spent years in Israeli prisons,* Gianluca Mezzofiore, "Israel names Hamas'
Marwan Qawasmeh and Amer Abu Aisha as Suspects in Kidnapped Teens
Search," *International Business Times,* June 27, 2014, http://www.ibtimes
.co.uk/israel-names-hamas-marwan-qawasmeh-amer-abu-aisha-suspects
-kidnapped-teens-search-1454389.

9 *Pronounced missing,* Max Blumenthal, "Netanyahu Government Knew Teens
Were Dead as It Whipped Up Racist Frenzy," *Electronic Intifada,* 8 July 2014,
http://electronicintifada.net/content/netanyahu-government-knewteens-wer.....

9 *The plan quickly unraveled,* Amos Harel, "Tapes reveal pleas of kidnapped
boy's father met with call center apathy," *Haaretz,* July 2, 2014, http://www
.haaretz.com/news/diplomacy-defense/.premium-1.602537.

9 *Shot the teens to death,* Shlomi Eldar, "Was Israeli Public Misled on Abductions?," *Al-Monitor,* July 3, 2014, http://www.al-monitor.com/pulse/originals
/2014/07/misleading-kidnapping-almoz-hamas-vengeance-hatred.html#.

9 *Buried their bodies,* Jodi Rudoren, "A Trail of Clues Leading to Victims and
Heartbreak," *New York Times,* July 1, 2014, http://www.nytimes.com/2014
/07/02/world/middleeast/details-emerge-in-deaths-of-israeli-teenagers.html.

9 *One of the killers,* Jake Edmiston, "Chilling new recording of Israeli teen's
emergency call to police may have captured the boys' last minutes alive,"
National Post, July 2, 2014, http://news.nationalpost.com/2014/07/02
/investigator-played-israeli-teens-panicked-police-call-for-his-mother-told
-her-not-to-be-alarmed-by-sound-of-gunfire-interview/.

10 *Blood and bullets were found,* Noam Sheizaf, "How the public was manipulated into believing the teens were alive," *+972 Magazine,* July 2, 2014,
http://972mag.com/how-the-public-was-manipulated-into-believing-the
-teens-were-alive/92865/.

10 *"I was naive,"* Yaakov Levi, "Bat-Galim Sha'ar: Failures Go Right to the
Top," *Arutz Sheva,* July 2, 2014, http://www.israelnationalnews.com/News
/News.aspx/182438#.VNz0nS5dVnJ.

10 *"All the details,"* Adam Horowitz and Philip Weiss and Scott Roth, Israel
maintains gag order in missing teens' case, leading to charge of media 'ma-
nipulation,'" *Mondoweiss,* June 23, 2014, http://mondoweiss.net/2014/06
/maintains-missing-manipulation.

10 *Rai Al Youm,* http://electronicintifada.net/content/netanyahu-government-
knew-teens-were-dead-it-whipped-racist-frenzy/13533.

10 *Going rogue,* see: Savadski, "It Turns Out Hamas May Not Have Kidnapped
and Killed the 3 Israeli Teens After All;" and Eldar, "Accused kidnappers are
rogue Hamas branch," *Al Monitor.*

11 *Prosor appeared at the UN,* UN Web TV, Ron Prosor on the abduction of three
Israeli teenagers in the West Bank, June 17, 2014, http://webtv.un.org/watch
/ron-prosor-israel-on-the-abduction-of-three-israeli-teenageers-in-the-west
-bank-security-council-media-stakeout-17-june-2014/3627317543001.

11 *Netanyahu mimics #BringBackOurGirls,* Allison Kaplan Sommer, "Move
over, Michelle Obama," *Haaretz,* June 20, 2014, http://www.haaretz.com
/blogs/routine-emergencies/.premium-1.600083.

12 *Yellow ribbons at synagogues,* Marc Shapiro, "Baltimore joins three ribbons campaign," *Baltimore Jewish Times,* June 26, 2014, http://jewishtimes.com /24729/baltimore-joins-three-yellow-ribbons-campaign/.

12 *Local politicians at pro-Israel rallies,* NYC prayer rally honors kidnapped Israeli teens, NBC, July 1, 2014, http://www.nbcnewyork.com/news/local /New-York-City-Rally-Killed-Israeli-Teens-West-Bank-265315581.html.

12 *Tributes to teens from US diplomats,* Philip Weiss, "Among US expressions of outrage and condolence, Obama, Kerry and Rice identify with Israeli parents," *Mondoweiss,* July 1, 2014, http://mondoweiss.net/2014/07/expressions -condolence-identify.

12 *Rachel Frenkel addresses UN,* Mother of Kidnapped Israeli Teenager Neftali Frankel Addresses UN, June 24, 2014, http://blog.unwatch.org/index.php/2014 /06/24/mother-of-kidnapped-israeli-teenager-neftali-frankel-addresses-un/.

12 *Gag order,* Greg Mitchell, "'New York Times' Admits It Agreed to 'Gag Orders' in Israel," *The Nation,* April 18, 2014, http://www.thenation.com/ blog/179406/new-york-times-admits-it-agreed-gag-orders-israel#.

13 *Rearrest of Adnan and Issawi prisoners,* Patrick Strickland, "Israeli forces rearrest hunger striker Samer Issawi," *Electronic Intifada,* June 23, 2014, http://electronicintifada.net/blogs/patrick-strickland/israeli-forces-rearrest -hunger-striker-samer-issawi. See also: Khader Adnan Returns to Administrative Detention amid Ongoing Mass Arrests and Massacres in Gaza, Samidoun: Palestinian Prisoner Solidarity Network, July 2014, http://samidoun .ca/2014/07/khader-adnan-returns-to-administrative-detent.....

13 *Closed off the area around Hebron,* "Hamas Will Pay," *Daily Mail,* July 1, 2014, http://www.dailymail.co.uk/news/article-2675451/Bodies-three-Jewish -settlers-went-missing-near-Hebron-near-West-Bank-city.html.

13 *Israel seizes flags,* Allison Deger, "Nighttime Israeli raid on Bir Zeit University yields — truck full of Hamas flags," *Mondoweiss,* June 19, 2014, http:// mondoweiss.net/2014/06/nighttime-israeli-university.

13 *Israel and PA coordinate raids,* Allison Deger, "One killed in protests as Israeli army takes control of Ramallah city center for first time since 2007," *Mondoweiss,* June 22, 2014, http://mondoweiss.net/2014/06/ramallah -palestinian-authority#sthash.2f9mEYUU.dpuf.

14 *"The People of Israel Demand Revenge,"* Sara C Nelson, "Facebook Page Calls For The Execution Of A Palestinian 'Terrorist' Every Hour Until Missing Israeli Teenagers Are Found," *Huffington Post,* June 16, 2014, http://www .huffingtonpost.co.uk/2014/06/16/facebook-page-israelis-kill-palestinian -terrorist-missing-teenagers-found_n_5499434.html.

14 *Volunteer searchers,* "Bodies of three kidnapped teens found; Netanyahu calls families," *Times of Israel,* June 30, 2014, http://www.timesofisrael.com /bodies-of-three-kidnapped-teens-found/

Notes to Chapter 2

15 *Netanyahu under mounting pressure,* "Netanyahu's approval ratings in a free-fall in light of latest Gaza cease-fire," *Jerusalem Post,* August 27, 2014, http://www.jpost.com/Arab-Israeli-Conflict/Netanyahus-approval-ratings- in-a-free-fall-in-light-of-latest-Gaza-cease-fire-372448.

15 *Bennett was gaining in polls,* "Poll: Jewish Home Party Gains Over Likud," *Hamodia*, July 3, 2014, http://hamodia.com/2014/07/03/poll-jewish-home -party-gains-likud/.

15 *Lieberman's attacks,* David Horowitz, "Lieberman's unacceptable war on Netanyahu," *Times of Israel*, July 15, 2014, http://www.timesofisrael.com /libermans-unacceptable-war-on-netanyahu/.

16 *Netanyahu's statement on teens' discovery,* Max Blumenthal, "Netanyahu Government Knew Teens Were Dead as It Whipped Up Racist Frenzy," *Electronic Intifada*, 8 July 2014, http://electronicintifada.net/content/netanyahu -government-knew-teens-were-dead-it-whipped-racist-frenzy/13533.

16 *This second poem helped radicalize,* https://books.google.com/books?id=7h aFhI2q2_YC&pg=PA187&lpg=PA187&dq=city+of+slaughter+jabotinsky &source=bl&ots=kOxIYANfE7&sig=jSwU07vhK9bfuJF8I9icechrz TE&hl=en&sa=X&ei=s1KTVPvhIZHbsASKm4HoBg&ved=0CC0Q6A EwAg#v=onepage&q=city%20of%20slaughter%20jabotinsky&f=false.

16 *Vladimir Jabotinsky,* Benzion Netanyahu obituary, *The Guardian*, May 1 2012, http://www.theguardian.com/world/2012/may/01/benzion-netanyahu.

17 *"Death to Arabs" mobs,* Blumenthal, "Netanyahu Government Knew," *The Electronic Intifada,* 8 July 2014.

17 *Ayelet Shaked's Facebook post,* Mira Bar Hillel, "Why I'm on the brink of burning my Israeli passport," *The Independent*, July 11, 2014, http://www .independent.co.uk/voices/why-im-on-the-brink-of-burning-my-israeli -passport-9600165.html.

17 *"Act with a heavy hand,"* "Ori Lewis, Israel mourns teenagers, strikes Hamas in Gaza," *Reuters*, July 1, 2014, http://www.reuters.com/article /2014/07/01/us-palestinians-israel-idUSKBN0F521P20140701.

17 *"Broad moral gulf,"* CNN, "Israel's Netanyahu says of slain teens: 'May God avenge their blood,'" July 1, 2014, http://www.cnn.com/2014/07/01 /world/meast/israel-teenagers-death/.

17 *Perel's call for vengeance,* Or Kashti, "World Bnei Akiva chief calls for price of "blood" for Israeli teens' murder," *Haaretz*, July 2, 2014, http://www .haaretz.com/jewish-world/jewish-world-news/.premium-1.602675.

18 *Circumstances of Abu Khdeir's murder,* "Mohammed Abu Khdeir murder," Lizzie Dearden, *The Independent*, July 14, 2014, http://www.independent .co.uk/news/world/middle-east/mohammed-abu-khdeir-murder-three-israeli -jews-admit-kidnapping-teenager-and-burning-him-to-death-9605371.html; Also: 'When my son died, I felt like my life was over', Tovah Lazaroff, *The Jerusalem Post*, July 9, 2014, http://www.jpost.com/National-News/Suha -Abu-Khdeir-When-my-son-died-I-felt-like-my-life-was-over-362037; Also: 'They took three of ours, so let's take one of theirs', Aviel Magnezi, Ynet, August 11, 2014, http://www.ynetnews.com/articles/0,7340,L-4557714,00.html.

19 *Yosef Chaim Ben-David had been arrested,* Robert Tait, "Six Arrested in Palestinian Teenager Murder Investigation," *The Telegraph*, July 6, 2014, http://www.telegraph.co.uk/news/worldnews/middleeast/israel/10949520/ Six-arrested-in-Palestinian-teenager-murder-investigation.html.

19 *Police sought to interrogate Abu Khdeir family,* Allison Deger, "Identities of Minors Who Admitted to Killing Mohammed Abu Khdeir to Be Revealed

Monday," *Mondoweiss*, 19 October 2014, http://mondoweiss.net/2014/10/identities-admittedmohammed#sthash.wU3Ta7q.....

19 *Gag order on Chaim David,* Yonah Jeremy Bob, "Supreme Court lifts gag order on lead alleged murderer of Abu Khdeir," *Jerusalem Post*, July 29, 2014, http://www.jpost.com/National-News/Supreme-Court-lifts-gag-order-on-lead-alleged-murderer-of-Abu-Khdeir-363599.

19 *Attempted to kidnap,* Omri Efraim, "Suspects in Murder of Palestinian Teen Attempted to Kidnap Young Boy Day Earlier," Ynet, 7 June 2014, http://www.ynetnews.com/articles/0,7340,L-4538687,00.html..

19 *"I am the Messiah!"* Lazar Berman, "Suspect in Abu Khdeir Killing Says He's 'the Messiah,'" *Times of Israel*, 27 July 2014, http://www.timesofisrael.com/man-suspect-in-abu-khdeir-killing-i-am-the-messiah/.

20 *Rioting had exploded in Shuafat,* Jodi Rudoren, "In Divided Jerusalem, Rail Line for Arabs and Jews Is Among the Fractures," the *New York Times*, July 13, 2014, http://www.nytimes.com/2014/07/14/world/middleeast/in-divided-jerusalem-rail-line-for-arabs-and-jews-is-among-the-fractures.html.

20 *Gunshots rang out,* Peter Beaumont, "Murdered Palestinian teenager's funeral draws thousands of mourners," *The Guardian*, July 4, 2014, http://www.theguardian.com/world/2014/jul/04/palestinian-funeral-jerusalem-mohammed-abu-khdeir.

20 *Twenty-five members thrown in jail,* Dan Cohen, "'I'm 100% certain we won't receive justice in this racist court': Abu Khdeir family awaits justice that will likely never come," *Mondoweiss*, September 5, 2014, http://mondoweiss.net/2014/09/certain-receive-justice.

20 *Tariq Abu Khdeir's arrest,* Caitlin Johnston and Jimmy Geurts, "Beaten Tampa teen, 15, released from Israeli jail," *Tampa Bay Times*, July 6, 2014, http://www.tampabay.com/news/publicsafety/tampa-teen-released-from-israeli-jail/2187376.

20 *Revenge raid on family,* Max Blumenthal, "Israeli police ransack Tariq Abu Khdier family and arrest relatives in apparent revenge raid," *Mondoweiss*, July 18, 2014, http://mondoweiss.net/2014/07/relatives-apparent-revenge.

22 *Shimon Peres' role in Qana,* Noam Sheizaf, "Blame Peres, not Bennett, for the Qana massacre," *+972mag*, January 7, 2015, http://972mag.com/blame-peres-not-bennett-for-the-qana-massacre/101046/.

22 *Death threats to Peretz,* Nir Hasson, "Death threats follow minister's condolence call to family of burned teen," *Haaretz*, July 9, 2014, http://www.haaretz.com/news/diplomacy-defense/.premium-1.604112.

23 *Racist killing of Amjad Abu Khdeir,* Jodi Rudoren, "Tensions high in Jerusalem as Palestinian teenager is given a martyr's burial," *The New York Times*, July 4, 2014, http://www.nytimes.com/2014/07/05/world/middleeast/israel.html.

23 *Beating of Shweiki and Mahfouz,* Nir Hasson, "10 Israeli Jews charged with attempted lynch of Palestinians," *Haaretz*, August 11, 2014, http://www.haaretz.com/news/national/1.609987.

26 *Gaza rockets on July 6,* Matan Tzuri and Yoav Zitun, "Gaza rockets continue to hit southern Israel," Ynet, July 6, 2014 http://www.ynetnews.com/articles/0,7340,L-4538739,00.html.

26 *Israel kills Hamas members on July 7*, Nidal Al-Mughrabi, "Israeli air strikes kill seven Gaza gunment, Hamas says," *Reuters*, July 7, 2014, http://uk .reuters.com/article/2014/07/07/us-palestinians-israel-airstrike-idUKKBN 0FB12I20140707.

26 *Hamas takes credit*, "Live updates, July 7, 2014: Rockets bombard south, Hamas claims responsibility," *Haaretz*, http://www.haaretz.com/news /diplomacy-defense/1.603472.

26 *Rockets to Jerusalem*, Yaakov Lappin and Herb Keinon, "Hamas rockets reach Jerusalem and Tel Aviv," *Jerusalem Post*, July 8, 2014, http://www .jpost.com/Operation-Protective-Edge/Iron-Dome-intercepts-second-rocket -over-greater-Tel-Aviv-361994.

26 *Israel planned Gaza assault in advance*, Marissa Newman, "Army prepared for Gaza campaign, defense minister says," *Times of Israel*, December 31, 2013 http://www.timesofisrael.com/army-prepared-for-gaza-campaign-defense -minister-says/.

Notes to Chapter 3

27 *Palestinian death toll*, "Photos of the week: Violence continues as hopes for ceasefire fade," Activestills *+972Mag*, July 17, 2014, http://972mag.com /a-week-in-photos-violence-continues-as-hopes-for-ceasefire-fade/93797/.

27 *Kaware family killing* "Israeli army says the killing of 8 Gazan family members was in error, Gili Cohen," Haaretz, July 10, 2014 http://www.haaretz .com/news/diplomacy-defense/1.604128.

27 *Fun Times Beach Cafe bombing*, "World Cup fans killed in Gaza as bomb hits cafe," *Middle East Eye*, July 10, 2014 http://www.middleeasteye.net /news/world-cup-fans-killed-gaza-bomb-hits-cafe-1394390500.

28 *Bakr boys killing*, "Witness to a shelling: first-hand account of deadly strike on Gaza port," Peter Beaumont, *The Guardian*, July 16, 2014 http://www .theguardian.com/world/2014/jul/16/witness-gaza-shelling-first-hand -account.

28 *Izz Ad-Din Al-Qassam background* Beverly Milton-Edwards, Stephen Farrell, *Hamas: The Islamic Resistance Movement*, John Wiley & Sons, 2010, 20–27.

29 *Al-Qassam's Black Hand cells*, ibid, 24–29.

29 *Al-Qassam Brigades had just a single rifle*, Zaki Chehab, *Inside Hamas: The Untold Story of the Militant Islamic Movement*, Nation Books, 2007, 44.

29 *Al-Qassam attacks were aimed at collaborators*, Jean-Pierre Filiu, *Gaza: A History*, Oxford University Press, 2014, 215.

30 *Imad Aqel and his assassination*, Chehab, *Inside Hamas*, 47–50.

30 *Assassination of Ayyash*, ibid, 59.

30 *Assassination of Shehadeh*, Suzanne Goldenberg, "12 dead in attack on Hamas," *The Guardian*, July 22, 2002, http://www.theguardian.com/world /2002/jul/23/israel1.

31 *"It has embarrassed the Palestinian Authority,"* Dr. Alon Ben-Meir, "The Assassination of Yahya Ayyash: Untimely and Unwise," Washington Report on Middle East Affairs, February/March 1996 http://www.wrmea.org/1996 -february-march/the-assassination-of-yahya-ayyash-untimely-and-unwise .html.

31 *killing of Shehadeh during truce,* Gideon Alon, "Ramon unveils Tanzim plan made before Shehadeh hit," *Haaretz,* July 30, 2002, http://www.haaretz .com/news/ramon-unveils-tanzim-truce-plan-made-before-shehadeh-hit -1.38323.

31 *Born as Mohammed Diab Ibrahim Al-Masri,* Qassem Qassem, "Who is Hamas's 'Phantom'?" *Al Akhbar English,* July 31, 2014, http://english.al -akhbar.com/node/20943.

31 *Closest it came to eliminating Deif,* Filiu *Gaza: A History,* 260.

31 *Deif and Jaabari,* Milton-Edwards and Farrell, *Hamas,* 126–129.

32 *Jaabari and Shalit operation,* Mohammed Budeir, "Jaabari: Hamas Military Chief and Mastermind of Shalit Operation," *Al Akhbar English,* November 15, 2012, http://english.al-akhbar.com/node/13758.

32 *Deif returns to Gaza,* Milton-Edwards and Farrell, *Hamas,* 126–129.

32 *Al-Ghoul's weapons development,* Chehab, *Inside Hamas,* 63–65.

32 *Hamas drones deployed,* Caroline Alexander, "Hamas Bragging Rights Grow With Drones Use Against Israel," *Bloomberg News,* July 16, 2014, http://www.bloomberg.com/news/articles/2014-07-16/hamas-bragging -rights-grow-with-drones-use-against-israel.

32 *Rockets struck Tel Aviv,* Nidal Al-Mughrabi, "Rockets hit near Tel Aviv as Gaza death toll rises," *Reuters,* November 15, 2012, http://www.reuters .com/article/2012/11/15/us-palestinians-israel-hamas-idUSBRE8AD0WP 20121115.

33 *"Bomb, Bomb Tel Aviv,"* "Tel Aviv Rockets Get a Song, Hot Arabic Music," November 17, 2012, http://hotarabicmusic.blogspot.com/2012/11/tel-aviv -rockets-get-song.html.

33 *"Zalzil Amna Israel" in Hebrew,* Song for Israel Zalzil Amna Israel (Hebrew), uploaded by Youtube user Suzika Chan on July 16, 2014, https:// www.youtube.com/watch?v=2EwFq20LdrM.

34 *"Here, We Prepare,"* Here, we have prepared for you, uploaded by Youtube user Truth Meteor on July 30, 2014 https://www.youtube.com/watch?v=pQ tmHjPoc1s.

34 *Background on Ramzi al-'Ak,* "Choir group of prisoners deported to Gaza," *Pal Times,* October 15, 2012, http://bit.ly/1EZ70TQ.

34 *"Your words are gunpowder!"* Abu Obeida, uploaded by Youtube user Paldf on December 15, 2011, https://www.youtube.com/watch?v=LLBE D97AXyA.

35 *Abu Obeida interview,* "An Interview with Abu Obaida-Part 2," Al-Qassam Media, October 7, 2009, http://www.qassam.ps/video-7-An_interview _with_Abu_Obaida_Part_2.html.

35 *Alsharq Al-Awsat profile of Abu Obeida,* Kifah Zuboun, *Alsharq Al-Awsat,* July 24, 2014, http://aawsat.com/home/article/144956.

35 *Obeida took to the airwaves,* Strong fiery speech by spokesman of the Qassam Brigades, Abu Obeida, uploaded by Youtube user Palestine Voice on July 11, 2014, https://www.youtube.com/watch?v=7h_gBxkWQBU.

36 *Hamas/Islamic Jihad ceasefire demands,* Ira Glunts, "Report: Hamas offers Israel 10 conditions for a 10 year truce," *Mondoweiss,* July 16, 2014, http:// mondoweiss.net/2014/07/report-israel-conditions.

37 *Derided by international observers,* David Kirkpatrick, "International Observers Find Egypt's Presidential Election Fell Short of International Standards," *The New York Times,* May 29, 2014, http://www.nytimes.com/2014/05/30 /world/middleeast/international-observers-find-fault-with-egypt-vote.html.

37 *Incited against Palestinian refugees,* Max Blumenthal, "The Egyptian Army and Palestinian Authority join forces to crush Gaza," *Mondoweiss,* July 10, 2013, http://mondoweiss.net/2013/07/the-egyptian-army-and-palestinian -authority-join-forces-to-punish-gaza.

37 *"They actually were suffocating Gaza too much,"* Adam Entous and Nicolas Casey, "Gaza Tension Stoked by Unlikely Alliance Between Israel and Egypt," *Wall Street Journal,* August 6, 2014, http://www.wsj.com/articles/unlikely -alliance-between-israel-and-egypt-stoked-gaza-tension-1407379093.

38 *"Hamas has a fundamental choice to make,"* Michael R. Gordon, "Kerry Says US Would Address Hamas Demands After Cease-Fire," *The New York Times,* July 22, 2014, http://www.nytimes.com/2014/07/23/world/middleeast/kerry -says-us-would-address-hamas-demands-after-cease-fire.html.

Notes to Chapter 4

39 *Leaked video of frogman raid,* Itay Blumental, "IDF probe of Protective Edge infiltration leaks," YNet, November 12, 2014, http://www.ynetnews.com/Ext/ Comp/ArticleLayout/CdaArticlePrintPreview/0,2506,L-4602652,00.html.

39 *"Hamas is in control of the agenda,"* Shirly Seidler, "Israeli army admits error in letting civilians return to south," *Haaretz,* August 11, 2014, http:// www.haaretz.com/news/national/1.609971.

39 *Accounts of Sudaniya battle,* "Al-Qassam Brigades ambushes Israeli naval forces, foils infiltration attempt Palestine Information Center," *Occupied Palestine,* July 13, 2014, https://occupiedpalestine.wordpress.com/2014/07 /13/al-qassam-brigades-ambushes-israeli-naval-forces-foils-infiltration-at- tempt-gazaunderattack/ Palestine Information Center is a Hamas backed news service. Its report was syndicated by the blog Occupied Palestine..

40 *Four Israeli soldiers "lightly wounded,"* "Israeli forces carry out rocket raid in Gaza Strip," *Associated Press,* July 12, 2014, http://www.washingtonpost .com/world/israeli-forces-carry-out-raid-on-rocket-base-in-gaza-strip/2014 /07/12/92bf92b2-0a37-11e4-a0dd-f2b22a257353_story.html; See also: "LIVE UPDATES: Operation Protective Edge Day 6," http://www.haaretz.com /news/diplomacy-defense/1.604714.

40 *A series of online graphics,* "Shuja'iya: Hamas' Terror Fortress in Gaza," Israel Defense Forces, July 20, 2014, http://www.idfblog.com/blog/2014/07 /20/shujaiya-hamas-terror-fortress-gaza/.

42 *Nothing more than improvised explosive devices,* Al Jazeera Arabic's Tamer Mishal interviewed Al Qassam veterans of Shujaiya in a feature length doc- umentary broadcast on August 6, 2014. In a tunnel shaft, one fighter dis- played explosive barrels marked, "Made in Gaza by the Qassam Brigades," describing receiving instructions to attack Israeli special forces with them. Israeli army Chief of Staff Benny Gantz also commented on the tactic: "To run up and try to put an explosive charge on a tank is the act of courageous people." Inna Lazareva, Israeli army chief praises "courageous Hamas fighters," *The*

Telegraph, October 14, 2014, http://www.telegraph.co.uk/news/worldnews
/middleeast/israel/11161445/Israeli-army-chief-praises-courageous-Hamas
-fighters.html The tactic was on display in the leaked Israeli army video of
Al Qassam's frogman infiltration of Kibbutz Zikim..

42 *Drove over the bodies,* "IDF releases details on Shejaiya battle in which 7
soldiers died July 20," *Times of Israel*, August 22, 2014, http://www.times
ofisrael.com/idf-releases-details-on-shejaiya-battle-in-which-7-soldiers
-died/.

43 *"More than what we caused"* Mohamed Najib, "Palestinian militants inflict
substantial casualties on Israeli forces in Gaza," *IHS Jane's Terrorism &
Insurgency Centre*, August 1, 2014, http://www.janes.com/article/41421
/palestinian-militants-inflict-substantial-casualties-on-israeli-forces-in-gaza.

43 *"An ambush from hell,"* Ian Black and Inigo Gilmore and Mitchell Prothero,
"The day Israel realized that this was a real war," *The Guardian*, July 29,
2006, http://www.theguardian.com/world/2006/jul/30/syria.israel1.

44 *"We gave them half an hour,"* Gili Cohen, "IDF: Bloodiest battle in Gaza
could have been much worse," *Haaretz*, July 28, 2014, http://www.haaretz
.com/news/diplomacy-defense/.premium-1.607496.

44 Over 120 *Shujaiya residents killed,* Peter Beaumont, "Gaza Crisis: Palestinian death toll climbs past 500 as hospital is hit," *The Guardian*, July 21,
2014, http://www.theguardian.com/world/2014/jul/21/gaza-crisis-obama
-ceasefire-fighting-goes-on.

45 *Details of the operation shocked US officials,* Mark Perry, "Why Israel's
bombardment of Gaza neighborhood left US officers 'stunned,'" *Al Jazeera
America*, August 27, 2014, http://america.aljazeera.com/articles/2014/8/26
/israel-bombing-stunsusofficers.html.

45 *"Hell of a pinpoint operation,"* Arthur Delany, "John Kerry's Hot Mic Reaction To Gaza: 'Hell Of A Pinpoint Operation,'" *Huffington Post*, July 25,
2014, http://www.huffingtonpost.com/2014/07/20/john-kerry-israel_n_56
03389.html.

45 *Report broadcast on Israel's Channel 2,* Female Soldiers of the Most Moral
Army—Shell Gaza Every 2 Minutes! uploaded by Youtube user boycott
apartheid BDS on August 9, 2014, https://www.youtube.com/watch?v=Jbrs
HszM3Xg.

47 *"What happened in the Dahiya quarter,"* "Israel warns Hizbullah war
would invite destruction," *Reuters*, March 10, 2008, http://www.ynetnews
.com/articles/0,7340,L-3604893,00.html.

47 *Maj. Gen. Eizenkot interview with Yedioth Ahronoth,* Israel warns Hizbullah war would invite destruction, Ynet, October 3, 2008, http://www
.ynetnews.com/Ext/Comp/ArticleLayout/CdaArticlePrintPreview/1,2506,L
-3604893,00.html.

47 *Col. Siboni's "Disproportionate Force,"* Ben White, "Israel: wedded to war?"
The Guardian, October 7, 2008, http://www.theguardian.com/comment
isfree/2008/oct/07/israelandthepalestinians.lebanon.

48 *Katz on "mowing the lawn,"* Yaakov Katz, "Analysis: Easy to start, hard to
end," *Jerusalem Post*, March 10, 2012, http://www.jpost.com/Defense/Analysis
-Easy-to-start-hard-to-end.

NOTES

48 *Inbar on "mowing the grass,"* Ephraim Inbar and Eitan Shamir, "Mowing the grass in Gaza" *Jerusalem Post*, July 22, 2014, http://www.jpost.com/Opinion/Columnists/Mowing-the-grass-in-Gaza-368516.

49 *B'tselem on Israeli military's open fire policy,* Black Flag: The legal and moral implications of the policy of attacking residential buildings in the Gaza Strip, Summer 2014, B'tselem report, January 2015 http://www.btselem.org/sites/default/files2/201501_black_flag_eng.pdf.

49 *Ninety families removed from the civil records,* "Israeli occupation exterminate 90 Palestinian families in Gaza," *Middle East Monitor*, August 25, 2014, https://www.middleeastmonitor.com/news/middle-east/13712-israeli-occupation-exterminate-90-palestinian-families-in-gaza; See also: Jack Khoury, "89 families killed in Gaza since hostilities began, Palestinians say," August 24, 2014, http://www.haaretz.com/news/diplomacy-defense/1.612255.

49 *Defense Department official reacted with shock,* Mark Perry, "Why Israel's bombardment of Gaza neighborhood left US officers 'stunned,'" *Al Jazeera America,* August 27, 2014.

51 *Denied Amnesty International and Human Rights Watch,* Amira Hass, "Israel bars Amnesty, Human Rights Watch workers from Gaza," *Haaretz*, August 18, 2014, http://www.haaretz.com/news/diplomacy-defense/.premium-1.611015.

56 *Refusal to coordinate with its first responders,* ICRC personnel were not able to enter Shujaiya until the morning of July 20, when Israel agreed with Hamas to a two hour humanitarian ceasefire. See: Israel, Hamas agree to two-hour truce in Gaza's Shejaiya, Agence France Press, July 20, 2014, http://news.yahoo.com/hamas-accepts-call-three-hour-humanitarian-truce-095802332.html.

56 *Targeted its ambulances,* Sharif Abdel Kouddous, "Massacre in Shejaiya," *The Nation,* July 20, 2014, http://www.thenation.com/article/180728/massacre-shejaiya# Kouddous reported: "Ambulances could not get in...one took a direct hit with a paramedic inside."

Notes to Chapter 5

58 *Rise in price tag violence* See: When Settlers Attack, The Jerusalem Fund for Education and Community Development, 2012 http://www.thejerusalemfund.org/ht/a/GetDocumentAction/i/32678.

58 *45 percent plunge in price tag violence during war* Tova Dvorin, Report: 45% decrease in "Price Tag" attacks in 2014, Arutz Sheva, February 13, 2015 http://www.israelnationalnews.com/News/News.aspx/191311#.VRCMHGTF9Hg.

58 *Graffiti on churches,* see: Christians in Israel and Palestine Fear Rise in Violence Ahead of Pope's Visit," Michael Craowford, *The Guardian* http://www.theguardian.com/world/2014/may/09/christians-israel-palestine-rise-violence-pope-visit.

59 *US NSA and Israel's Unit 8200* James Bamford, Israel's NSA Scandal, New York Times, September 16, 2014 http://www.nytimes.com/2014/09/17/opinion/israels-nsa-scandal.html?_r=0.

60 *Eran Efrati on red "execution line"* Eran Efrati, Facebook post, July 28, 2014 https://www.facebook.com/eran.efrati.9/posts/10204269146351996;

also see Efrati's testimony at the Russell Tribunal on Palestine, September 24, 2014 https://www.youtube.com/watch?v=Y8XuwLGLDrQ. My Russell Tribunal testimony, also on September 24, 2014, includes display and analysis of the Israeli military map I retrieved in Shujaiya: https://www.youtube.com/watch?v=iWrOuGNrzZc.

62 *Video of Salem Shamaly execution* Robert Mackey, Palestinian family finds missing son in YouTube video of his shooting, New York Times, July 22, 2014 http://www.nytimes.com/2014/07/23/world/middleeast/palestinian-family-finds-missing-son-in-youtube-video-of-his-shooting.html.

63 *UN schools sheltering Gazans,* Raya Jalabi, "Gaza Crisis: a closer look at Israeli strikes on UNRWA schools," *The Guardian*, August 8, 2014, http://www.theguardian.com/world/2014/aug/08/-sp-gaza-israeli-strikes-unrwa-schools.

64 *NBC clip about Salem Shamaly,* http://www.nbcnews.com/nightly-news/his-family-loved-him-father-searches-son-ruins-n165851.

Notes to Chapter 6

68 *Army firing on Khuza'a farmers:* For a video look at violent attacks on Khuza'a farmers prior to Operation Protective Edge see Palestinian filmmaker Fida Qishta's documentary, Where Should The Birds Fly? http://whereshouldthebirdsfly.org/.

68 *July 22 attack on Khuza'a,* Sharif Abdel Kouddous, "The Tank Shells Fell Like Rain", *The Nation*, July 25, 2014, http://www.thenation.com/article/180782/tank-shells-fell-rain-survivors-attack-unrwa-school-report-scenes-carnage-and-destruc#.

68 *Givati Brigade in Khuza'a,* Amos Harel, "Netanyahu's Hamas Dilemma," *Haaretz*, July 28, 2014, http://www.haaretz.com/news/diplomacy-defense/1.607597.

68 *Ofer Winter's letter,* Ali Abunimah, "Israeli commander declares "holy war" on Palestinians," *Electronic Intifada*, July 11, 2014, http://electronicintifada.net/blogs/ali-abunimah/israeli-commander-declares-holy-war-palestinians#letter.

69 *Giant Viper:* The Giant Viper is a British-made, trailer mounted mine clearance system. The device launches a barrel filled with C4 explosives, which detonate across areas containing mines, triggering their explosive charges. Its apparent use in densely populated civilian areas in Khuza'a suggests it was not employed for mine clearance. Video of Giant Viper in action uploaded by YouTube user Jaglavak Military on September 5, 2009 can be seen here: https://www.youtube.com/watch?v=HtB0QnfviXQ.

69 *Bound and blindfolded Palestinian men as human shields,* Samer Badawi "Palestinian teen: I was used as a human shield in Gaza," *+972 magazine,* August 21, 2014, http://972mag.com/palestinian-teen-i-was-used-as-a-human-shield-in-gaza/95800/.

70 *Khalil Al-Najjar's humiliation,* Mohammed Omer, "Horror, then degradation, confront Gaza residents," *Middle East Eye*, August 16, 2014, http://www.middleeasteye.net/news/horror-then-degradation-confront-gaza-residents-2127590906.

71 *"I felt...sorry for the iman,"* Mohammed Omer's testimony at Russell Tribunal on Palestine, Brussels, Belgium, September 24, 2014, https://www.youtube.com/watch?v=xWQm8MO_dRI.

71 *Ebad Al-Rahman mosque detonation,* Video: Israeli soldiers cheer as explosives flatten mosque in Gaza, France 24, August 5, 2014, http://observers.france24.com/content/20140805-video-israeli-soldiers-cheer-explosives-flatten-mosque-gaza.

72 *Meshal Khuza'a documentary;* Documentary is available with English and Italian subtitles at "Khuzaa attack and Aftermath con sottotitoli in italiano #GazaUnderAttack" uploaded by YouTube user Carpe Diem on August 21, 2014, https://www.youtube.com/watch?v=9gp6qb3Njwo

74 *Rosenfeld's interview,* Jesse Rosenfeld, "Did Israel execute jihadists in Khuza'a?" *The Daily Beast,* September 7, 2014, http://www.thedailybeast.com/articles/2014/09/07/did-israel-execute-jihadists-in-gaza.html

78 *Ghadir Rujeila's body found,* Al Jazeera's Tamer Mishal was the first reporter to come upon Ghadir Rujeila's body at the gate of Khuza'a. The scene of his discovery appears at 26:50 in "Khuza'a: Attack and Aftermath." https://www.youtube.com/watch?v=9gp6qb3Njwo.

80 *Post Traumatic Stress Disorder among Gaza youth,* Trauma and PTSD among civilians in the Middle East, PTSD Research Quarterly, Fall 2010, http://www.ptsd.va.gov/professional/newsletters/research-quarterly/v21n4.pdf.

Notes to Chapter 7

86 *Spot and Strike system,* Richard Silverstein, "Female IDF drone jockeys kill Gazans remotely," *Tikkun Olam,* April 20, 2014, http://www.richardsilverstein.com/2014/04/20/female-idf-drone-jockeys-kill-gazans-remotely/; Also see: Anshel Pfeffer, "Lethal joysticks," *Haaretz,* July 2, 2010, http://www.haaretz.com/weekend/week-s-end/lethal-joysticks-1.299650; Hanan Greenberg, IDF deploys new anti-terror system around Gaza, YNet, March 24, 2008, http://www.ynetnews.com/articles/0,7340,L-3523125,00.html.

86 *Attack on UNRWA school in Beit Hanoun,* Jesse Rosenfeld, "Inside the Gaza Schoolyard Massacre," *The Daily Beast,* July 26, 2014, http://www.thedailybeast.com/articles/2014/07/26/inside-the-gaza-schoolyard-massacre.html.

88 *Wahadans abducted,* Israeli forces confine Gaza family to home, occupants later killed in attack, Defense of Children International — Palestine, October 29, 2014, http://www.dci-palestine.org/documents/israeli-forces-confine-gaza-family-home-occupants-later-killed-attack.

89 *Rami Wahadan abducted, family killed in Jabalia* ibid.

90 *"I cry a thousand times a day"* ibid; DCI Palestine confirmed my initial reporting on the incident: Max Blumenthal, "Gaza residents share allegations of abuse, claim Israeli soldiers used them as human shields," *Alternet,* August 26, 2014, http://www.alternet.org/world/gaza-residents-share-monstrous-allegations-abuse-israeli-soldiers.

90 *Summary execution in 1956,* Joe Sacco, *Gaza: A Graphic Novel,* Henry Holt and Company, 2010, Footnotes.

90 *Campaign of home razing*, Razing Rafah: Mass Home Demolitions in the Gaza Strip, Human Rights Watch, October 18, 2004, http://www.hrw.org /reports/2004/10/17/razing-rafah.

90 *Scavengers at Arafat airport*, "Scavengers collect rubble of Gaza's bombed out airport," *The Associated Press*, August 17, 2010, http://www.haaretz .com/news/world/scavengers-collect-rubble-of-gaza-s-bombed-out-airport -1.308533.

93 *Murder holes*, Dan Lamothe, "Marine scout snipers use "murder holes" in Afghanistan," *Marine Corps Times*, October 26, 2012, http://battlerattle .marinecorpstimes.com/2012/10/26/marine-scout-snipers-use-murder-holes -in-afghanistan/.

Notes to Chapter 8

95 *Ceasefire and Kerry on "defensive operations,"* US Department of State, http://www.state.gov/secretary/remarks/2014/08/230072.htm; See also: Ruth Pollard, "Ceasefire brings Israeli-Palestinian bloodshed to a pause for Cairo talks," *Sydney Morning Herald*, August 1, 2014, http://www.smh.com .au/world/ceasefire-brings-israelipalestinian-bloodshed-to-a-pause-for-cairo -talks-20140801-zzibi.html.

95 *Qassam Twitter reports of battle*, Max Blumenthal and Allison Deger, "Who broke the ceasefire? Obama blames Hamas against all evidence," *Alternet*, August 1, 2014, http://www.alternet.org/world/who-broke-ceasefire-obama -blames-hamas-against-all-evidence.

96 *Gag order on Goldin and Yaalon*, Tova Dvorin, "Slain soldier Lt. Hadar Goldin was Ya'alon's close relative," *Arutz Sheva*, August 3, 2014, http:// www.israelnationalnews.com/News/News.aspx/183647#.VN6e57B4qZs.

96 *Goldin and Yaalon*, "Ya'alon mourns loss of relative, Lt. Hadar Goldin: I knew him his whole life," *Jerusalem Post*, August 3, 2014, http://www.jpost .com/Operation-Protective-Edge/Yaalon-mourns-loss-of-relative-Lt-Hadar -Goldin-I-knew-him-his-whole-life-369870.

97 *Obama condemns Hamas for Goldin*, Rebecca Shabad, "Obama condemns Hamas for breaking cease-fire," *The Hill*, August 1, 2014, http://thehill.com /policy/healthcare/214094-obama-condemns-hamas-for-breaking-ceasefire.

97 *Kerry condemns Hamas*, Mark Tran and Tom McCarthy, "Obama sees "very hard" path to "put a ceasefire back together"—as it happened," *The Guardian*, August 1, 2014, http://www.theguardian.com/world/live/2014 /aug/01/gaza-crisis-israel-palestinians-ceasefire-begins-live-updates.

97 *"Barbaric violation"* "US calls Hamas attack "barbaric violation' of cease-fire," CNN, *Reuters*, August 1, 2014, http://www.reuters.com/article/2014 /08/01/us-mideast-gaza-whitehouse-idUSKBN0G143S20140801.

97 *Kerry blames Hamas for three teenagers' kidnapping*, Barak Ravid, "Kerry points to Hamas role in Israelis' kidnapping," *Haaretz*, July 15, 2014, http:// www.haaretz.com/news/diplomacy-defense/.premium-1.598941.

97 *"Purposely playing politics,"* Michael Wilner, "Kerry slams Hamas for bucking ceasefire with Israel," *Jerusalem Post*, July 15, 2014, http://www.jpost .com/Operation-Protective-Edge/Kerry-cancels-trip-to-Cairo-relying-on -Egyptian-brokered-ceasefire-instead-362853.

98 *The Hannibal Directive,* Max Blumenthal, "The Hannibal Directive: How Israel killed its own troops and massacred Palestinians to prevent soldier's capture," *Alternet,* September 2, 2014, http://www.alternet.org/hannibal -directive-how-israels-secret-military-doctrine-deliberately-killed-soldiers -and-massacred.

98 *Kasher denied Hannibal's existence,* "Shots across the bow," Haaretz, May 8, 2003, http://www.haaretz.com/shots-across-the-bow-1.10755.

98 *Kasher defends Hannibal's implementation,* Rania Khalek, "Killing 40 civilians in one go is "reasonable," says Israel army ethicist," *Electronic Intifada,* December 31, 2014, http://electronicintifada.net/blogs/rania-khalek/killing -40-civilians-one-go-reasonable-says-israel-army-ethicist.

98 *"You cannot throw a grenade"* Eamon Murphy, "You're shooting like retards": Rafah recordings reveal IDF's Hannibal directive in action, January 8, 2015, http://mondoweiss.net/2015/01/shooting-recordings-directive.

98 *Amidror conceded,* Mitch Ginsburg, "Has the Hannibal Protocol run its course?" *Times of Israel,* August 12, 2014, http://www.timesofisrael.com /has-the-hannibal-protocol-run-its-course/.

99 *Yakir Ben Melech killing,* Jonathan Cook, "Israelis shot mental patient 'under controversial military directive,'" *The National,* December 10, 2009, http://www.thenational.ae/news/world/israelis-shot-mental-patient-under -controversial-military-directive.

99 *"Painful as it is, it's better this way,"* Dimi Reider, "Captive soldier would have been better off if we shot him," +*972Mag,* August 10, 2014, http:// 972mag.com/leader-of-rescue-squad-captive-soldier-wouldve-been-better -off-if-we-shot-him/95276/.

99 *Israeli army recordings from Rafah,* Mitch Ginsburg, "Recordings shed harrowing new light on IDF's response to Gaza abduction," *Times of Israel,* December 30, 2014, "Killing 40 civilians in one go is 'reasonable,'" says Israel army ethicist, http://www.timesofisrael.com/gaza-abduction-comes-to -life-in-recordings/; Also see: Eamon Murphy, "You're shooting like retards": Rafah recordings reveal IDF's Hannibal directive in action, January 8, 2015, http://mondoweiss.net/2015/01/shooting-recordings-directive.

100 *Law banning prisoner releases,* Knesset adopts law that effectively bans release of Palestinian prisoners, i24 News, November 4, 2014, http://www .i24news.tv/en/news/israel/49758-141104-knesset-adopts-law-that-effectively -bans-release-of-palestinian-prisoners.

101 *"Simply called fascism,"* Uri Arad, "Hannibal Directive is the beginning of fascism in Israel," YNet, August 12, 2014 http://www.ynetnews.com/articles /0,7340,L-4557951,00.html.

101 *"That's why we used all this force,"* Karin Laub and Ibrahim Barzak, "Israeli fire on Gaza town raises war crimes claim," *Associated Press,* August 31, 2014, http://www.csmonitor.com/World/Latest-News-Wires/2014/0831/Did -Israel-commit-war-crimes-in-Rafah.

101 *121 lay dead,* The Gaza-based Al Mezan Center for Human Rights produced a comprehensive list of the names and ages of those killed on August 1 and 2 in Rafah. See: Laub and Barzak, *Associated Press,* "Israeli fire on Gaza town raises war crimes claim."

106 *Omer on "the corpses of children,"* Mohammed Omer, "Butchery in Rafah. The dead are kept in vegetable refrigerators," *Middle East Eye*, August 2, 2014, http://www.middleeasteye.net/news/gazans-forced-keep-dead-bodies -vegetable-refrigerators-1006544969.

106 *Children in ice cream coolers,* Dan Bloom and Richard Spillett, "Gaza's dead children are kept in ice cream freezers," *The Daily Mail*, August 3, 2014, http://www.dailymail.co.uk/news/article-2714575/Humanitarian-crisis -Gaza-half-million-homeless.html.

107 *DIME use in Gaza since 2006,* Rory McCarthy, "Gaza doctors say patients suffering mystery injuries after Israeli attacks," *The Guardian*, October 17, 2006, http://www.theguardian.com/world/2006/oct/17/israel1; White phos- phorous and Dense Inert Metal Explosives: Is Israel using banned and experi- mental munitions in Gaza?, *Democracy Now!*, January 14, 2009 http://www. democracynow.org/2009/1/14/white_phosphorous_and_dense_inert_metal Rania Khalek, Israel firing experimental weapons at Gaza's civilians, say doc- tors, *Electronic Intifada*, July 15, 2014 http://electronicintifada.net/blogs/rania -khalek/israel-firing-experimental-weapons-gazas-civilians-say-doctors.

107 *Winter objecting to female singer,* Mazal Mualem, "An inside look at IDF's "faith-driven" warriors," *Al Monitor*, August 12, 2014, http://www.al -monitor.com/pulse/originals/2014/08/israel-idf-army-religious-zionism -ofer-winter-ethos-god.html#; See also: Matan Tzuri, Army colonel tells re- ligious troops to stay put for women's performance, Ynet, August 19, 2014, http://www.ynetnews.com/articles/0,7340,L-4560048,00.html.

108 *Winter's Yedioth interview,* Rania Khalek, "Israeli officer admits ordering lethal strike on own soldier during Gaza massacre," *Electronic Intifada*, September 10, 2014, http://electronicintifada.net/blogs/rania-khalek/israeli -officer-admits-ordering-lethal-strike-own-soldier-during-gaza-massacre.

108 *Rise of religious nationalism in army.* According to Eyal Press in the *New York Review of Books*, "Not only are some 30 percent of officers openly orthodox but an estimated 50 percent of soldiers in officer training colleges are now religious.".

108 *Eliyahu on Mama Rochel,* Jerusalem — Former Chief Rabbi: Mama Rochel Gaza Miracle Story True, uploaded by YouTube user Gruntig2008 on Jan- uary 20, 2009, https://www.youtube.com/watch?v=_-eGYOJP2_U.

Notes to Chapter 9

111 *"Politicide,"* Baruch Kimmerling, *Politicide*, London; New York: Verso, 2003, 4–7.

112 *Israeli Jewish support for segregation, apartheid, forced removal,* Dahlia Scheindlin, "Majority of Israeli Jews support bus segregation, survey finds," *+972Mag*, December 11, 2014, http://972mag.com/majority-of-israeli-jews -support-bus-segregation-poll-finds/99941/; See also: Gideon Levy, Survey: "Most Israeli Jews wouldn't give Palestinians vote if West Bank was an- nexed," *Haaretz*, October 23, 2012, http://www.haaretz.com/news/national /survey-most-israeli-jews-wouldn-t-give-palestinians-vote-if-west-bank-was -annexed.premium-1.471644. More findings from 2012 Dialog poll: "A third of the Jewish public wants a law barring Israeli Arabs from voting for

the Knesset and a large majority of 69 percent objects to giving 2.5 million Palestinians the right to vote if Israel annexes the West Bank. A sweeping 74 percent majority is in favor of separate roads for Israelis and Palestinians in the West Bank. A quarter - 24 percent - believe separate roads are "a good situation" and 50 percent believe they are "a necessary situation." According to Haaretz's Levy, "Almost half - 47 percent - want part of Israel's Arab population to be transferred to the Palestinian Authority and 36 percent support transferring some of the Arab towns from Israel to the PA, in exchange for keeping some of the West Bank settlements."

112 *Lack of opposition to disproportionate force*, Mirren Gidda, "Poll: 92% of Israeli Jews say Operation Protective Edge was justified," *Time*, August 19, 2014; Also see: Gil Hoffman, "Poll finds Israelis don't believe charges of excessive force," *Jerusalem Post*, July 29, 2014, http://www.jpost.com/Operation-Protective-Edge/Poll-Over-96-percent-of-Israeli-Jews-do-not-believe-the-IDF-is-using-excessive-force-in-Gaza-369283.

113 *Death to Arabs at Subliminal/Shadow shows*, Mark Levine, *Heavy Metal Islam: Rock, Resistance, and the Struggle for the Soul of Islam*, New York: Three Rivers Press, 2008, 127..

113 *Subliminal on Zoabi*, Richard Silverstein, "Israeli Hip Hop Celebrity Says Palestinian MK 'Fucks Us in the Ass,'" *Tikun Olam*, 30 June 2014, http://www.richardsilverstein.com/2014/06/30/israeli-palestinian-mk-gets.....

114 *"Looking for Traitors,"* Lia Tarachansky, "Inside Israel's Pro-War Nationalist Camp," *The Real News*, Real News Network, 3 August 2014, http://therealnews.com/t2/index.php/index.php?option=com_content&task=vi.....

114 *Kahane's enduring influence*. See: Max Blumenthal, *Goliath: Life and Loathing in Greater Israel*, Nation Books, 2013, Chapter 60: "When Kahane Won," 325.

114 *Ben-Ari and anti-African rallies*, David Sheen and Max Blumenthal, "Israel's New Racism: The Persecution of African Migrants in the Holy Land," *The Nation*, October 21, 2013, http://www.thenation.com/video/176762/israels-new-racism-persecution-african-migrants-holy-land. Also see Israeli independent journalist David Sheen's extensive collection of documentary videos and articles on anti-African racism in Israel, which highlight the role of Ben-Ari and other Israeli politicians in the organized campaign of incitement and violence: http://www.davidsheen.com/racism/.

114 *Lehava and anti-miscegenation politics in Israel*. See: Max Blumenthal, *Goliath: Life and Loathing in Greater Israel*, Chapter 58: The Daughters of Israel and Chapter 59: Children Whose Hearts Were Unmoved, Nation Books, 2013.

114 *Lehava and Abu Khdeir*, Max Blumenthal, "Netanyahu Government Knew Teens Were Dead as It Whipped Up Racist Frenzy," *Electronic Intifada*, 8 July 2014, http://electronicintifada.net/content/netanyahu-government-knewteens-wer....

115 *Maccabi ultras t-shirt slogans*, Ofer Aderet, "Right-wing demonstrators in Tel Aviv wore neo-Nazi shirts," *Haaretz*, July 15, 2014, http://www.haaretz.com/news/national/.premium-1.605234

115 *Shadow, Ben Ari storm anti-war demo,* Lia Tarachansky, "Inside Israel's Pro-War Nationalist Camp," *The Real News,* Real News Network, 3 August 2014, http://therealnews.com/t2/index.php/index.php?option=com_content &task=vi.

115 *Assad beaten in Haifa,* Rocky (Chicky) Arad, Right-wingers beat Haifa deputy mayor during anti-war protest, *Haaretz,* July 20, 2014, http://www .haaretz.com/news/national/.premium-1.606240.

115 *Campaign against Zoabi.* See: Max Blumenthal, *Goliath: Life and Loathing in Greater Israel,* pp. 136-39, Nation Books, 2013. The Central Elections Commission ban of Zoabi's party in 2009, herself in 2012 and in 2015 were supported by members of the Labor Party. See: ibid and Moran Azulay, Center-left Zionist Camp supports bid to ban MK Zoabi, Baruch Marzel, Ynet, February 12, 2015, http://www.ynetnews.com/articles/0,7340,L-46258 40,00.html.

116 *Activists followed home,* Lia Tarachansky, "Inside Israel's Pro-War Nationalist Camp," *The Real News,* Real News Network, 3 August 2014, http:// therealnews.com/t2/index.php/index.php?option=com_content&task=vi.....

116 *Dozens lost their jobs,* Orli Santo, "How Freedom of Speech Was Crushed During Protective Edge,"+972 *Magazine,* August 31, 2014, http://972mag .com/how-freedom-of-speech-was-crushed-during-protective-ed....

117 *Radical left self-defense groups,* Haggai Matar, "Facing increased right-wing violence, Israeli leftists learn to fight back," +972*Mag,* October 14, 2014, http://972mag.com/facing-increased-right-wing-violence-israeli-leftists -learn-to-fight-back/97486/.

118 *Aharonovitz bans demonstrations,* Orli Santo, "How Freedom of Speech Was Crushed During Protective Edge,"+972 *Magazine,* August 31, 2014, http://972mag.com/how-freedom-of-speech-was-crushed-during-protective -ed.....

118 *"Despicable deeds,"* Gideon Levy, "Lowest deeds from loftiest heights," *Haaretz,* July 15, 2014, http://www.haaretz.com/opinion/.premium-1.605 001.

118 *Threats against Levy,* Jennie Matthew, "Witch hunt" against Israel's war critics, Agence France Press, August 15, 2014, http://news.yahoo.com/witch -hunt-against-israels-war-critics-134302477.html.

119 *Feiglin's plan to "concentrate,"* "Knesset Member: Retake Gaza, but civilians in 'tent camps'" *Times of Israel,* August 5, 2014, http://www.timesof israel.com/knesset-member-retake-gaza-put-civilians-in-tent-camps/ and Ali Abunimah, "'Concentrate'and'Exterminate': Israel Parliament Deputy Speaker's Gaza Genocide Plan," *Electronic Intifada,* August 3, 2014, http:// electronicintifada.net/blogs/ali-abunimah/concentrate-and-exterminate-israel -parliament-deputy-speakers-gaza-genocide-plan.

119 *"Exterminating the enemy,"* "West Bank Rabbi Dov Lior: Jewish Law Permits Destruction of Gaza," *Jewish Telegraphic Agency,* July 24, 2014, http:// www.jta.org/2014/07/24/news-opinion/israel-middle-east/west-bank-....

119 *Kedar's rape proposal,* Or Kashti, "Israeli Professor's 'Rape as Terror Deterrent' Statement Draws Ire," *Haaretz,* July 22, 2014, http://www.haaretz .com/news/national/.premium-1.606542..

119 *Israeli teens annihilationist tweets,* David Sheen, "Terrifying tweets of pre-Army Israeli teens," *Mondoweiss,* July 10, 2014, http://mondoweiss.net /2014/07/terrifying-tweets-israeli and https://www.facebook.com/Updates fromPalestine/posts/298194307019399.

119 *Lieberman on summer vacation,* Israeli official says likelihood of Gaza invasion "very high," *The Dallas Morning News,* July 16, 2014, http://www .dallasnews.com/news/headlines/20140716-israeli-official-says-likelihood -of-gaza-invasion-very-high.ece.

120 *95% support for war,* Yifa Yaakov, "Over 90 percent of Jewish Israelis Say Gaza Op Justified," *Times of Israel,* July 29, 2014, http://www.timesofisrael .com/over-90-of-jewish-israelis-say-gaza-op-just.....

120 *Ban on Al Jazeera,* "Foreign Minister Avigdor Lieberman Seeks to Ban Al Jazeera from Operating in Israel," *Newsweek,* July 21, 2014, http://www .newsweek.com/israeli-foreign-minister-avigdor-lieberman-seeks-ban-al -jazeera-operating-260178.

120 *Lieberman as "leftist,"* "Lieberman jabs at "hysterical" Likud, Jewish home," *Times of Israel,* December 14, 2014, http://www.timesofisrael.com /liberman-jabs-at-hysterical-likud-jewish-home/.

120 *Bennett benefits from war,* Tzvi Ben-Gedalyahu, "Poll: Netanyahu and Bennett Benefit from War at the Expense of Lapid," *Jewish Press,* August 14, 2014, http://www.jewishpress.com/news/breaking-news/poll-netanyahu -andbennett-.....

120 *Final destruction of Hamas,* Barak Ravid, "Bennett: Destruction of tunnels not enough — Hamas must be completely defeated," *Haaretz,* July 29, 2014, http://www.haaretz.com/news/diplomacy-defense/1.607836

Notes to Chapter 10

121 *Deadly mortar attack,* Ben Hartman, "Mortar shell attack kills four IDF soldiers in Eshkol on Gaza border," *Jerusalem Post,* July 29, 2014, http:// www.jpost.com/Operation-Protective-Edge/Mortar-shell-attack-wounds-10 -in-southern-Israel-369179.

121 *Qassam Nahal Oz operation,* Hamas footage on the infiltration via tunnel to Nahal Oz village, Israel, uploaded by YouTube user pm on July 29, 2014, https://www.youtube.com/watch?v=i9NNunTsO1c Also see: Qassam releases details of Nahal Oz operation that killed 5 soldiers, *Ma'an News,* July 29, 2014 http://www.maannews.com/eng/ViewDetails.aspx?id=716795.

122 *Israeli army's cover-up attempt,* Amos Harel and Chaim Levinson, "Hamas video exposes IDF blunder in deadly border infiltration," *Haaretz,* July 31, 2014, http://www.haaretz.com/news/diplomacy-defense/.premium-1.608 095.

122 *Israeli casualties over 60,* Griff Witte, "Israelis regard soldier deaths in Gaza as a price that must be paid," *Washington Post,* August 3, 2014, http://www .washingtonpost.com/world/middle_east/israelis-regard-soldier-deaths-in -gaza-as-a-price-that-must-be-paid/2014/08/03/89460053-50a8-430d-bfec -95dbdde84761_story.html.

122 *Palestinian death toll in Gaza,* IOF War Crimes Expose International Complacency: Al Mezan Warns about further Crimes in Rafah as Death toll rises

to 1,828; 81.8% Civilians; 413 Children and 229 Women, Al Mezan Center for Human Rights, August 4, 2014, http://reliefweb.int/report/occupied-palestinian -territory/iof-war-crimes-expose-international-complacency-al-mezan -warns. UN OCHA report published on August 10 provides similar numbers: 1,948 Palestinians killed in the Gaza Strip with 9,806 wounded, including 5,238 women and children. See: Occupied Palestinian Territory: Gaza Emergency Situation Report, OCHA OPT, August 10, 2014, http://www.ochaopt.org/documents/ocha_opt_sitrep_10_08_2014.pdf.

123 *Peres on ground invasion*, Ilana Curiel, "Peres: Give Gaza back to Abbas, end the war," YNet, July 30, 2014, http://www.ynetnews.com/articles/0,73 40,L-4552247,00.html.

123 *"We have been dragged,"* Nahum Barnea, "Paying the price of a justified war," Ynet, July 29, 2014, http://www.ynetnews.com/articles/0,7340,L-455 1558,00.html.

123 *"Punched hard in the gut,"* Itay Blumenthal, "Soldiers criticize lack of safety measures outside battlefield," Ynet, July 30, 2014, http://www.ynetnews .com/articles/0,7340,L-4552042,00.html.

124 *The "intimidation meeting,"* Barak Ravid, "Netanyahu tried to scare off ministers to get Gaza occupation off the table," *Haaretz*, August 6, 2014, http://www.haaretz.com/news/diplomacy-defense/1.609152.

124 *Deif addresses the public,* Al-Qassam brigades footage of infiltration to Nahal Oz and Killing 10 Israeli soldiers, Al Jazeera Arabic, July 29, uploaded by YouTube user InnerDanger on July 29, 2014, https://www.youtube .com/watch?v=-30lmLsAups.

125 *"He's a dead man,"* "Lapid says Hamas commander Mohammad Deif 'a dead man,'" *Jerusalem Post*, July 30, 2014, http://www.jpost.com/Operation -Protective-Edge/Lapid-says-Hamas-commander-Mohammad-Deif-a-dead -man-369412.

126 *Obama on "heartbreaking" images,* Press Conference by the President, The White House, August 1, 2014, http://www.whitehouse.gov/the-press-office /2014/08/01/press-conference-president.

126 *"Not to ever second-guess me again [on Hamas],"* Matt Lee, "Netanyahu to US: Don't second guess me on Hamas," *Associated Press*, August 2, 2014, http://news.yahoo.com/netanyahu-us-dont-second-guess-hamas-091032793 --politics.html?vp=1.

126 *Israeli army claim Hamas ordered residents to stay,* David Blair, "Gaza conflict: Broken by Israeli barrage, the people of Shejaiya flee as homes are laid waste," *Telegraph UK*, July 20, 2014, http://www.telegraph.co.uk/news /worldnews/middleeast/israel/10979389/Gaza-conflict-Broken-by-Israeli -barrage-the-people-of-Shejaiya-flee-as-homes-are-laid-waste.html.

127 *Rockets found in school,* Cache of rockets found in UN school in Gaza, UNRWA, July 29, 2014, http://www.unrwa.org/newsroom/press-releases /cache-rockets-found-un-school-gaza.

127 *US rearms Israeli army,* Luis Martinez, US has sold ammunition to Israel since start of Gaza conflict, ABC News, July 30, 2014, http://abcnews.go .com/blogs/politics/2014/07/u-s-has-sold-ammunition-to-israel-since-start -of-gaza-conflict/.

127 *$1.2 billion stockpile,* Chistopher Haress, During war in Gaza, "Israel gets ammunition from US stockpile," *International Business Times,* August 1, 2014, http://www.ibtimes.com/during-war-gaza-israel-gets-ammunitions-us -weapons-stockpile-1646590.

127 *Bennett and tunnel destruction,* Amos Harel, "Tunnels, kugel and war: Israel's young right-wing minister and his secret army contacts," *Haaretz,* September 17, 2014, http://www.haaretz.com/news/diplomacy-defense/.premium -1.616278.

128 *Rontski dismissed,* "Ex-IDF chief rabbi denies leaking info to Bennett," *Times of Israel,* September 16, 2014, http://www.timesofisrael.com/ex-idf -chief-rabbi-denies-leaking-info-to-bennett/.

128 *"That's unacceptable,"* Ya'alon calls Bennett's actions during war "anarchy," Arutz Sheva, October 15, 2014, http://www.israelnationalnews.com/News /News.aspx/186200#.VOyHxbPF9Hi.

128 *"Hit Hamas without mercy,"* William Booth and Ruth Eglash, "Israelis support Netanyahu and Gaza war despite rising deaths on both sides," *Washington Post,* July 29, 2014, http://www.washingtonpost.com/world/middle _east/israelis-support-netanyahu-and-gaza-war-despite-rising-deaths-on -both-sides/2014/07/29/0d562c44-1748-11e4-9349-84d4a85be981_story .html.

128 *"If it takes a month, we'll take it,"* Barak Ravid, Bennett: "Destruction of tunnels not enough — Hamas must be completely defeated," *Haaretz,* July 29, 2014, http://www.haaretz.com/news/diplomacy-defense/1.607836.

129 *"Brother Naftali,"* Joshua Mitnick, "Israeli voters flock to "brother" Naftali Bennett — but not all his policies," *Christian Science Monitor,* January 17, 2013, http://www.csmonitor.com/World/Middle-East/2013/0117/Israeli-voters -flock-to-brother-Naftali-Bennett-but-not-all-his-policies.

129 *"Disproportionate Force,"* Gabi Siboni, Disproportionate Force: Israel's concept of response in light of the Second Lebanon war, INSS, October 2, 2008, http://www.inss.org.il/index.aspx?id=4538&articleid=1964.

Notes to Chapter 11

131 *Army blog on rocket attacks,* Rocket attacks on Israel from the Gaza Strip, *IDFBlog.com,* 2014 http://www.idfblog.com/facts-figures/rocket-attacks -toward-israel/.

131 *Sderot mayor protests,* "Sderot mayor blasts Ya'alon as "resounding failure" for continued Gaza rocket fire," *Jerusalem Post,* August 8, 2014, http:// www.jpost.com/Operation-Protective-Edge/Sderot-mayor-blasts-Yaalon-as -resounding-failure-for-continued-Gaza-rocket-fire-370520.

131 *"Israel cannot afford a war of attrition,"* Jason Burke and Patrick Kingsley and Orlando Crowcroft, "Gaza conflict: Israel and Hamas agree to extend ceasefire by five days," *The Guardian,* August 13, 2014, http://www.theguard ian.com/world/2014/aug/13/gaza-conflict-israel-hamas-extend-ceasefire.

132 *US taxpayers subsidize Iron Dome,* Amos Harel, "Iron Dome defense system gets new backer: Barack Obama," *Haaretz,* May 13, 2010, https://web.archive .org/web/20100516032351/http://www.haaretz.com/news/diplomacy-defense/ iron-dome-defense-system-gets-new-backer-barack-obama-1.290226.

132 *2014 Iron Dome authorization,* Molly O'Toole, "Senate defense bill doubles Obama's request for Israel's Iron Dome," *Defense One,* July 15, 2014, http://www.defenseone.com/politics/2014/07/senate-defense-bill-doubles-obamas-request-israels-iron-dome/88804/.

132 *Criticism of Iron Dome,* Alex Gatopoulos, "How successful was Israel's Iron Dome?" *Al Jazeera,* September 8, 2014, http://www.aljazeera.com/news/middleeast/2014/08/israel-iron-dome-gaza-rockets-201481712494436388.html.

132 *Number and lethality of Gaza rockets,* Rashid Khalidi, The Dahiya Doctrine, Proportionality, and War Crimes, *Journal of Palestine Studies,* Vol. 44 2014-2015, http://www.palestine-studies.org/jps/fulltext/186668.

132 *Depriving Bedouins services, Iron Dome,* May Guarnieri, "Israel's Bedouin: Civilians in death alone," +*972Mag,* July 20, 2014, http://972mag.com/israels-bedouin-civilians-in-death-alone/93965/.

133 *Wounded kibbutz owl,* Lazar Berman, "Owl hurt by Hamas fire recovering," *The Times of Israel,* July 25, 2014, http://www.timesofisrael.com/owl-hurt-by-hamas-fire-recovering/.

133 *Killing of Najam family,* Hamza Hendawi, "In Gaza war, violent death part of daily life," *Associated Press,* August 5, 2014, http://bigstory.ap.org/article/gaza-war-violent-death-part-daily-life.

133 *"bits of debris,"* ibid.

133 *Abu Saif's wartime diary,* Atef Abu Saif, "Eight Days in Gaza: A wartime diary," *The New York Times,* August 4, 2014, http://www.nytimes.com/2014/08/05/opinion/atef-abu-saif-life-and-death-in-gaza-strip-jabaliya-refugee-camp.html?_r=0.

134 *Rafah school shelled, US condemns,* Annie Robbins, "Israel shells another UN school — and even the US is 'appalled,'" *Mondoweiss,* August 3, 2014, http://mondoweiss.net/2014/08/attacked-another-appalled.

135 *408 children killed,* Lizzie Dearden, "Israel-Gaza conflict: Names of 373 children killed by bombing released in charity plea for permanent ceasefire," *Independent UK,* August 6, 2014, http://www.independent.co.uk/news/world/middle-east/israelgaza-conflict-names-of-373-children-killed-by-bombing-released-in-charity-plea-for-permanent-ceasefire-9651400.html.

135 *Associated Press investigation,* Karin Laub and Fares Akram and Mohammed Daraghmeh, "High civilian death toll in Gaza house strikes," *Associated Press,* February 13, 2015, http://hosted2.ap.org/APDEFAULT/cae69a7523db45408eeb2b3a98c0c9c5/Article_2015-02-13-ML--Israel-Striking%20Homes/id-5ddc81151d2e46c9bc9f43232606dd50.

135 *Ironside on child deaths,* Tom Miles, "UNICEF laments Gaza child casualties warns of task ahead," *Reuters,* August 5, 2014, http://in.reuters.com/article/2014/08/05/mideast-gaza-unicef-idINKBN0G51WL20140805.

135 *Abu Murad's estimate of Israeli munitions,* "Unexploded munitions add to Gaza risks," *Al Jazeera,* August 10, 2014, http://www.aljazeera.com/video/middleeast/2014/08/unexploded-munitions-add-gaza-risks-201481003251688388.html.

135 *Murad killed,* Nora Barrows-Friedman, "Head of Gaza bomb squad killed as 1,000 tons of Israeli munitions remain," *Electronic Intifada,* August 13,

NOTES

2014, http://electronicintifada.net/blogs/nora-barrows-friedman/head-gaza
-bomb-squad-killed-1000-tons-israeli-munitions-remain.

135 *Abunimah on Murad's estimate,* Ali Abunimah, "How many bombs has Israel
dropped on Gaza?" *Electronic Intifada,* August 19, 2014, http://electronic
intifada.net/blogs/ali-abunimah/how-many-bombs-has-israel-dropped-gaza.

136 *Haaretz on total ammo cost,* ibid.

136 *Gal-On criticizes Netanyahu,* Larry Derfner, "In ceasefire talks, Netanyahu
is letting Hamas win Gaza war," *+972Mag,* August 15, 2014, http://972mag
.com/in-ceasefire-talks-netanyahu-is-letting-hamas-win-gaza-war/95540/.

137 *Abbas slams Hamas,* "Abbas slams Gaza rocket fire on Israel," Ynet, July
11, 2014, http://www.ynetnews.com/articles/0,7340,L-4541732,00.html.

137 *The "big loser,"* Grif Witte and William Booth, "Fight in Gaza has no clear
winners but one big loser," *Washington Post,* July 12, 2014, http://www
.washingtonpost.com/world/rockets-from-both-gaza-and-lebanon-strike
-israel/2014/07/11/2ee312f2-f558-41ac-a945-e38c73e39abe_story.html.

137 *Israeli intransigence,* Adnan Abu Amer, "Hamas warns Gazans 'have nothing
to lose,'" *Al Monitor,* August 11, 2014, http://www.al-monitor.com/pulse
/originals/2014/08/truce-gaza-war-israel-hamas-demands.html.

138 *"This document did not respond to any of our requests,"* "Operation Protective Edge, day 32," *Haaretz,* August 9, 2014, http://www.haaretz.com
/news/diplomacy-defense/1.609571.

138 *"Discussions had returned to square one,"* Gaza conflict: Peace talks continue as deadline looms, BBC News, August 18, 2014, http://www.bbc.com
/news/world-middle-east-28836572.

140 *Camp Breakerz,* Dan Cohen, "Gaza's Camp Breakerz crew struggles against
the siege," *Mondoweiss,* August 21, 2014, http://mondoweiss.net/2014/08
/breakerz-struggles-against.

Notes to Chapter 12

144 *2012 attack on Dalou home, Israel's changing story,* Alex Kane, "Israeli
military changes story about al-Dalou airstrike — for the fourth time,"
Mondoweiss, December 12, 2012, http://mondoweiss.net/2012/12/israeli
-military-changes-story-about-al-dalou-airstrike-for-the-fourth-time.

144 *Widad Asfoura background,* Hani Ibrahim, "Families of al-Qassam Brigades
keep the dream of the Resistance alive," *Al Akhbar English,* August 23,
2014, http://english.al-akhbar.com/node/21248.

145 *Asfoura's letter to Deif,* Hadeel Attallah, "Love in the time of Gaza: The story
of Mohamed Al-Deif and his late wife Widad Asfoura," *Felesteen,* translated
and republished by *Middle East Monitor* on September 3, 2014, https://www
.middleeastmonitor.com/articles/middle-east/13908-love-in-the-time-of-gaza
-the-story-of-mohamed-al-deif-and-his-late-wife-widad-asfoura.

147 *"You're not brave enough to kill Mohammed Deif,"* The speech of Abu
Obeida in response to the attempted assassination of the leader Mohammed
Deif, uploaded by YouTube user Al Madar on August 20, 2014, https://
www.youtube.com/watch?v=ieMuaZRLl-Y&feature=youtu.be Al Qassam
titled Obeida's speech: "The speech of the Qassam Brigades on the 45th day
of battle." It was originally aired on Al Aqsa TV on August 19, 2014.

147 *Assassination attempt on Deif,* Nidal Al-Mughrabi and Maayan Lubell, "Has Hamas military chief, Mohammed Deif, escaped death again?" *Reuters,* August 20, 2014, http://www.reuters.com/article/2014/08/20/us-mideast-gaza-deif-idUSKBN0GK1OW20140820.

147 *FAA flight ban,* Josh Levs and Ben Brumfield and Dana Ford, "US extends ban on flights to Ben Gurion Airport," CNN, July 23, 2014, http://www.cnn.com/2014/07/23/travel/israel-flights-suspended/.

147 *Scores of flights cancelled,* Ola Attalah, "Hamas fires rocket at Israel's Ben Gurion airport," *The Daily Star,* August 21, 2014, http://www.dailystar.com.lb/News/Middle-East/2014/Aug-21/267969-hamas-fires-rocket-at-israels-ben-gurion-airport.ashx.

149 *Attacking Gaza's sewage infrastructure,* Marian Houk, "Israel may have deliberately attacked sewage infrastructure," *Electronic Intifada,* March 30, 2009, http://electronicintifada.net/content/israel-may-have-deliberately-attacked-sewage-infrastructure/8159 Israel attacked a major sewage station in Gaza during Operation Protective Edge. See also: "Israel airstrike bombs major water line, sewage station and water wells in Gaza," *International Solidarity Movement,* July 13, 2014, http://palsolidarity.org/2014/07/israel-airstrike-bombs-major-water-line-sewage-station-and-water-wells-in-gaza/.

149 *Scabies in Gaza,* Mohammed Omer, "Gaza's new plague: Scabies," *Middle East Eye,* August 11, 2014, http://www.middleeasteye.net/news/gaza-s-new-plague-scabies-331974707.

150 *3300 children wounded by August 24,* Jack Khoury, "89 families killed in Gaza since hostilities began, Palestinians say," *Haaretz,* August 24, 2014, http://www.haaretz.com/news/diplomacy-defense/1.612255.

150 *"Self-genocide,"* Hezki Ezra, "Bennett: Hamas committing "self-genocide," *Arutz Sheva,* July 17, 2014, http://www.israelnationalnews.com/News/News.aspx/183007.

152 *Strike on Kallab's home to kill Attar, et al,* Asma al-Ghoul, "After assassination of military leaders, Hamas targets spies," *Al Monitor,* August 25, 2014, http://www.al-monitor.com/pulse/originals/2014/08/hamas-execute-spies-israel-assassination-qassam-brigades.html.

152 *Background on Attar, Shamaleh, Barhoum,* Bayan Abdel Wahad and Islam Sakka, "Hamas loses three great leaders, vows a thousand leaders to come," *Al Akhbar English,* August 22, 2014, http://english.al-akhbar.com/node/21230.

152 *Raba Abu Shamaleh,* Message of Raba the daughter of the martyred leader Mohammed Abu Shamaleh, uploaded by YouTube user Palestinian Media Observatory on August 21, 2014, https://www.youtube.com/watch?v=A5Oo BJ6Z0Rw&feature=youtu.be.

155 *"World-wide network of militant Islamists,"* Ari Yashar, "Netanyahu shows in pictures how 'Hamas is ISIS,'" *Arutz Sheva,* September 30, 2014, http://www.israelnationalnews.com/News/News.aspx/185652#.VOMJTbB4qZs.

155 *Unit 8200 and NSA,* James Bamford, "The most wanted man in the world," *Wired,* August, 2014, http://www.wired.com/2014/08/edward-snowden / Also see: "NSA and Israeli intelligence: memorandum of understanding" — full document, *The Guardian,* September 11, 2013, http://www.theguardian

.com/world/interactive/2013/sep/11/nsa-israel-intelligence-memorandum
-understanding-document.

155 *Unit 8200 letter,* "Israeli intelligence veterans' letter to Netanyahu and military chiefs" — in full, *The Guardian*, September 12, 2014, http://www
.theguardian.com/world/2014/sep/12/israeli-intelligence-veterans-letter
-netanyahu-military-chiefs.

156 *Netanyahu thanks Cohen,* Avaneesh Pandey, "Netanyahu thanks Shin Bet for the deaths of senior Hamas commanders"; "17 killed in Gaza Thursday," *International Business Times*, August 21, 2014, http://www.ibtimes
.com/netanyahu-thanks-shin-bet-deaths-senior-hamas-commanders-17-killed
-gaza-thursday-1664764.

156 *"Netanyahu the hero,"* Amos Harel, "Assassinations of Hamas commanders could make Netanyahu the hero", *Haaretz*, August 21, 2014, http://www
.haaretz.com/news/diplomacy-defense/.premium-1.611791

Notes to Chapter 13

157 "knock on the roof," rocket to Zafer 4 Israeli military flattens Gaza tower block, Channel 4 UK, August 24, 2014, http://www.channel4.com/news
/gaza-israel-tower-block-destroyed-attacks-air-strikes. For video and background on Israel's "knock on the roof" tactic, see: Philip Weiss, Terror in Gaza: 57 after "warning," Israel destroys a house, *Mondoweiss*, July 11, 2014, http://mondoweiss.net/2014/07/seconds-warning-destroys.

158 *Fatah officials and members in Zafer Ali* Abunimah, "Gaza's 9/11": Israel destroys high-rise building in Gaza - video, *Electronic Intifada*, August 23, 2014, http://electronicintifada.net/blogs/ali-abunimah/gazas-911-israel
-destroys-high-rise-building-gaza-video.

159 *Saftawi's lifestream, recorded strike* Missile Strike on Gaza Jehad Saftawi's Neighbour, uploaded by YouTube user FreakyVidsDaily on July 28, 2014, https://www.youtube.com/watch?v=Y34LMcmRO-U During the 51 Day War, Saftawi operated his live stream at http://www.ustream.tv/channel/jehadels.

159 *Drop in Netanyahu's support* Massive drop in support for Netanyahu — poll, *Times of Israel*, August 25, 2014, http://www.timesofisrael.com/massive
-drop-in-support-for-netanyahu-poll/.

160 *Grief over Tragerman's death* Shirly Seidler, " 'May peace come of your death,' mother of four-year-old Israeli mortar victim says," *Haaretz*, August 24, 2014, http://www.haaretz.com/news/national/.premium-1.612162.

160 *"Nothing is immune,"* Amnesty International, "Nothing is Immune:" Israel's destruction of landmark buildings in Gaza, p. 8, 2014, http://www.amnesty.
nl/sites/default/files/public/nothing_is_immune.pdf. Amnesty International's report determined that "the attacks [on Gaza's landmark towers and three other buildings] are of great significance because they are examples of what appears to have been deliberate destruction and targeting of civilian buildings and property on a large scale, carried out without military necessity. The timing of these attacks and statements by Israeli officials suggest that these were instances of collective punishment, ones with long- term impact on the already perilous economic situation of Palestinian civilians in Gaza."

160 *leaflet warnings,* ibid.

160 *Attack on Rafah commercial comple,x* Amnesty International, "Nothing is Immune:" Israel's destruction of landmark buildings in Gaza, pp. 9-11, 2014, http://www.amnesty.nl/sites/default/files/public/nothing_is_immune.pdf.

160 *"You are warned,"* Dan Cohen, Translation of Israel's threat to Gazans disseminated via a takeover of al Aqsa television channel, Twitter, August 23, 2014, https://twitter.com/dancohen3000/status/503288192204689408.

161 *Marzouk suggests stalemate,* "Operation Protective Edge, day 47," *Haaretz,* August 23, 2014, http://www.haaretz.com/news/diplomacy-defense/1.612036.

161 *Islamic Jihad supports ceasefire Roi Kais,* Palestinian source: Hamas prepared to accept ceasefire, Ynet, August 25, 2014, http://www.ynetnews.com /articles/0,7340,L-4563584,00.html.

161 *Bombed the Rafah terminal,* "Rafah crossing continues to function amidst Israeli attacks," IMEMC, August 25, 2014 http://www.imemc.org/article /68952.

161 *Attack on Italian tower,* Amnesty International, "Nothing is Immune:" Israel's destruction of landmark buildings in Gaza, pp. 15–17, 2014, http:// www.amnesty.nl/sites/default/files/public/nothing_is_immune.pdf.

162 *Attack on Basha Tower,* ibid, pp. 17–21.

163 *Omer on GBU's,* Mohammed Omer, "Gaza outraged at Israel's use of GBU-28 missile," *Middle East Eye,* August 20, 2014, http://www.middleeasteye .net/news/gaza-outraged-israel-s-use-gbu-28-missile-1699621250.

163 "Israel receives GBU shipment Michael B. Kelley, Israel is set to receive 5,000 US bunker buster bombs after delaying its attack on Iran," *Business Insider,* December 13, 2012, http://www.businessinsider.com/the-us-sale-of -5000-bunker-buster-bombs-to-israel-israel-bunker-busters-in-exchange-for -not-striking-iran-2012-12. Israel first used GBU-39 small diameter bombs in the Gaza Strip during Operation Cast Lead in January 2009. See: Yaakov Katz, GBU-39: "Israel uses new US-supplied smart bomb to attack Hamas," *Jerusalem Post,* January 28, 2009, http://www.huffingtonpost.com/2008/12 /28/gbu39-israel-uses-new-uss_n_153840.html.

164 *"the transfer should be handled quietly,"* "US embassy cables: Israel seeks to block US planes for Saudi," *The Guardian,* November 28, 2010, http:// www.theguardian.com/world/us-embassy-cables-documents/235359.

165 *"without military necessity,"* Amnesty International, "Nothing is Immune:" Israel's destruction of landmark buildings in Gaza, 2014, http://www .amnesty.nl/sites/default/files/public/nothing_is_immune.pdf.

165 *16 journalists killed in Gaza,* "Families of 16 journalists killed in Gaza demand justice," *Maan News,* September 25, 2014, http://www.maannews .com/eng/ViewDetails.aspx?id=729989.

165 *Journalists killed on camera.* Palestinian journalist killed in Shujaiya while wearing vest marked "PRESS" can be seen at 5:22 mark of: URGENT: Battle of Shujaiya market - an unforgivable crime of the Zionist entity — painful and inhumane scenes, uploaded by YouTube user Channel Nine on July 30, 2014, https://www.youtube.com/watch?v=zPw3bdsua8k.

165 *Saud Abu Ramadan's work for Bloomberg,* Ramadan's Bloomberg archive can be viewed at: http://www.bloomberg.com/authors/APxnm69cxF4/saud -abu-ramadan.

165 *Morsi halts Israeli assassinations,* Ian Black, "Israel-Hamas ceasefire: how much has been achieved in the past week?", *The Guardian,* November 21, 2012, http://www.theguardian.com/world/2012/nov/21/israel-hamas-ceasefire -how-much-has-been-achieved.

166 *Netanyahu boasts of ceasefire deal,* Hezki Ezra and Ari Yashar, "Netanyahu boasts, 'Terror towers in Gaza fell,' " *Arutz Sheva,* August 28, 2014, http:// www.israelnationalnews.com/News/News.aspx/184527#.VOPUMLB4qZs.

167 *Civilian targets in Gaza,* mortar attack, "surrender to terrorism" Operation Protective Edge, day 50, *Haaretz,* August 27, 2014, http://www.haaretz .com/news/diplomacy-defense/1.612468.

Notes to Chapter 14

169 *Injuries during celebrations,* Nasouh Nazzal, "Woman killed, 50 injured by celebrations," *Gulf News,* August 27, 2014, http://m.gulfnews.com/news /region/palestinian-territories/woman-killed-50-injured-by-celebratory -gunfire-1.1377184.

171 *"Gaza into Ramallah,"* Allison Deger, "With ceasefire set to expire, Palestinians aim to life the siege while Israel wants to turn 'Gaza into Ramallah,'" *Mondoweiss,* August 18, 2014, http://mondoweiss.net/2014/08/ceasefire -palestinians-ramallah.

172 *"We will build a seaport,"* Hamas: "We will build a seaport and an airport. We don't need anyone's approval for that," *Islamic Invitation Turkey,* August 27, 2014 http://www.islamicinvitationturkey.com/2014/08/27/hamas -we-will-build-a-seaport-and-an-airport-we-dont-need-anyones-approval -for-that/.

172 *"attack the ports,"* Palestinians don't need permission to build a seaport and airport, *Middle East Monitor,* August 27, 2014, https://www.middleeast monitor.com/news/middle-east/13757-palestinians-dont-need-permission -to-build-a-seaport-and-airport.

173 *Haniyeh victory speech,* Speech by leader Ismail Haniyeh in Gaza victory ceremony, uploaded by YouTube user Eboumhmed on August 27, 2014, https://www.youtube.com/watch?v=rV1UqyjtpTQ.

176 *Abu Obeida victory speech,* Full speech of Abu Obeida: his victory speech, uploaded by Youtube user EHNATV on August 28, 2014, https://www.youtube .com/watch?v=jAQx66s4e9o.

177 *PA won't pay Hamas employees,* "Hamas asks PA to pay Gaza government salaries," *AFP/Al Akhbar,* June 5, 2014, http://english.al-akhbar.com/node /20053.

178 *Meshal's pieces widely viewed,* Mishal's Al Jazeera exclusive report on Al Qassam, which saw him gain access to fighters in active tunnels during the war, generated headlines in Israeli media. See: Roi Kais, "Hamas fighter: We have more weapons, can hit more Israeli cities," Ynet, August 7, 2014, http://www.ynetnews.com/articles/0,7340,L-4555937,00.html. Mishal's Qassam documentary can be viewed in Arabic at: Al Jazeera documentary tears and triumph / Qassam tunnels and operations, uploaded by YouTube user Hittin Irbid Division II on August 24, 2014, https://www.youtube.com /watch?v=PvY2bEy8Kk0.

NOTES

Notes to Chapter 15

180 *Ahed Zakhout killed,* Dave Zirin, "His name was Ahed Zaquout: Former Palestinian soccer star killed in Gaza," *The Nation,* August 1, 2014, http://www.thenation.com/blog/180870/his-name-was-ahed-zaqout-former-palestinian-soccer-star-killed-gaza#.

180 *Al-Zameli killed,* Four Palestinian athletes killed in Gaza onslaught, Press TV, July 25, 2014, http://www.presstv.com/detail/2014/07/25/372715/four-palestinian-athletes-killed-in-gaza/.

180 *Twenty athletes killed,* Mohamed Harb, "Future of Palestinian football slowly fades away," *FootyOnions.com,* August 19, 2014, http://www.footynions.com/2014/08/19/future-palestinian-football-slowly-fades-away/.

180 *Rosenfeld on execution,* Jesse Rosenfeld, "Who is behind Gaza's mass execution?" *The Daily Beast,* August 1, 2014, http://www.thedailybeast.com/articles/2014/08/01/who-is-behind-gaza-s-mass-execution.html.

181 *Al Aqsa deliberately targeted,* David Carr, "Using war as cover to target journalists," *The New York Times,* November 25, 2012, http://www.nytimes.com/2012/11/26/business/media/using-war-as-cover-to-target-journalists.html?_r=0 Also see: Two al-Aqsa TV journalists among 6 killed in Gaza, *Al Arabiya News,* November 20, 2012, http://english.alarabiya.net/articles/2012/11/20/250829.html.

181 *Army warning to journalists,* Advice to reporters in #Gaza, just like any person in Gaza: For your own safety, stay away from #Hamas positions and operatives, @IDFSpokesperson, Twitter, November 18, 2012, https://twitter.com/IDFSpokesperson/status/270141407015079936.

183 *Killing of Anwar Al Zaaneen,* Al Mezan condemns killing its member Anwar Al Zaaneen in Beit Hanoun and calls for immediate investigation into this crime, Al Mezan Center for Human Rights, August 10, 2014, http://www.mezan.org/en/details.php?id=19309&ddname=IOF&id_dept=9&p=center.

Notes to Chapter 16

187 *40,000 depend on fishing industry,* Restrictions threaten Gaza fishermen's livelihood, UN Office for the Coordination of Humanitarian Affairs, April 19, 2007, http://electronicintifada.net/content/restrictions-threaten-gaza-fishermens-livelihoods/3214.

190 *Germany sells cruisers to Israel,* Ilan Ben Zion, "Israel buying 4 new warships from Germany, PM confirms," *Times of Israel,* December 25, 2014, http://www.timesofisrael.com/israel-buying-4-new-warships-from-germany-pm-confirms/.

194 *18 shooting incidents at sea,* Ben White, "NGO: More than one Israeli attack on Gaza per day in September," *Middle East Monitor,* October 24, 2014, https://www.middleeastmonitor.com/blogs/politics/14842-ngo-more-than-one-israeli-attack-on-gaza-per-day-in-september.

194 *Zero rockets from Gaza,* Gili Cohen, "False rocket sirens sound in Israel's south," *Haaretz,* October 19, 2014, http://www.haaretz.com/news/diplomacy-defense/1.621470

194 "A fragile calm," Isabel Kershner and Irit Pazner Garshowitz, "Stabbing on Tel Aviv bus breaks a fragile calm," *The New York Times,* January 21,

2015, http://www.nytimes.com/2015/01/22/world/middleeast/middle-east
-violence.html

Notes to Chapter 17.

195 *Gaza uninhabitable by 2020,* Gaza in 2020: A livable place?, UNRWA,
August 28, 2012, http://www.unrwa.org/newsroom/press-releases/gaza-2020
-liveable-place.

195 *Some 2200 killed, 70% civilians* 50 days of death & destruction: Israel's
"Operation Protective Edge," Institute for Middle East Understanding, September 10, 2014, http://imeu.org/article/50-days-of-death-destruction-israels
-operation-protective-edge From IMEU's report: According to the United
Nations, between July 7 and August 26, at least 2131 Palestinians were
killed in Gaza as a result of Israel's "Operation Protective Edge." According
to Al Mezan Center for Human Rights, a total of 2168 Palestinians were
killed, while the Palestinian Center for Human Rights (PCHR) put the total
number of Palestinian fatalities at 2191. (NOTE: Updated February 2015
to reflect revised PCHR figures). According to the UN, at least 1473 of the
dead were civilians, including 501 children and 257 women, with another
379 individuals yet to be identified. According to PCHR, 1660 Palestinian
civilians were killed, including 527 children and 299 women, while Al
Mezan reported that 1666 of the dead were civilians, including 521 children
and 297 women.

195 *400+ businesses damaged,* From IMEU's report: According to the Palestinian Federation of Industries, 419 businesses and workshops were damaged,
and 128 totally destroyed by Israeli attacks. The overall unemployment rate
in Gaza prior to Israel's latest assault was 45 percent (70 percent for those
aged 20–24). According to the UN: "It is expected that labour market conditions in Gaza will further deteriorate following the conflict, exacerbating
the impact of the blockade and the longstanding access restrictions imposed
by Israel which have been preventing any meaningful economic activity."
According to the UN Conference on Trade and Development (UNCTAD),
Gaza's economy was in a "state of total collapse" even prior Israel's latest
attack, warning on September 3 of "grave consequences" if Israel's siege and
blockade aren't lifted.

195 *Attacks on medical facilities* From IMEU's report: At least 24 medical facilities were damaged and at least 16 health care workers were reportedly killed in Israeli attacks. Notable examples of attacks on medical
facilities include: On July 23, the Israeli military shelled the Wafa Rehabilitation Hospital east of Gaza City seriously damaging the building. Between
July 11 and July 17, Israeli forces attacked the hospital on three occasions,
injuring four patients and staff. On July 21, Israel attacked the Al-Aqsa
Hospital in central Gaza, killing four people and injuring 40 others. On July
12, an Israeli airstrike killed two residents of a special needs facility in Beit
Lahiya in northern Gaza and seriously wounded several others. The dead
were 31-year-old Ola Washahi and 47-year-old Suha Abu Saada, who both
suffered from severe mental and physical handicaps. Also see: Wafa Hospital, Mechan Keneally, Inside a Gaza hospital under Israeli rocket fire, July

16, 2014, http://abcnews.go.com/International/inside-gaza-hospital-israe-li-rocket-fire/story?id=24592141.

195 *Al-Omari mosque bombed,* "In photos: Israel bombs destroy historic al-Omari mosque in Jabalia," *Maan News,* August 2, 2014, http://www.maannews.com/eng/ViewDetails.aspx?id=717666.

195 *Amin Muhammad mosque destroyed,* Max Blumenthal, "Inside Gaza City's Amin Muhammad mosque. It was locked and empty when hit," Twitter, August 15, 2014, https://twitter.com/maxblumenthal/status/500438356421918721.

196 *Destruction of only power plant,* Harriet Sherwood, "Gaza's only power plant destroyed in Israel's most intense air strike yet," *The Guardian,* July 29, 2014, http://www.theguardian.com/world/2014/jul/29/gaza-power-plant-destroyed-israeli-airstrike-100-palestinians-dead.

196 *180,000 housing units destroyed or damaged,* 50 days of death & destruction: Israel's "Operation Protective Edge," Institute for Middle East Understanding, September 10, 2014, http://imeu.org/article/50-days-of-death-destruction-israels-operation-protective-edge. From IMEU's report: According to the UN, 18,000 housing units were totally destroyed or severely damaged by Israeli attacks, leaving approximately 108,000 of Gaza's 1.8 million Palestinians homeless. Prior to this latest assault, there were 12,000 Palestinians still displaced from Israel's 2008-09 attack, "Operation Cast Lead," and a shortage of 71,000 housing units, according to the UN. (See http://www.ochaopt.org/documents/gazacrisisatlas_2014.pdf for UN Gaza Crisis Atlas, showing satellite images and geographic distribution of attacks.) According to the UN, at the peak of Israel's assault, an estimated 485,000 people (approximately 28% of Gaza's population) were displaced..

197 *"Singapore or Darfur,"* Gil Hoffman, "Israeli minister: World may be wasting its money on Gaza," *Jerusalem Post,* October 12, 2014, http://www.jpost.com/Israel-News/Politics-And-Diplomacy/Israeli-minister-World-may-be-wasting-its-money-on-Gaza-378683.

197 *"considerable donor fatigue,"* "Donor "fatigue" at "intractable" conflict as Gaza aid conference kicks off in Cairo," *Middle East Eye,* October 12, 2014, http://www.middleeasteye.net/news/donor-fatigue-intractable-conflict-gaza-aid-conference-kicks-cairo-964384961.

198 *Schaar on futility,* "Analysis: Donors threaten to withhold Gaza aid," *IRIN News,* October 7, 2014, http://www.irinnews.org/report/100690/analysis-donors-threaten-to-withhold-gaza-aid.

198 *30 percent of the government's budget* New US report shows excessive spending on PA security services, Missing Peace, February 6, 2013 http://missingpeace.eu/en/2013/02/new-us-report-shows-excessive-spending-on-pa-security-services/.

198 *Kerry at conference,* Full text of US Secretary of State John Kerry's speech at Gaza donors conference, *Jerusalem Post,* October 12, 2014, http://www.jpost.com/Middle-East/Full-text-of-US-Secretary-of-State-John-Kerrys-speech-at-Gaza-donors-conference-378657.

199 *Sisi's massacres,* "All According to Plan: The Rab'a massacre and mass killing of protesters in Egypt," *Human Rights Watch,* August 12, 2014, http://www.hrw.org/reports/2014/08/12/all-according-plan-0.

199 *40,000 political prisoners,* Ben Norton, "Australian journalist released from Egyptian jail, but 40,000 political prisoners remain," *Middle East Monitor,* February 2, 2014, https://www.middleeastmonitor.com/articles/africa/167 26-australian-journalist-released-from-egyptian-jail-but-40000-political -prisoners-remain. From Norton's report: WikiThawra, a project conducted by the Egyptian Centre for Economic and Social Rights, estimated that, between July 2013 and mid-May 2014, over 40,000 Egyptians were detained or indicted. The independent Cairo-based NGO holds that today there are still so many political prisoners languishing in Egyptian prisons; some of them are children. A representative of UNICEF-Egypt told the Global Post that the UN body had "recorded over 700 cases of children who have been detained in multiple locations in Egypt in connection with political events."

199 *US helicopters to Sisi,* Sisi: US will send Apache helicopters next month, Middle East Memo, https://www.middleeastmonitor.com/news/africa/14658 -sisi-us-will-send-apache-helicopters-next-month.

199 *Kerry on "restoring democracy"* Egypt army 'restoring democracy', says John Kerry, BBC, August 1, 2013 http://www.bbc.com/news/world-middle -east-23543744.

199 *Sisi's destruction of Rafah, Egypt,* Egypt prepares to destroy 1200 homes for Rafah border zone, *Maan News,* December 27, 2014, http://www.maannews .com/eng/ViewDetails.aspx?id=749939.

199 *Israel bars rebuilding materials,* Israel bars building materials from Gaza, *Middle East Monitor,* October 7, 2014, https://www.middleeastmonitor.com /news/middle-east/14545-israel-bars-building-materials-from-gaza.

199 *"Positive steps,"* Full text of US Secretary of State John Kerry's speech at Gaza donors conference, *Jerusalem Post,* October 12, 2014, http://www .jpost.com/Middle-East/Full-text-of-US-Secretary-of-State-John-Kerrys -speech-at-Gaza-donors-conference-378657.

200 *Rollout of Initiative for the Palestinian Economy,* Max Blumenthal, "Kerry and Blair's $4 billion mystery plan for Palestine: Crony capitalism under the guise of peace?" *Mondoweiss,* May 31, 2013, http://mondoweiss.net/2013 /05/billion-palestine-capitalism.

200 *Blair's corruption,* ibid.

200 *Blair advising Sisi,* Seumas Milne, "Tony Blair to advise Egypt president Sisi on economic reform," *The Guardian,* July 2, 2014, http://www.theguardian. com/politics/2014/jul/02/tony-blair-advise-egypt-president-sisi-economic -reform.

201 *Kerry and Masri, Collins,* Max Blumenthal, "Kerry and Blair's $4 billion mystery plan for Palestine: Crony capitalism under the guise of peace?" *Mondoweiss,* May 31, 2013, http://mondoweiss.net/2013/05/billion-palestine -capitalism.

201 *The paper on Initiative for the Palestinian Economy can be read in full at:* Max Blumenthal, International community promises to rebuild Gaza... with sweatshops to exploit Palestinian workers, *Alternet,* October 16, 2014, http:// www.alternet.org/world/international-community-promises-rebuild-gaza -sweat-shops-exploit-palestinian-workers.

202 *Not a single dollar for Northern Gaza Emergency Sewage Treatment plant,* A report on the World Bank website titled, Northern Gaza Emergency Sewage Treatment plant, notes that US $0.00 has been committed to fulfill the $43.05 million cost of building the plant. The project was approved on September 7, 2004. http://www.worldbank.org/projects/P074595/northern -gaza-emergency-sewage-treatment-ngest-project?lang=en.

203 *"One thousand Palestinian mothers crying"* Gil Hoffman, "Israeli minister: World may be wasting its money on Gaza," *Jerusalem Post*, October 12, 2014, http://www.jpost.com/Israel-News/Politics-And-Diplomacy/Israeli -minister-World-may-be-wasting-its-money-on-Gaza-378683.

203 *"The next stage of Israel's blockade,"* Ali Abunimah, "Under cover of reconstruction, UN and PA become enforcers of Israel's Gaza siege," *Electronic Intifada*, October 17, 2014, http://electronicintifada.net/blogs/ali-abunimah /under-cover-reconstruction-un-and-pa-become-enforcers-israels-gaza-siege.

204 *"Cutting edge SuperMax facility,"* Dimi Reider, *Middle East Eye*, October 11, 2014, http://www.ynetnews.com/articles/0,7340,L-4579502,00.html.

204 *"The conflict management approach,"* Ron Ben Yishai, "Easing Gaza restriction is the new two state solution," Ynet, October 11, 2014, http:// www.ynetnews.com/articles/0,7340,L-4579502,00.html.

204 *"Submerged in despair," plan rejected by Gaza,* Ali Abunimah, "Top UN official aloof as Gaza is 'submerged in despair,'" *Electronic Intifada*, November 28, 2014, http://electronicintifada.net/blogs/ali-abunimah/top-un-official -aloof-gaza-submerged-despair

204 *"We need a government,"* Ori Lewis, "Palestinian political stalemate is stalling Gaza rebuilding - UN envoy," *Reuters*, January 29, 2015, http://af.reuters .com/article/idAFL6N0V86L120150129.

204 *UNRWA funds dry up,* Tovah Lazaroff, "The war left more than 100,000 Palestinians homeless, over half of whom are children," said UNRWA, *Jerusalem Post*, January 20, 2015, http://www.jpost.com/Middle-East/UNRWA -By-months-end-well-be-out-of-funds-to-repair-Gaza-homes-388374. Also see: "Gaza donations fall way short of pledges," *Al Jazeera*, February 19, 2015, http://www.aljazeera.com/news/2015/02/gaza-donations-fall-short -pledges-150218060136423.html.

204 *42,000 unpaid employees,* Megan O'Toole, "Hamas warns of unpaid staff taking to streets," *Al Jazeera*, December 26, 2014, http://www.aljazeera.com /news/middleeast/2014/12/hamas-warns-unpaid-staff-taking-streets-201412 26162534518621.html.

205 *Israel refuses Turkish electricity for Gaza,* Israel reportedly rejects Turkish maritime electricity for Gaza, *Haaretz*, December 1, 2014, http://www.haaretz .com/news/diplomacy-defense/1.629484.

205 *Death of Abu Khesi,* Ayman Mohyeldin, "Father finds five-month-old son frozen to death in Gaza," NBC News, January 20, 2015, http://www.nbc news.com/storyline/middle-east-unrest/father-finds-five-month-old-son -frozen-death-gaza-n289371. Also see: "Fifth child dies from exposure to freezing temperatures in war-torn Gaza," *Mondoweiss*, January 21, 2015, http://mondoweiss.net/2015/01/exposure-freezing-temperatures.

Notes to Chapter 18

207 *Gaza Writes Back, Gaza Writes Back: Short stories from young writers in Gaza, Palestine,* Just World Books, 2014, http://justworldbooks.com/gaza-writes -back/.

209 *Sarah Ali blocked from Gaza Writes Back tour,* Israel blocks Gazan writer from attending US tour, *World Bulletin,* May 8, 2014, http://www.world bulletin.net/palestine/135834/israel-blocks-gazan-writer-from-attending-us -tour.

211 *Weapons development center,* Gazans report destruction as search for Goldin continues, Agence France Presse, August 2, 2014, http://www.timesofisrael .com/gazans-report-destruction-as-search-for-goldin-continues/.

211 *"Hath not a Palestinian eyes?"* Refaat Alareer, "There are no poems of mass destruction," *Middle East Eye,* August 4, 2014, http://www.middleeasteye .net/columns/there-are-no-poems-mass-destruction-246613520.

216 *Capsizing of refugee boat,* Shlomi Eldar, "Escaping Gaza, hundreds of Palestinians drown," *Al Monitor,* September 19, 2014, http://www.al-monitor .com/pulse/originals/2014/09/tragedy-sea-boat-smugglers-gaza-despair -young-people.html.

216 *"This has never happened before,"* Bettina Marx, "The back of the Gazan economy has been broken," *Qantara,* 2014, http://en.qantara.de/content /rebuilding-gaza-the-back-of-the-gazan-economy-has-been-broken.

217 *Omer kidnapped,* Lina Alsaafin, "Gaza group linked to IS kidnaps MEE correspondent," *Middle East Eye,* February 4, 2015, http://www.middleeasteye .net/news/islamic-state-group-kidnap-3-gaza-including-mee-correspondent -54280400.

217 *Wave of mysterious bombings,* Asmaa al-Ghoul, "Who keeps bombing the French Cultural Center in Gaza?" *Al Monitor,* December 17, 2014, http:// www.al-monitor.com/pulse/originals/2014/12/gaza-bombing-french-consulate -accusations-hamas.html#.

217 *"The only way to act against it is with force,"* Yonatan Mendel, "War on Gaza: A promise Israeli politicians can keep," *+972Mag,* January 9, 2015, http://972mag.com/war-on-gaza-a-promise-israeli-politicians-can-keep /101141/.

217 *"A fourth operation on Gaza is inevitable,"* Attila Somfalvi, "Lieberman: Third Lebanon war is inevitable," Ynet, February 2, 2015, http://www.ynetnews .com/articles/0,7340,L-4621448,00.html.

ACKNOWLEDGMENTS

Alessandra Bastagli presided over the production of this book with diligence, patience, and meticulous care. I was proud to work with Nation Books on this project and especially grateful to the Nation Institute for their support. Anna Stein provided expert counsel and invaluable input. Also thanks to Annie Stricklin and Melissa Raymond.

The reporting that comprises this book would not have been possible without the participation of Dan Cohen. His dedication to reporting from the Gaza Strip and sensitivity to its residents is a source of inspiration. The assistance and insight of Ebaa Rezeq was essential. Thanks also to Allison Deger, Jesse Rosenfeld, David Sheen, Jehad Saftawi, Lara Aburamadan, Belal Dabour, Refaat Alareer, Meera Albaba, Ahmed Rezeq, Mohammed Suliman, Thawra Abu Khdeir, Lazar Simenov, Dima Sarsour, Ali Abunimah, Rania Khalek, and Philip Weiss.

Jan Frel and Don Hazen of Alternet have provided a home for my reporting and unequivocal backing for it. The generosity of Reza Amin, Scott Roth, Patrick Lannan and the Lannan Foundation has been pivotal. My parents and my brother, Paul, provided thoughtful input and unwavering support throughout this project.

INDEX

INDEX

INDEX

INDEX

INDEX

politicide against Palestinians in,
111–112
propaganda blitz of, 11–12
public frustration with Netanyahu,
136–137
quelling of dissent in, 112
restrictions on Gaza by, 6
right-wing and left-wing politics in,
113–120
in second battle of Shujaiya, 40–44
targeted reporters for assassination, 181
teens' murder reactions in, 17–18
truce agreements from, 165–167
view of Palestinians, 3
Israel Defense Forces (IDF), 45, 114, 118,
128, 135
Israel Democracy Institute, 120
Israeli Air Force, 118
Israeli Merkava tank, 42, 46, 86, 208
Israeli military, 6
airstrike on al-Dalou family, 144–145,
147, 149, 150
athletes attacked by, 180
attack on Khuza'a, 68–72
Al-Basha Tower attack by, 162–165
Beit Hanoun onslaught by, 86–94
cemeteries and schools bombing in
Gaza, 133–137
civilian targets of, 122, 125
criticism of atrophy of, 123
Gaza Strip occupation by, 2, 15
Gazan fishermen attacked by, 193–194
Gaza's infrastructure pulverized by,
195–197
Hannibal Directive in, 98–101, 103,
108, 122
Italian Compound attack by, 161–162
level of firepower of, 136
maps of Shujaiya used by, 58, 59
(photo), 60
media silencing by, 162–165
mosques bombed by, 195, 196 (photo)
munitions replenishment by U.S., 127,
163–164
Nahal Oz surprise attack on, 121–122
naval patrol ships in, 190–191, 193
in Rafah, 90–94, 96–107
red line use by, 60
Shamaly family encounter with, 61–65
violence toward farmers of Khuza'a, 68
Zafer 4 and Zafer 1 towers attack by,
157–159
Israeli Military Industries (IMI), 73

Israeli Northern Command, 47
Israibi, Saleh, 93
Israibi, Suleiman (father), 94
Italian Compound, Israeli military attack
on, 161–162
Izz Ad-Din Al-Qassam Brigades. *See*
Al-Qassam Brigades

Jaabari, Ahmad, 32, 39, 145, 153
Jabalia, 89, 90, 133, 195
Jabotinsky, Vladimir, 16
al-Jarrah, Abu Obeida, 35
Al Jazeera America, 44, 49
Al Jazeera Arabic, 72, 120, 178
Jerusalem, 18, 23–24, 26, 28, 109, 114
Jerusalem Post, 47
Jewish Home Party, 8, 15, 17, 120, 127
Jewish National Fund, 29
Jibril Agreement, 98
JP Morgan, 200

Kach Party, 114
Kahane, Meir, 114–115
al-Kahlout, Hozaifa Samir Abdullah. *See*
Obeida, Abu
Kallab, Abu Hussein, 152
Kasaa'a, Bilal, 145
Kasher, Asa, 98
Katz, Yaakov, 47–48
Katz, Yisrael, 197, 203
Kaware family, 27
Kedar, Mordechai, 119
Kerry, John, 12, 37, 38, 45, 95, 97,
198–203
Khan Younis, 27, 73, 74, 76–77
Khuza'a, 107, 112, 133
atrocities in, 72–74
escaping, 74–76
Israeli military attack on, 68–72
main water tower of, 67 (photo), 71, 81
Palestinian Red Crescent volunteers
story of, 79–80
Rujeila family story of, 77–78
violence toward farmers of, 68
walking through, 80–83
Kibbutz Nirim, 133
Kimmerling, Baruch, 111–112
Kiryat Arba, 119
Knesset, 113–116, 131
Kramer, Martin, 3
Krav Maga, 117
Kuuza Mosque, 69, 71
Kuwaiti Hospital, 105, 150

INDEX

INDEX

The Nation Institute

NATION BOOKS

Founded in 2000, **Nation Books** has become a leading voice in American independent publishing. The inspiration for the imprint came from the *Nation* magazine, the oldest independent and continuously published weekly magazine of politics and culture in the United States.

The imprint's mission is to produce authoritative books that break new ground and shed light on current social and political issues. We publish established authors who are leaders in their area of expertise, and endeavor to cultivate a new generation of emerging and talented writers. With each of our books we aim to positively affect cultural and political discourse.

Nation Books is a project of The Nation Institute, a nonprofit media center dedicated to strengthening the independent press and advancing social justice and civil rights. The Nation Institute is home to a dynamic range of programs: the award-winning Investigative Fund, which supports ground-breaking investigative journalism; the widely read and syndicated website TomDispatch; the Victor S. Navasky Internship Program in conjunction with the *Nation* magazine; and Journalism Fellowships that support up to 25 high-profile reporters every year.

For more information on Nation Books, The Nation Institute, and the *Nation* magazine, please visit:

www.nationbooks.org

www.nationinstitute.org

www.thenation.com

www.facebook.com/nationbooks.ny

Twitter: @nationbooks